Lab Manual for
Criminalistics
An Introduction to Forensic Science

Eleventh Edition

Clifton E. Meloan
Richard E. James (deceased)
Thomas Brettell
Richard Saferstein

PEARSON

Boston Columbus Indianapolis New York San Francisco Upper Saddle River
Amsterdam Cape Town Dubai London Madrid Milan Munich Paris Montréal Toronto
Delhi Mexico City São Paulo Sydney Hong Kong Seoul Singapore Taipei Tokyo

Editorial Director: Vernon R. Anthony	*Art Director:* Diane Y. Ernsberger
Executive Editor: Gary Bauer	*Cover Designer:* Wee Design Group, Wanda Espana
Development Editor: Elisa Rogers, 4development	*Cover Image:* (Clockwise from top left) © Jochen Tack/Alamy, © rsdphotography/Alamy, © Timothy Evans/Alamy, © Simon Belcher/Alamy
Program Manager: Alicia Ritchey	
Editorial Assistant: Lynda Cramer	
Director of Marketing: David Gesell	*Media Project Manager:* Leslie Brado
Marketing Manager: Mary Salzman	*Media Project Coordinator:* April Cleland
Senior Marketing Coordinator: Alicia Wozniak	*Full-Service Project Management:* Shyam Ramasubramony, S4Carlisle Publishing Services
Marketing Assistant: Les Roberts	
Team Lead for Project Management: JoEllen Gohr	*Composition:* S4Carlisle Publishing Services
Project Manager: Jessica H. Sykes	*Printer/Binder:* Edwards Brothers Malloy/Jackson
Procurement Specialist: Deidra M. Skahill	*Cover Printer:* Edwards Brothers Malloy/Jackson
Creative Director: Design Development Services, Andrea Nix	*Text Font:* Adobe Garamond Pro 11/12

Credits and acknowledgments borrowed from other sources and reproduced, with permission, in this textbook appear on the appropriate page within text.

Microsoft® and Windows® are registered trademarks of the Microsoft Corporation in the U.S.A. and other countries. Screen shots and icons reprinted with permission from the Microsoft Corporation. This book is not sponsored or endorsed by or affiliated with the Microsoft Corporation.

Copyright © 2015, 2011, 2007 by Pearson Education, Inc. All rights reserved. Manufactured in the United States of America. This publication is protected by Copyright, and permission should be obtained from the publisher prior to any prohibited reproduction, storage in a retrieval system, or transmission in any form or by any means, electronic, mechanical, photocopying, recording, or likewise. To obtain permission(s) to use material from this work, please submit a written request to Pearson Education, Inc., Permissions Department, One Lake Street, Upper Saddle River, New Jersey 07458, or you may fax your request to 201-236-3290.

Many of the designations by manufacturers and sellers to distinguish their products are claimed as trademarks. Where those designations appear in this book, and the publisher was aware of a trademark claim, the designations have been printed in initial caps or all caps.

10 9 8 7 6 5 4 3 2 1

ISBN 10: 0-13-345889-X
ISBN 13: 978-0-13-345889-3

Contents

Preface vii

Acknowledgments ix

Experiment 1 Practice in Making Laboratory Measurements 1
   Part A: Density of Rectangular Solids 2
   Part B: Densities of Cylindrical Solids 3
   Part C: Densities of Irregularly Shaped Solids 3
   Part D: Cleanup, Calculations, and Questions 4

Experiment 2 Density of Glass by Flotation and Density Gradient Columns 7
   Part A: Physical Matching 8
   Part B: Edge Thickness 9
   Part C: Density Comparison by Flotation 9
   Part D: Density Comparison by Density Gradient Tubes (Advanced) 9

Experiment 3 Practice in the Use of the Microscope 19
   Part A: The Compound Microscope 20
   Part B: The Stereoscopic Microscope 23
   Part C: Comparison of Paint Chips 24
   Part D: Comparison of Paper Matches 25

Experiment 4 Forensic Paint Analysis: Microscopic Analysis and Solvent Testing 29
   Microscopic Examination 30
   Solvent Testing 31

Experiment 5 Refractive Index (RI) of Glass Fragments 35
   Part A: The Becke Line Concept 38
   Part B: Refractive Index of Automotive Glass (Advanced) 38

Experiment 6 Powder Residues on Fabrics 43
   Part A: Bullet Holes in Fabric 44
   Part B: Sodium Rhodizonate Test for Lead Residues 45

Contents

Experiment 7 Shooting Reconstruction by iPhone 49
   Calibration 49
   Trajectory Angle Measurement 50

Experiment 8 Satellite Imaging Lab 57

Experiment 9 Blood Identification and Typing 61
   Part A: Is it Really Blood? 62
   Part B: Presumptive Testing with Kastle-Meyer Reagent 63
   Part C: Presumptive Testing with Hemastix® 64
   Part D: Confirmation for Blood 65
   Part E: Incompatibility Relationships in the ABO System 66

Experiment 10 Fingerprinting 73
   Part A: Making a Latent Fingerprint Visible 75
   Part B: Lifting a Latent Print 75
   Part C: Fluorescent Dusting Powder (Advanced) 76
   Part D: Obtaining an Inked Print 77
   Part E: Matching Prints 77

Experiment 11 Fingerprinting (Advanced) 87
   Part A: Obtaining Fingerprints From Paper by Means of Ninhydrin 88
   Part B: The Silver Nitrate Method 89
   Part C: The Use of Super Glue 90
   Part D: Enhancement of Super Glue Fingerprints by Dusting and Fluorescence (Advanced) 92

Experiment 12 Comparison of Tool Marks and Casting 97
   Part A: Making a Cast of a Tool Imprint 98
   Part B: Individual Characteristics of Tool Marks 99
   Part C: Plaster of Paris Casts of Footprints and Tire Treads 99
   Part D: Making a Cast From a Mold (Advanced) 100

Experiment 13 Reproducing Bite Marks 107

Experiment 14 Restoring Serial Numbers on Metals 111

Experiment 15 Restoring Bloody Shoe Prints 117
   Part A: Coomassie Blue Processing 118
   Part B: Leucocrystal Violet Processing 119

Experiment 16 Examination of Hair and Textile Fibers by Microscopy 123
   Part A: General Internal Characteristics 125
   Part B: Scale Patterns 126
   Part C: Hair Color 126
   Part D: Making Cross Sections of Fibers (Advanced) 126

Experiment 17 Drug Analysis: Microchemical Spot Tests for General Classes 133

Experiment 18 Drug Analysis: Microcrystalline Tests 143
   Part A: Testing of Known Samples 144
   Part B: Testing of Unknown Samples 145

Experiment 19   Separation of Drugs Using Thin-Layer Chromatography   149
  Development Sequence   152

Experiment 20   Identification of Drugs and Poisons by Infrared Spectroscopy (Advanced)   155

Experiment 21   Salicylates in Blood by Visible Spectroscopy   161
  Part A: Basic Spectrophotometry   162
  Part B: Salicylates in Blood Serum (Advanced)   163
  Crime Scene   163

Experiment 22   Salicylates in Blood by Fluorometry (Advanced)   167
  Calculations   169

Experiment 23   Quinine in Urine by Fluorometry (Advanced)   173
  Calculations   174

Experiment 24   Analysis of Blood Alcohol by Gas Chromatography Using a Thermal Conductivity Detector   177

Experiment 25   Analysis of Blood Alcohol by Gas-Liquid Chromatography Using a Flame Ionization Detector   185

Experiment 26   Separation of Ink Dyes Using Thin-Layer Chromatography   191

Experiment 27   Seminal Stains by Human Prostatic Acid Phosphate   197
  Part A: Suspected Stains on Clothing or Bedding   198
  Part B: Examination of Swabs   199
  Part C: Vaginal Washings   199
  Part D: Location of Seminal Stains by their Phosphorescence (Advanced)   199

Experiment 28   Arson Detection: The Recovery of Flammable Liquids   203
  Part A: Headspace Analysis   204
  Part B: Vapor Concentration on Charcoal (Advanced)   205

Experiment 29   Metal Residues on Hands from Guns, Knives, and Other Metal Weapons   209
  Part A: The 8-Hydroxyquinoline Method   209
  Crime Scene   210
  Part B: The Ferrozine Method   211

Experiment 30   The Emission Spectrum of Elements   215
  Part A: Obtaining Flame Emissions   216
  Part B: The Spectroscope   216
  Part C: The Emission Spectra of Elements   217

Experiment 31   Determination of Blood-Spatter Angles of Impact   221
  Part A: Obtaining Blood Spatters   222
  Part B: Measuring Angles of Impact   223

Experiment 32   Electrophoretic Analysis of Blood for Human Origin (Advanced)   229

Experiment 33   Nuclear DNA Extraction   235
  Part A: Isolation of Chromosomal DNA from *E. Coli*   238
  Part B: Isolation of DNA from Vegetable Sources   238

vi   Contents

Part C: Staining of DNA for Visualization   239
Alternate Experiments   239

Experiment 34   DNA Fingerprinting: EDVO-Kit # 109   243

Experiment Objective   249
Gel Requirements   249
Preparing the Gel Bed   250
Casting Agarose Gels   250
Practice Gel Loading   253
Electrophoresis Samples   253
QuickStrip™ Samples   254
Staining of DNA   256
Destaining and Visualization of DNA   257
Liquid Staining and Destaining of DNA   258
Laboratory Notebook Recordings   258

Experiment 35   PCR Amplification of DNA for Fingerprinting: EDVO-Kit # 130   261

Experiment Brief Description   264
Experiment Objective   265
Gel Requirements   265
Laboratory Safety   266
Preparing the Gel Bed   266
Casting Agarose Gels   266
Preparing the Gel for Electrophoresis   268
Practice Gel Loading   269
Electrophoresis Samples   270
QuickStrip™ Samples   270
Staining of DNA   272
Destaining and Visualization of DNA   273
Liquid Staining and Destaining of DNA   274
Laboratory Notebook Recordings   275
Study Questions   276

Experiment 36   The Comparison Microscope   277

Part A: Comparison of Toolmark Scratches   278
Crime Scene   278
Part B: Comparison of Shell Cases and Slugs   279
Part C: Photomicrographs   280

Experiment 37   Burglaries and Murders: The Final Exam   285

Part A: A Bungled Burglary   285
Part B: Campsite Crime   286
Part C: A Parking Ramp Rumble   288
Part D: A Household Homicide   289
Part E: A Love Triangle?   291

Appendix 1   Glossary   293

Appendix 2   The Metric System   297

Preface

NEW TO THIS EDITION

New experiments added to this edition of the manual are:

1. Forensic Paint Analysis: Microscopic Analysis and Solvent Testing (Experiment 4).
2. Shooting Reconstruction by iPhone (Experiment 7).
3. Satellite Imaging Lab (Experiment 8).
4. Separation of Drugs Using Thin-Layer Chromatography (Experiment 19).

PREFACE TO THE FIRST EDITION

When lawyers present their cases before the courts, they often engage in debate. Another word for debate, when applied to the judicial process, is forensics (L. *forensis*, market or forum). Over the years, the increasing application of scientific principles to difficult court cases has given rise to the general field of *forensic science*, or science as applied to law. Forensic science includes all areas of scientific endeavor, such as medicine, psychiatry, psychology, geology, physics, chemistry, and biology. The particular area of forensic science that describes the services normally provided by crime laboratories is known as *criminalistics*.

The one statement that perhaps most clearly epitomizes the pursuits of the criminalist is that made by Edmund Locard, who said, "Every contact leaves a trace." Many years ago such a statement was merely a dream, but modern technology now permits many traces of contact to be detected, and the future holds the promise of more to come. Even Locard would be amazed by the fact that it is now possible to take fingerprints from the throat of a strangled person, determine a smoker's blood type from the remains of a cigarette butt, and, through the use of holography, to measure the size of an invisible shoeprint left on a carpet. Certainly every contact leaves a trace; it is up to us to find a way to detect it. The following experiments show how numerous contacts are detected. We hope that students will find them interesting and gain a better appreciation of what a criminalist does, and that the experiments might also capture students' imaginations so that in the future they may well discover how to detect a new type of contact.

It must be clearly understood that this set of experiments is intended as an introduction to the analyses performed in a forensic laboratory. The experiments are an attempt to acquaint nonscience students with the investigation of physical evidence through the use of scientific procedures. They are written at an introductory level, using terms that can be understood by nonscience students. The experiments are actual procedures, modified to fit the background of students.

Advanced-level experiments are also included for science-oriented students. These experiments are designed to familiarize these students with basic criminalistic techniques, such as the application of electrophoresis, the typing of bloodstains, and the determination of the index of the refraction of glass specimens using of the Becke line technique.

The specific objectives of this set of laboratory experiments are as follows:

1. To provide a first set of laboratory experiments for criminal justice and general science students who have had little or no previous science laboratory experience.

2. To show beginning students in criminal justice and general science the significance of physical evidence at the scene of a crime.

3. To demonstrate what happens to physical evidence when it is sent to the laboratory so that students will know what is needed, how much is needed, and how to prepare it.

4. To educate students in basic laboratory practices so that they can ask and/or answer questions more intelligently in a court of law.

5. And probably most important, to educate students so that they will not unintentionally destroy physical evidence at a crime scene, and will in fact try to preserve it for the trained forensic scientist.

We emphasize that these experiments, while being actual laboratory analyses, are designed to provide students with an overview of what can be done, not to make them polished forensic scientists.

The views expressed in this manual are those of the authors.

PREFACE TO THIS EDITION

A student once made the following comment: "I have learned a lot in this class, but since I'm not going to be a police officer, I have no idea how I might use it." The answer was, "In your lifetime you might be the first person at the scene of a crime. Now that you know what constitutes physical evidence and how important it is to obtain it in its original state, you can keep the crowd of onlookers away from it until the police arrive. This can be an invaluable service."

In this edition, we continue to include selected references from the literature but have eliminated most of the old references prior to 1995. Every now and then a student wants to know more, and the teachers need to know more to make their lectures and discussions more accurate. We limit our suggestions to selections from two main forensic journals most likely to be in libraries: the *Journal of Forensic Science* (American), and *Science and Justice* (British, until 1995 titled *Journal of the Forensic Science Society*). The web page address for the *Journal of Forensic Science* is **http://www.aafs.org**.

Instructors should remember that this is an introductory course; therefore, the students taking it have had very little science background.

Acknowledgments

We wish to thank the following people and organizations for providing technical information for the writing of these laboratory experiments for this and the previous editions:

Mr. James Rhodes, Supervisor of the Laboratory of the Minnesota Bureau of Criminal Apprehension

Mr. Leslie Loch, Crime Investigator based in St. Cloud, Minnesota

Captain Richard Witschen, St. Cloud Police Department, St. Cloud, Minnesota

Corporal Mike Lofgren, Minnesota Highway Patrol, expert on automobile lamp glass fragmentation and speed determination

Mr. Ronald Jones and Mr. Robert Olsen, the Kansas Bureau of Investigation Criminalistics Laboratory at Topeka, Kansas

Lt. Patrick B. Glynn, Wichita, Kansas, Criminalistics Laboratory

Lt. Al Riniker, Riley Co., Kansas, Police Department

Chief Kenneth Dickinson, Waite Park Police Department, Waite Park, Minnesota

Dr. Jeffrey Payne, 3M Co., Minneapolis, Minnesota

Laura Anne Roselli, Biotechnology Department, Burlington County College, Mt. Laurel, New Jersey

Edward E. Hueske, Forensic Training & Consulting, LCC, Palestine, TX 75803, www.edhueske.com

Morgan Mills, Cedar Crest College

Miss Nikki James, for the final exams

Annina Carter, Adirondack Community College, for reviewing the manual

The *Journal of Forensic Science* and *Science and Justice* were consulted at great length to determine updated criminalistics procedures, particularly those at a level that could be understood by nonscience majors.

Clifton Meloan
Richard James
Thomas Brettell
Richard Saferstein

Practice in Making Laboratory Measurements

EXPERIMENT 1

This is an introductory laboratory exercise intended to prepare you for Experiment 2, which deals with the analysis of glass fragments. You will become more familiar with measurements using the metric system and learn to use a laboratory balance. In this exercise you will determine the density of several objects by various methods. Do the parts of this exercise slowly and carefully so that you fully understand what is required and what the results indicate.

Density is a physical property of matter that is specific to the sample being measured and that may be used as a means of identification or comparison, whichever is required. The equation for density is:

$$\text{Density} = \frac{\text{Mass of Object}}{\text{Volume of Object}} \text{ expressed as either } \frac{g}{cm^3} \text{ or } \frac{lb}{ft^3} \qquad (1-1)$$

The utility of this type of determination may be made clearer to you by the following example. Suppose that a man has a body volume of 3 cubic feet and weighs 198 lb. What is his density? The calculation would be done by application of equation 1–1.

$$\text{Density} = \frac{\text{Weight}}{\text{Volume}}$$

$$= \frac{198 \text{ lb}}{3 \text{ ft}^3} = 66 \text{ lb/ft}^3$$

Water weighs 62.4 lb/ft^3. Therefore, if the man jumps into a lake or swimming pool, he will sink unless he knows how to swim or to keep himself afloat by holding air in his lungs. In other words, an object placed in a fluid sinks if its density is greater than that of the surrounding fluid and floats if its density is less than that of the surrounding fluid.

THE TOP-LOADING BALANCE

A top-loading balance is an instrument that is used to measure the mass of an object. An object to be weighed is placed on a metal pan and the mass is measured in the S.I. unit gram, usually indicated by a digital readout. Figure 1–1 shows one such balance. Although a balance technically compares weights, not masses, the weight of an object is proportional to its mass. The standard weights used with balances are usually labeled in mass units (grams). Most top-loading balances measure mass to two decimal places (0.01 g).

FIGURE 1-1 A top-loading balance.

EQUIPMENT

- 1 Balance, top-loading (capable of an accuracy to ±0.01 g)
- 1 Beaker, 250 mL
- Rectangular metal solids
- Cylindrical solids (wooden rods)
- 1 pr Goggles, safety
- 1 Graduated cylinder (1,000 mL is best)
- Irregular metal objects
- 1 Meter stick or metric ruler
- 1 pr Scissors
- String, 60–90 cm long

METHOD

PART A: DENSITY OF RECTANGULAR SOLIDS

In this part of the exercise you will determine the density of an object by applying the relationship

$$\text{Density} = \frac{\text{Mass of Object (g)}}{\text{Volume of Object (cm}^3)}$$

See Table 1–1 for the densities of various common materials.

1. Obtain a rectangular solid from the sample supply.

2. Measure the three dimensions of the object with a ruler, using the centimeter as the unit of measurement, and record the values on the data sheet.

3. Determine the volume by applying the following formula:

$$V = \text{length} \times \text{width} \times \text{height} \tag{1-2}$$

   The volume will then be derived in units of cubic centimeters.

4. Determine the mass of the object by use of the laboratory balance.

5. Measure the mass of the object to the nearest 0.01 g, and record the mass on the data sheet for this exercise.

6. Determine the density of the object by applying the formula given at the beginning of this section, and record the value on the data sheet.

TABLE 1-1	Densities of Various Common Materials (g/cm³)		
Material	Density	Material	Density
Cork	0.22–0.26	Glass, flint	2.9–5.9
Bone	1.7–2.0	Iron	7.86
Glass, window	2.47–2.56	Brass, yellow	8.44–8.70
Flint	2.63	Lead	11.34
Aluminum	2.70	Gold	19.3

PART B: DENSITIES OF CYLINDRICAL SOLIDS

1. Obtain a cylindrical solid from the sample supply, measure its mass in the same manner as done previously, and record the value. Because this object is not of the same shape as the rectangular solid, you will have to determine its volume using a different mathematical relationship. The formula to be used in this case is

   $$\text{Volume} = \pi r^2 h \tag{1-3}$$

   where $\pi = 3.14$
   $r =$ radius
   $h =$ height or length of the object

   The height and radius of a cylinder are shown in Figure 1–2.

2. Measure the diameter in cm, and divide by 2 to obtain the radius.

3. Measure the height or length of the object in centimeters.

4. Record these values, and determine the volume of the object.

5. Enter this value on the data sheet.

6. Determine the value for the density of the object using the relationship

   $$D = \frac{M}{V}$$

   and record this value.

PART C: DENSITIES OF IRREGULARLY SHAPED SOLIDS

1. Obtain an irregularly shaped solid from the sample supply. Because it would be very difficult to obtain the volume of this object by measurement, we will approach this determination in a different manner.

2. Measure the mass of the object by using the balance as you did in Part A.

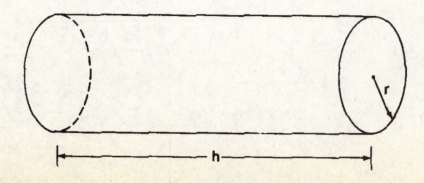

FIGURE 1–2 Diagram of a cylinder showing the measurements needed.

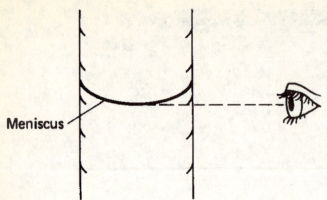

FIGURE 1-3 Illustrating a meniscus and proper eye level.

3. Obtain a graduated cylinder from the equipment supply and fill it with water to one of the graduations. The volume of water is read by noting the position of the bottom of the curve (meniscus) of the liquid level, as shown in Figure 1-3.

4. Record this value.

5. Tie a piece of string around the object. Gently lower the irregular object into the graduated cylinder so that it is entirely immersed (submerged) below the water level. Note that the water level has risen in the graduated cylinder. (This method would not be used for an object that would absorb water or dissolve in it.)

6. Read the level of the meniscus and record it.

7. Subtract the first value from the second value for the water level, and you have the volume of the object by a method known as **water displacement**. Record this value also.

You may now find the density of the object by applying the following reasoning. The volume of the object has been indirectly determined and is expressed in milliliters of water, its equivalent volume. A relationship exists in the metric system between units of volume of liquids and units of volume of solids. This relationship is

$$1 \text{ mL} = 1 \text{ cm}^3 \tag{1-4}$$

Thus, all that is necessary to express the volume in cubic centimeters is the volume in milliliters.

8. Determine the density by applying the equation in step B-6. Record this value.

9. Repeat the steps in Part C using the rectangular or cylindrical solid sample, and record the values for the mass, volume, and density of this object.

PART D: CLEANUP, CALCULATIONS, AND QUESTIONS

Dry all glassware, return all materials to the place from which you obtained them, and clean up your work area. Complete the data sheet, answer the questions, and hand your completed papers to your laboratory instructor.

EXPERIMENT 1 Name _____

DATA SHEET Date _____

PRACTICE IN MAKING LABORATORY MEASUREMENTS

Part A: Density of Rectangular Solids

Mass

Volume

Density

Calculations:

Part B: Density of Cylindrical Solids

Mass

Volume

Density

Calculations:

Part C: Density of Irregularly Shaped Solids

1. Irregular solid

    Mass

    Volume of water with solid immersed

    Volume of water initially

    Volume of solid

    Density

Calculations:

Experiment 1

2. Rectangular or cylindrical solid   Calculations:

   Mass

   Volume of water with solid immersed

   Volume of water initially

   Volume of solid

   Density

Questions

1. Compare the density of a single solid object obtained by various methods. Which methods do you think give the most accurate values? Why?

2. Could you have used the method in Part C for determining the volume of any wooden solid object? What would you have to change in the apparatus to permit the value for the volume to be more accurately obtained?

Density of Glass by Flotation and Density Gradient Columns

The objective of glass comparison is to associate one glass fragment with another while minimizing or eliminating the possible existence of other sources. Glass will have its greatest evidential value when it can be individualized to one source. Such a determination, however, can only be made when the suspect and crime-scene fragments are assembled and physically pieced together (a physical match). The possibility that two pieces of glass originating from different sources will fit exactly together is so unlikely as to exclude all other sources from practical consideration. If this effort fails, the forensic examiner will compare the glasses to determine whether they do or do not have the same densities and refractive indices. This experiment will allow you to become familiar with laboratory techniques employed for comparing the densities of glass. The purpose of such an analysis is to establish the possibility or impossibility of any glass fragments having a common origin.

The simplest comparative-density technique is known as **flotation** (not floatation). It is based on the observation that a solid particle will float in a liquid medium of greater density, sink in a liquid of lower density, or remain suspended in a liquid of equal density. A second comparative-density technique is the **density gradient** method. A standard density gradient tube is made up of layers of two liquids mixed in varying proportions so that each layer has a different density value. When completed, a density gradient tube will usually have six to ten original layers, in which the bottom layer has the heaviest density and the top layer the lightest density. After standing for 24 hours these layers will diffuse into one continuous gradient. A solid particle added to the tube will sink until its density is the same as the surrounding liquid and then remain suspended at that level. Furthermore, if absolute density values are desired, the gradient tube can be calibrated by adding to it solids of known densities. Densities for glass and similar materials are listed in Table 2–1.

CRIME SCENE

During a mugging, the attacker drops his glasses and one lens breaks. He picks up the pieces and flees. The victim, however, observes this incident and when the police officer arrives, describes it to him. The officer, upon careful searching, finds a few very small pieces of glass. These have been given to you. Once the suspect is apprehended, you try to match the glass fragments.

Experiment 2

TABLE 2–1	Crystals of Different Densities (g/cm³)		
Compound	Density	Compound	Density
$KC_2H_3O_2$	1.57	KF	2.48
$Na_2B_4O_7 \cdot 10H_2O$	1.73	$NaClO_3$	2.49
$Na_2C_4H_4 \cdot 2H_2O$	1.82	$KClO_4$	2.52
$K_3Fe(CN)_6$	1.85	$CuCl_2 \cdot 2H_2O$	2.54
KNO_2	1.91	NaF	2.56
KCl	1.98	$MgSO_4$	2.66
KNO_3	2.10	$K_2Cr_2O_7$	2.67
$NaCl$	2.16	$KMnO_4$	2.70
$NaNO_3$	2.26	Na_2CrO_4	2.72
$KClO_3$	2.32	$AgClO_4$	2.80

EQUIPMENT

- 8 Beakers, 250 mL (for knowns and unknowns)
- 1 Brush, test tube
- 1 Buret holder
- 4 Rubber stoppers, small
- 1 Forceps
- 1 Funnel, glass, 35 mm
- 1 Pipet bulb
- 1 Pipet, Mohr, 5 mL
- 1 Rack, test tube
- 1 Ring stand
- 1 Ruler (metric)
- Samples of small glass fragments, eyeglass, windowpane, headlight
- 2 Glass tubes, 30 cm × 1 cm (closed at one end)
- 1 pr Goggles, safety
- 1 Medicine dropper
- 1 Micrometer, optional
- 1 Mortar and pestle, small
- 1 Pencil, grease
- 1 pr Scissors
- 1 Spatula
- 1 Stirring rod, glass, 4 m × 15 cm
- 5 Test tubes, 10 cm
- 21 Vials, to hold compounds from Table 2–1

MATERIALS

Bromobenzene (d = 1.52)
Bromoform (d = 2.89)
Several small crystals of a few of the compounds listed in Table 2–1

METHOD

Obtain a glass fragment from each of four beakers labeled "unknown" and those labeled "known." The unknowns are numbered 1, 2, 3, and 4. The knowns are lettered A, B, C, and D. The object is to determine whether the numbered and lettered fragments have a common origin. In some instances, this cannot be done with absolute certainty. Do the very best you can.

PART A: PHYSICAL MATCHING

Try to obtain a physical match between fragments if possible; that is, match letters, if present, on two fragments by fitting together any scratches on the fragments or by some other piecing together of the fragments. Such a fracture match—a physical match of two fragments—is conclusive proof that they were once the same piece of glass. Record any physical match on the data sheet.

PART B: EDGE THICKNESS

Compare the fragments by measuring the thickness of the edges of the fragments. Truly accurate measurement requires a micrometer. However, a visual comparison of pieces of glass placed side by side is fairly reliable. Although the results may not be conclusive in themselves, they may help the decision-making process later. Record any similarity in edge thickness on the data sheet. Use the metric scale or a ruler for better comparison of edge measurements.

PART C: DENSITY COMPARISON BY FLOTATION

1. Before adding the glass fragments to the test tube, it is important that each piece of glass be carefully examined and briefly sketched. This will allow the examiner to identify each fragment when placed in the mixture of bromoform and bromobenzene.

2. A cleaned and dried sample of an unknown glass particle is placed in a test tube containing 1–2 mL of bromoform. The glass will float on the liquid's surface. This indicates that the density of the liquid is greater than that of the glass. Slowly add a less dense liquid (bromobenzene) dropwise, with stirring, until the particle is exactly suspended. If too much bromobenzene is added, so that the glass particle begins to sink, gradually add more of the heavier liquid.

3. Add a similarly sized, cleaned, and dried sample of the known glass. If the two glasses are similar in density, each will remain suspended in the liquid. Otherwise, one particle will tend to rise or sink relative to the other.

4. Systematically compare all the unknown glasses to the known glasses, attempting to match up a lettered fragment with a numbered glass.

PART D: DENSITY COMPARISON BY DENSITY GRADIENT TUBES (ADVANCED)

An alternative technique of comparing the densities of glass particles is to use density gradient tubes. In this experiment we not only compare glass, but also show you an easy way to calibrate the density column so that a fairly accurate estimate of density can be made. This is done by adding to the density column small crystals of ionic salts whose densities are known, but that are insoluble in the organic liquid.

METHOD

You will prepare three identical density columns, add a few crystals of known density to each column to calibrate them, and then add the small fragments of glass. You should be able to measure the density and determine if the suspect glass matches that found at the scene.

1. Place five test tubes in a test tube rack.

2. Prepare mixtures b–f by pipetting bromoform and bromobenzene into the five test tubes.

    The ratios are as follows:

    a. Pure bromoform
    b. 0.5 mL of bromobenzene, 2.5 mL of bromoform
    c. 1.0 mL of bromobenzene, 2.0 mL of bromoform
    d. 1.5 mL of bromobenzene, 1.5 mL of bromoform
    e. 2.0 mL of bromobenzene, 1.0 mL of bromoform
    f. 2.5 mL of bromobenzene, 0.5 mL of bromoform
    g. Pure bromobenzene

3. Place a buret holder on a ring stand.

4. Mark off seven equal spaces along each of three glass tubes.

5. Place the columns (marked glass tubes) in the buret holder, being sure the bottoms are securely closed, with waxed-in or taped-in rubber stoppers if necessary.

6. Carefully add the solutions in the order listed in step 2 (bromoform on the bottom).

7. With a forceps, carefully select one of the more dense crystals listed in Table 2–1 and add it to one of the columns. Repeat this process until you have added at least seven different crystals to each column. Record which ones you use.

8. Allow the crystals to settle for about 10 minutes and measure their height from the bottom of the tube with a metric ruler.

9. Carefully add a few of the glass fragments (suspect and scene) found to match in Part C to their respective columns and allow the columns to stand overnight.

10. Record the height of the marker crystals in each column.

11. Plot density versus height for the marker crystals in each column.

12. Determine the height of the glass in each column.

13. From the graph plotted in step 11, determine the density of the glass in each column.

14. Clean out the columns, and pour the solutions into the recycle bottle.

SELECTED SOURCES FOR ADDITIONAL INFORMATION

Curran, J. M., Triggs, C. M., Buckleton, J. S., Walsh, K. A. J., and Hicks, T., "The interpretation of elemental composition measurements from forensic glass evidence, I," *Sci. & Just.*, 37 (4), (1997), 241.

Curran, J. M., Triggs, C. M., Buckleton, J. S., Walsh, K. A. J., and Hicks, T. "The interpretation of elemental composition measurements from forensic glass evidence, II," *Sci. & Just.*, 37 (4), (1997), 245.

Curran, J. M., Triggs, C. M., Buckleton, J. S., Walsh, K. A. J., and Hicks, T., "Assessing transfer probabilities in a Bayesian interpretation of forensic glass evidence," *Sci. & Just.*, 38 (1), (1998), 15.

Fong, W., "Value of glass as evidence," *J. Forens. Sci. Soc.*, 18, (1973), 398.

Heye, C. L., Rios, F. G., and Thornton, J. I., "Density characterization of armor piercing ammunition," *J. Forens. Sci.*, 40 (3), (1995), 401.

Hicks, T., Vanina, R., and Margot, P., "Transfer and persistence of glass fragments on garments," *Sci. & Just.*, 36 (2), (1996), 101.

Lambert, J. A., Satterthwaite, M. J., and Harrison, P. H., "A survey of glass fragments from clothing of persons suspected of involvement in crime," *Sci. & Just.*, 35 (4), (1995), 273.

EXPERIMENT 2

DATA SHEET

Name _____

Date _____

DENSITY OF GLASS BY FLOTATION AND DENSITY GRADIENT COLUMNS

Part A: Physical Matching

Set No. _____

Part B: Edge Thickness

1. Measurement of the edges of the fragments (thickness)

    A   1

    B   2

    C   3

    D   4

2. Tentative comparisons

Part C: Density Comparison by Flotation

A. _____

B. _____

C. _____

D. _____

12 Experiment 2

Part D: Density Comparison by Density Gradient Tubes (Advanced)

a. Record the crystals used for calibration here.

	Column 1			**Column 2**			**Column 3**	
Crystal	Init ht	Final ht	Crystal	Init ht	Final ht	Crystal	Init ht	Final ht

1.

3.

2.

4.

5.

6.

7.

8.

9.

10.

b. Plot density versus height for each column on the graph paper provided.

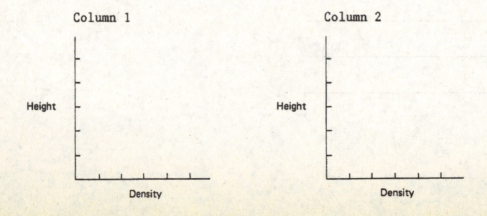

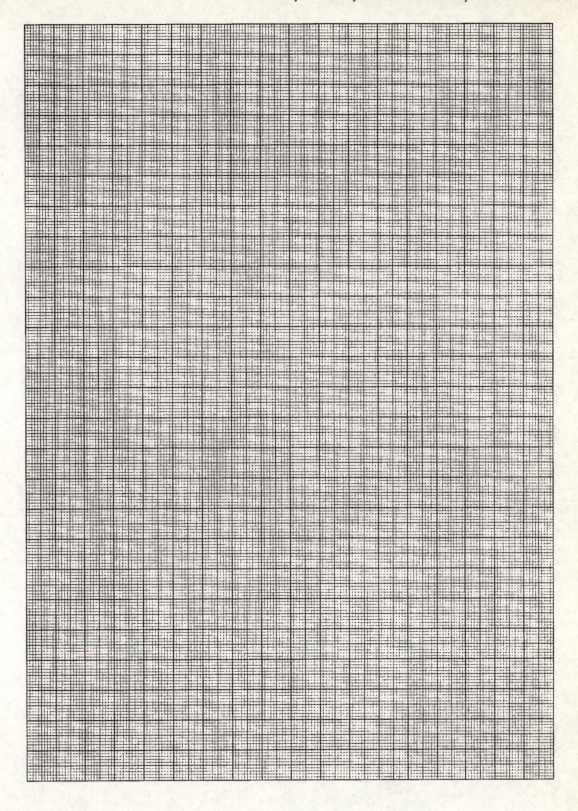

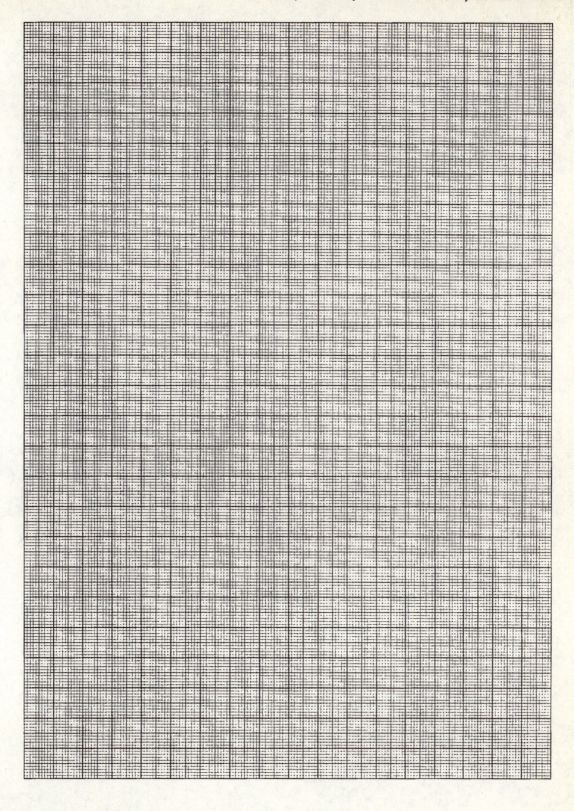

c. Indicate on the graphs in step b where the glass particles are in each column.

d. What are your conclusions? Which glass samples match, if any?

Questions

1. If your density profiles are not the same, what would you do the next time that you make this type of column?

2. Now that you know the density of glass fairly well, you could make a density gradient column covering 0.1 density units from the top to the bottom of the column. What mixtures of bromoform and bromobenzene would you use to make such a column?

3. How certain are you that the fragments you have matched do have a common origin? Give your reasons.

EXPERIMENT 3

Practice in the Use of the Microscope

The microscope is one of the most valuable tools of forensic scientists. They use it to study hair, fibers, seeds, soils, metals, paints—anything and everything involved in a crime. It is believed that engravers used glass globes filled with water as magnifying glasses at least 3,000 years ago. The simplest microscope is called a **magnifying glass**. Optical microscopes magnify because light rays reflected from an object bend (refract) as they pass through one or more lenses.

How big you can make the object depends on the refractive index (bend power) of the glass in the lens. Hand lenses are 3× to 10×. Because the light rays are spread out when an object is magnified, the magnified object is not as bright as the original. To make it as bright as it was originally, additional light must be used. This is the purpose of having a mirror under the lens of the microscope. It collects sunlight or light from an auxiliary lamp. The **condenser** focuses the light collected by the mirror onto the sample.

Suppose that you took a small section of a magnified object and placed a second lens over it. This magnified section could then be further magnified and we would have a **compound microscope**. Dutch spectacle maker Zacharias Janssen is credited with discovering this principle and making the first compound microscope in 1590. Since then, there have been many improvements, although the basic concept has remained essentially unchanged. Magnification up to about 400× is possible with ordinary illumination. With a substage condenser to focus more light on the object and with better lenses, it is possible to go to 1000× magnification. About the highest magnification that can be obtained with a compound microscope is 2500×.

The quality of a microscope resides in the lenses. Slight imperfections can cause large distortions in the object that is viewed. In addition, various colors refract at different angles, so correcting lenses must be added. Expensive microscopes have excellent correcting lenses, whereas less expensive microscopes may not even have correcting lenses.

In working with a compound microscope, you will find the following terms useful:

Working distance—the distance between the specimen and the tip of the objective lens. In general, the higher the magnification, the shorter the working distance.

Depth of focus—the thickness of the object that is simultaneously in focus. The higher the power of magnification, the less is the depth of focus.

Field of view—the area or diameter of the specimen that is in view. The higher the power of magnification, the less is the field of view.

Magnification—to determine the magnification of a microscope, **multiply the magnification of the eyepiece by the magnification of the nosepiece**.

Figure 3–1 shows the basic parts of a compound microscope.

20 Experiment 3

EQUIPMENT

   1 Auxiliary light (for the stereoscopic microscope)
1 bx Cover glasses
1 pr Forceps
1 pr Goggles, safety
1 bx Lens paper
   1 Medicine dropper
   1 Microscope, compound

   1 Microscope, stereoscopic
1 bx Microscope slides
   1 Razor blade
1 pr Scissors
  10 Vials, glass, 6 dram, to hold paint chips and matches
   1 White card, 7.5 × 10 cm

MATERIALS

Modeling clay
Newspaper
Paint chips from several cars, available at a salvage yard
Paper matches, from at least three different books
Tea
Tobacco

PART A: THE COMPOUND MICROSCOPE

1. Obtain an assigned compound microscope from the cabinet and carry it back to your seat at the lab table.
2. With a piece of lens paper, lightly wipe any dust and grease from all the exposed glass surfaces. Never use anything else to do this job.
3. Spend the next few minutes becoming familiar with the names and locations of the various important parts of the instrument; Figure 3–1 will help.

    Several important rules are to be noted in connection with the foregoing procedures:

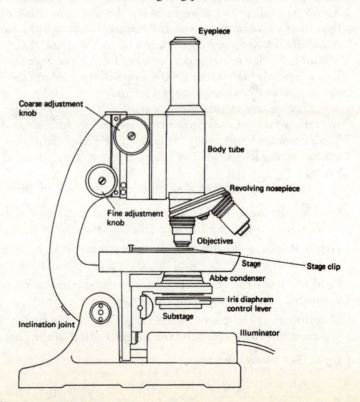

FIGURE 3–1 General structure of a compound microscope.

a. To find an object, **always start your examination with the low-power objective, never with the high**. The low-power objective reveals an area of the slide some 20 times larger than does the high-power objective, making it 20 times easier to locate the desired object.
b. To bring the object into focus, **always focus upward**, with the coarse adjustment. (NOTE: Some microscopes focus by moving the stage up and down rather than the body tube. In such cases the focusing is downward—away from the nonmovable parts.) You want to focus upward because when your eye is at the ocular (eyepiece), it is impossible to determine how far down or up the tip of the objective has traveled. In focusing down, carelessness might result in crushing the specimens.
c. When the high-power objective is being used, never use the coarse adjustment.

KOHLER ILLUMINATION

Anyone can eventually adjust a microscope to view an object placed on a slide. However, if you want to do it the best way possible to get the brightest image with the best focus possible, then you should use **Kohler illumination**. This is a method to align the optics and focus all of the components so as to minimize distortion and to obtain uniform brightness. It should be done with every sample, particularly if a photomicrograph is to be made. It can be done in less than five minutes once you know how to do it. An uncentered lamp filament will usually not show up until a photomicrograph is taken, and then the photo will be unevenly exposed. It has been estimated that 90% of the people who use a microscope do not use Kohler illumination, because they either do not know what it is or do not know how to make the adjustments. Because a microscope is a major component of a criminalistics laboratory and because many photomicrographs are taken, it is desirable that you should know the basics of how to establish Kohler illumination. A comparison can be made between a finely tuned engine and one that needs a tune up. Both will run and both will do the job, but to get the best performance and have the greatest peace of mind, you use the one that is properly tuned.

The components that need to be adjusted are: (a) the **light source**, (b) the **field diaphragm**, (c) the **condenser**, (d) the **objective lens**, and (e) the **iris diaphragm**. Whereas all of these can be adjusted on a high-quality microscope, usually only the condenser and the iris diaphragm can be adjusted on student-type microscopes. The following directions are for use with a high-quality microscope. Your instructor will tell you how many you can do with your microscope.

1. Place the **fixed objective** lens in place. This is usually a $10\times$ objective lens. Adjust its height to be about 2–3 mm above the stage with the coarse focusing adjustment.

2. Turn on the lamp. If it has an adjustable intensity control, adjust the intensity to be bright but not cause you to squint. Feel comfortable.

3. If the microscope is binocular (two eyepieces), adjust their separation to fit your eyes.

4. Place a slide, with a specimen on it, on the stage and center it.

5. Open both the field and iris diaphragms completely so the specimen can be viewed. You should have a full field of view with an unfocused specimen close to the center.

6. Bring the specimen into focus by focusing up, first with the coarse adjusting knob, then with the fine adjusting knob.

7. Close the field diaphragm (the one just in front of the lamp) completely or until about all you can see is a fuzzy circle around your specimen. Almost the entire field will be black except for a small white circle of light around your specimen, and the separation between the black and white will usually be fuzzy and multicolored. Keep your specimen inside of the light area, or at least so you can see part of it.

8. Move the condenser up or down to focus the edge of the diaphragm. You should now be able to see that the circle is actually a polygon.

9. Your specimen should be in the center of the lighted area. If it is not, and you have condenser controls (usually two adjusting screws with handles on them just under the stage), adjust the condenser so your specimen is in the center of the bright area.

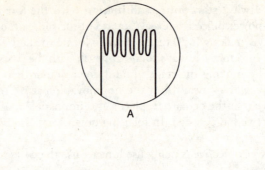
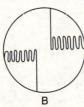
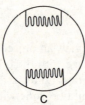
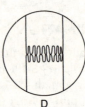

FIGURE 3–2 (A) A diagram of the image of the filament of a quartz-iodine bulb as seen in the plane of the aperture diaphragm of the condenser. (B) One possible appearance when the lamp system is out of adjustment. Two images of the filament (one inverted and produced by the mirror behind the lamp) are not coincident. (C) The filament images have not been aligned. (D) The final correct adjustment when the images are both aligned and made contiguous. *(Courtesy of S. Bradbury,* An Introduction to the Optical Microscope, *Oxford, UK: Oxford University Press, 1984).*

10. You should be able to move any other higher-power objective in place and the specimen should still be in the center. If it is not, then there are inset adjusting screws at the base of each objective lens where it fastens onto the turret. These can be adjusted to center the specimen. **Only the instructor should do this if it is necessary**.

11. Open the field iris until the lighted area just fills the circular field. You should be able to see a polygon perfectly inscribed and just touching the outer rim of the field of view.

12. Remove one of the eyepiece oculars so you can look down the body tube.

    If you have a high-quality microscope with a lamp adjustment, then do step 13. If not, go to step 14. Refer to Figure 3–2.

13. Focus an image of the lamp filament on the objective back focal plane by moving the lamp with its adjusting screws.

14. Open or close the iris diaphragm (right under the stage) until the polygon fills about 70–80% of the field of view. This provides for good image contrast, a flatter field, and better depth of field.

15. Replace the eyepiece ocular. You now have Kohler illumination. Unless you did step 10, you should repeat this each time the objective is changed.

METHOD

1. Cut the letter "h" from a newspaper. Place it on a clean slide, and with a medicine dropper, place one drop of water on the letter.

2. Wait a moment before covering it with a cover slide. Hold the cover slide at about a 45° angle to the support slide, and then slowly lower it. Gentle tapping will usually remove any bubbles that may be present.

3. Place the slide on the stage and clamp it down. Move the slide so that the letter is in the middle of the hole in the stage. Make certain that the low-power objective is in place. Viewing the stage from the side, use the coarse adjustment wheel to lower the objective until either the stop is reached or the objective is approximately 2 cm from the cover slide.

4. Turn on the substage illuminator of your microscope if it has one or the auxiliary lamp if the lighting is separate.

5. Now, looking through the ocular, slowly raise the tube with the coarse adjustment knob until the letter "h" is in focus. If you cannot see the object, center the slide more carefully and repeat the whole procedure. The focus may be made sharper by a slight turn on the fine adjustment knob.

6. Open and close the iris diaphragm by turning the diaphragm handle, which projects laterally from the lower portion of the condenser. The iris diaphragm controls the amount of light reaching the specimen. Adjust it to make the image as sharp as possible (maximum definition).

7. The image is in focus 3 to 4 mm above the eyepiece. **Thus, there is no reason to press one's eye to the ocular**. Some students who wear glasses find it advisable to remove them, while others to keep them on, as determined by experience.

8. To change to high power, make sure that you have focused sharply under low power on the object and centered it in the field. Then **carefully** swing the high-power objective into place. The microscopes are **parfocal**. This means that once the image is brought into sharp focus under low power, it will remain in focus when the high-power objective is turned into position. The high-power objective should not strike the slide, although it will come very close. A few turns of the fine adjustment knob, either up or down, should suffice to bring the "h" into sharp focus. If it does not, go back to step 3 and begin again. Once the image has been brought into sharp focus, it may be necessary to readjust the diaphragm opening, as discussed in step 8 in the Kohler illumination section.

EXERCISES

1. Examine the "h" under the low-power objective.
    a. Is the image right-side up?
    b. Move the slide to the left: Which way does the image seem to move?

2. Under high power, examine the letter "h."
    a. Note the many clear spaces **within** the letter; these are obviously caused by imperfect contact between the press and paper. The high-power lens is able to resolve these imperfections. The microscope, then, does two things: it enlarges (magnifies) the object, and it **resolves** distinctly between closely situated structures in the object (note that magnification and resolution are not the same).
    b. Take particular note of the fibrous texture of the newspaper. When you focus on different levels by turning the fine focus knob, you will notice that some fibers go out of view and others come in view. This is a maneuver for which you will find frequent use and that will enable you to determine whether a particular object is located above, below, or in the same plane as another object.
    c. The total magnification of the image formed by the microscope is determined by multiplying the individual magnifications of the ocular and the objective. The magnifying powers of these lenses are clearly marked as 10×, 40×, and so on. What is the magnification of the image at low power?
    d. What is the magnification at high power?

3. Repeat these exercises using the letter "e."

PART B: THE STEREOSCOPIC MICROSCOPE

Obtain an assigned stereoscopic microscope, and carefully carry it back to your desk or bench. Familiarize yourself with the parts of the microscope.

1. Place the previously prepared "h" slide onto the microscope stage. Illuminate the slide from above with an illuminator or any available light source.

2. Set the magnification knob to the highest power (2× or 3×). Look through the right eyepiece and adjust the focusing knob until the letter "e" is sharp.

3. Reset the magnification knob to the lowest power (1× or 0.7×). Without touching the focusing knob, look through the left eyepiece, and, using only the left eye, turn the eyepiece adjusting ring clockwise or counterclockwise until the image is sharp. Make sure that the eyepiece maintains contact with the

24 Experiment 3

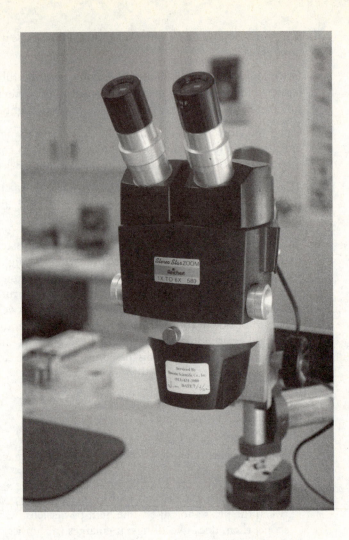

FIGURE 3–3 A stereomicroscope.
© Mikael Karlsson/arrestingimages.com

adjusting ring. The adjusting ring is set in the position that best accommodates each viewer's eyes. Once set, it should not be changed.

4. The magnification knob allows you to change the power continuously to exactly the best magnification for a given specimen. The stereoscopic microscope allows you to scan an object at a lower power and then to concentrate on some particular detail by increasing the power gradually to the desired value.

EXERCISES

1. Examine the previously prepared "h" and "e" slides under the set stereoscopic microscope. Is the image right-side up? Move the slide to the left: which way does the image seem to move?

2. Examine tea and/or cigarette tobacco under both low- and high-power magnification.

3. Examine the tips of your fingers under the stereoscopic microscope. Locate the ridges that form a fingerprint. Locate the sweat pores that exist on these ridges.

PART C: COMPARISON OF PAINT CHIPS

There are very few objects that do not have some sort of lacquer, varnish, or paint as a protective coating. When these objects are involved in a crime, the protective coating is often broken loose. A close examination of paint flakes may well be of use. Generally, several layers of paint are applied to an object. The color of an undercoat or primer usually differs from that of the final coats, and if the object has been painted several times, there will then be several layers of different thickness and color. If a paint chip is placed on edge and viewed under a microscope, these layers are readily visible.

Under a stereoscopic microscope, the number of layers, the color, and the relative thickness from a suspect paint chip can be matched with the reference paint.

CRIME SCENE

A hit-and-run accident has occurred in which a parked car has been sideswiped. A witness was able to get only two numbers of the license number. The police have found three cars that fit the general description of auto style, color, and license number. All three are older cars that have many scratches and dents on them, so no definitive conclusion can be drawn. Each driver has denied any responsibility for the accident. The police have obtained a chip of paint from each car and from the vehicle that was hit. These have been given to you, and your job is to see if a match can be made.

METHOD

1. Place a white plate or piece of white cardboard on the stage of the stereoscopic microscope.

2. Obtain a piece of clay about the size of a small marble, and press it into the plate so that it looks like a small pyramid.

3. Using a razor blade, make a small V cut in the top of the clay about half as deep as the paint chip is wide.

4. With forceps, carefully place the paint chip from the victim's car in the V cut so that the edge of the paint chip is up. Press the clay together to hold the chip.

5. Turn on the illuminator and direct it onto the paint specimen. Using the lowest power on the microscope, focus on the edge of the paint chip. Use your fingers to press the clay to position the paint chip so that the cut edge is horizontal and in focus over as much of its length as possible.

6. Repeat steps 1 through 5 with one of the comparison paint chips.

7. See if you can match the paint chips. Record what you see.

8. Repeat steps 1 through 6 with each of the suspect paint chips to see if you can make a match.

9. Clean up the area and put the clay back in the package.

PART D: COMPARISON OF PAPER MATCHES

From time to time a forensic laboratory may be asked to see whether a torn-out paper match comes from a partially used book, usually taken from an accused person.

Cursory examination of any matchbook will reveal that it contains two pieces of cardboard secured in the book with a staple. The individual match body is formed by a series of partial cuts in this cardboard; thus each layer of matches was originally a single piece of cardboard.

The obvious first attempt to match a torn-out match to a partially filled matchbook requires physically fitting the torn edges of the match to the corresponding portion of the torn book. Barring success in this attempt, a forensic examiner will then try to compare the suspect match with matches remaining in the book in order to establish an adjacent relationship.

Such a comparison can be conducted under a stereoscopic microscope. The most significant features to look for in the comparison of paper matches are:

1. Color, width, and thickness.

2. Inclusions. Most matches are made from reprocessed cardboard. Examination of the match edges may reveal inclusions consisting of a large variety of colored fibrous material, aluminum foil, and other contaminants that were involved in the production of the cardboard. A side-by-side examination of

matches for comparable inclusions is probably the easiest and most significant feature to look for in match comparisons.

3. Continuous fibers. Another feature for comparison is the presence of continuous fibers between adjacent matches. These fibers may exist on the upper and lower surfaces of the matches.

CRIME SCENE

A burglary has been committed, and apparently, in addition to the burglars inside the building, a lookout was posted. The detective at the scene noticed a few cigarette butts by the back door, as well as a few paper matches. He picked these up as possible evidence. A few days later, three suspects are apprehended. A search of the clothing in their apartments yields a book of matches in the trouser pocket of one of the suspects. Your job is to see if the match found at the back door is from the book recovered from the suspects.

METHOD

1. You will be given two matches for comparison.

2. Compare the matches' color, width, and thickness.

3. Under the highest power of the stereoscopic microscope, hold the edges of the matches side by side, and compare them for any matching characteristics.

4. Holding the upper surfaces of the matches side by side, compare them for any matching characteristics under the stereoscopic microscope. Repeat this examination for the underside of the matches. Are the matches alike? How certain can you be that they originated from the same book?

SELECTED SOURCES FOR ADDITIONAL INFORMATION

Grieve, M. C., "New man-made fibers under the microscope: Lyocell fibres and Nylon-6 block co-polymers," *Sci. & Just.*, 36 (2), (1996), 71.

Kopchick, K. A., and Bommarito, C. R., "Color analysis of apparently achromatic automotive paints by visible microspectrophotometry," *J. Forens. Sci.*, 51 (2), (2006), 340.

McDermott, S. D., and Willis, S. M., "A survey of the evidential value of paint transfer evidence," *J. Forens. Sci.*, 42 (6), 1997, 1012.

Platek, S. F., Keisler, M. A., Ranieri, N., Reynolds, T. W., and Crowe, J. B., "A method for the determination of syringe needle punctures in rubber stoppers using stereoscopic light microscopy," *J. Forensic. Sci.*, 47 (5), (2002), 986.

Suzuki, E. M., "Infrared spectra of US automobile original topcoats (1974–1989) V: Identification of organic pigments used in red non-metallic and brown non-metallic and metallic monocoats: DPpredBO and thioindigo Bordeaux," *J. Forens. Sci.*, 44 (2), (1999), 297.

Suzuki, E. M., "Infrared spectra of US automobile original topcoats (1974–1989) VI: Identification and analysis of yellow organic automotive paint pigments: Iisoindolinone yellow 3R, isoindoline yellow, anthrapyrimidine yellow and miscellaneous yellows," *J. Forens. Sci.*, 44 (6), (1999), 1151.

Suzuki, E. M., and McDermot, M. X., "Infrared spectra of US automobile original finishes. VII. Extended range FT-IR and XFR analysis of inorganic pigments in situ nickel titanate and chrome titanate," *J. Forens. Sci.*, 51 (3), (2006), 574.

Wiggins, K. G., Holness, J., and March, B. M., "The importance of thin layer chromatography and UV microspectrophotometry in the analysis of reactive dyes released from wool and cotton fibers," *J. Forens. Sci.*, 50 (2), (2005), 364.

Zieba-Palus, J., "Selected cases of forensic paint analysis," *Sci. & Just.*, 39 (2), (1999), 123.

EXPERIMENT 3

DATA SHEET

Name _____

Date _____

PRACTICE IN THE USE OF THE MICROSCOPE

Part A: The Compound Microscope

1. Sketch what an "h" looks like when viewed under this microscope.

Part B: The Stereoscopic Microscope

1. Sketch what an "h" looks like when viewed under this microscope.

Part C: Comparison of Paint Chips

1. Sketch the edge of the paint chip that you examined.

28 Experiment 3

Part D: Comparison of Paper Matches

1. Sketch the fiber patterns observed when the two matches are viewed broadside.

2. Sketch the fiber patterns observed when the two matches are viewed on edge.

Forensic Paint Analysis: Microscopic Analysis and Solvent Testing

EXPERIMENT 4

Paint as physical evidence is most frequently encountered in hit-and-run motor vehicle cases and burglary cases. Most commonly, a chip of dried paint or a paint smear may be transferred to the clothing of a hit-and-run victim from impact with a motor vehicle. Paint may also be transferred onto a tool used during the commission of a breaking-and-entering or burglary case. Confirming the transfer of paint from one surface to another can be of forensic significance. In most situations, the forensic scientist will compare two or more paint samples to establish the source of the paint chip or smear. Such a comparison can associate or link an individual with a suspect motor vehicle. Likewise, a paint comparison could link a tool used in a breaking-and-entering case to the crime scene.

PAINT COMPOSITION

Paint applied to a surface will dry into a hard film that consists of pigments and additives suspended on the binder. The most common types of paint examined in the crime laboratory involve automobile coatings. Automobile manufacturers normally apply a variety of layers to the body of an automobile. The wide diversity of automotive paint contributes to the forensic significance of an automobile paint comparison.

Paint samples are characterized by a number of different physical characteristics that include color; layer structure, thickness, and sequence; and surface and layer characteristics, among other features. Chemical composition varies because of different pigments, polymers, additives, and solvents that are used by different manufacturers. Color and layer structure are the most important characteristics of a paint chip. The more layers, the more the evidential value of the paint sample.

PAINT EXAMINATION

The properties described above for paint samples can be examined using microscopy, chemical, and instrumental methods. Microscopy is the most important technique for paint examination. Questioned and known paint samples are best compared side by side using a stereomicroscope. Color, surface texture, and color layer sequence should be examined and documented. A forensic paint examiner's primary goal is to assess the significance of any differences between the samples. The importance of layer structure for evaluating the evidential significance cannot be overemphasized. The potential for physical matches between questioned and known paint samples must also be considered. A physical match between two samples is the most conclusive type of examination that can be performed and would confirm the link between such samples.

Solvent tests have been used to discriminate between paint samples of differing composition that are otherwise similar in appearance. Solvent tests are destructive and should be applied first to known samples in order to evaluate their effectiveness with a specific sample, and they should be used only in situations with an adequate available questioned sample. Solvent tests should be conducted on both questioned and known materials at the same time.

CRIME SCENE

A pedestrian was hit by an automobile while crossing a rural road. There were no witnesses. Crime scene investigators collected paint chips found at the scene and paint smears from the victim's clothes. Several leads were developed concerning possible cars involved in the accident. Paint samples were collected from the suspect vehicles and submitted to the crime laboratory for comparison.

SAFETY

For all laboratory work, follow the safety procedures that have been outlined for your institution. If you are unsure how to handle a particular chemical, consult the Material Safety Data Sheet (MSDS) information or ask your instructor for assistance. **All solubility testing must be performed in a fume hood.**

EQUIPMENT, SUPPLIES AND REAGENTS:

Samples of questioned paint chips from scene and victim

Samples of known paint films from suspect automobiles

Stereomicroscope

Scalpel

Tweezers

Clay or some other device or adhesive to hold paint chips

Porcelain spot plates

Acetone

Xylene

Diphenylamine (acidified with sulfuric acid)

METHOD
MICROSCOPIC EXAMINATION

1. Place each paint sample flat on a sheet of white paper. Be sure to keep the samples organized and separated.

2. One by one, place each paint sample flat under a stereomicroscope with a 40× magnification. Note color and other marks or observations (such as striae).

3. Attempt to identify any possibility of a physical match between any of the questioned or known paint samples. If you identify a physical match, sketch the match on your worksheet.

4. Using a scalpel make an oblique cut (cut at an angle). This will give more exposure to all of the layers of the paint chip by increasing the surface area of all the layers.

5. Place the paint chip flat on a piece of clay (or other adhesive). Two-sided tape or picture adhesive tape will also work well.

6. Examine the paint chip while it is lying flat and note the layers. Turn the chip at different angles and observe the layer structure.

7. Determine the number, sequence, color, and thickness of the layer structure of the paint chips. Document your results in tabular form on the worksheet.

8. Compare the questioned samples to the known samples. Can you identify the suspect vehicle?

SOLVENT TESTING

1. Place a small piece of each paint sample in separate wells of a clean porcelain spot plate. Be sure to keep the samples organized. Mark the top of each well with an identifier.

2. Place one drop of acetone in each well. Observe the results. Reactions such as softening, swelling, curling or wrinkling, dissolution, effervescence, and color changes are some observations that may be noted. Document observations on your worksheet.

3. Repeat steps 1 and 2 with xylene. Document observations on your worksheet.

4. Repeat steps 1 and 2 with diphenylamine reagent. Document observations on your worksheet.

SELECTED SOURCES FOR ADDITIONAL INFORMATION

Crown, D. A., *The Forensic Examination of Paints and Pigments*, Springfield, IL: Charles C. Thomas, 1968.

Maehly, A., and Stromberg, L., *Chemical Criminalistics*, New York, NY: Springer-Verlag, 1981.

Nielsen, H. K. R., "Forensic Analysis of Coatings," *J. Coat. Tech*, 56 (718), (1984), 21–32.

Saferstein, R., *Criminalistics: An Introduction to Forensic Science*, 10th ed., Upper Saddle River, NJ: Prentice Hall, 2011.

Scientific Working Group on Materials Analysis, "Forensic Paint Analysis and Comparison Guidelines," www.swgmat.org (accessed 16 Nov. 2013).

Stoecklein, W., "Forensic Science: Paints, Varnishes and Lacquers," *Encyclopedia of Analytical Science*, New York: Academic Press, 1995, 1625–1635.

Thornton, J. I., "Forensic Paint Examination," *Forensic Science Handbook*, Vol. 1, Saferstein, R., Ed., Upper Saddle River, NJ: Prentice-Hall, 1982, 529–571.

EXPERIMENT 4 Name _____

DATA SHEET Date _____

FORENSIC PAINT ANALYSIS: MICROSCOPIC ANALYSIS AND SOLVENT TESTING

1. Sketch any physical matches of paint samples here.

2. Results of stereomicroscopic examination of color and layer structure.

Sample	# of Layers	Color and Striae Observations			
		Layer 1	Layer 2	Layer 3	Layer 4
Q-1					
Q-2					
Q-3					
K-1					
K-2					
K-3					

Experiment 4

3. Results of solvent testing.

Sample	Acetone	Xylene	Diphenylamine
Q-1			
Q-2			
Q-3			
K-1			
K-2			
K-3			

4. Can you come to any conclusions about your questioned samples?

5. Do you think a different solvent would improve the differentiation of the paint samples?

6. What types of other tests should be performed to compare the paint samples?

Refractive Index (RI) of Glass Fragments

EXPERIMENT 5

The analysis of glass chips sometimes involves measurement of the refractive index of the glass. **Refractive index is a measure of the bending of a ray of light as it passes from air into a solid or liquid.** Every material has its own characteristic refractive index. This measurement either provides additional data for the determination of the possible common origin of two glass samples or helps to disprove this possibility.

IMMERSION METHODS

When a transparent object such as a glass chip is immersed in a liquid, it is seen by the unaided eye or under a microscope as having a dark or colored boundary, a sort of "halo." This is called the **Becke line**. The intensity of this visible boundary around the glass depends on the difference in refractive index between the glass and the liquid. In general, the greater the difference between the refractive index of a specimen and that of a surrounding medium, the more distinct is the Becke line. As the refractive indices of the specimen and liquid approach equality, the Becke line will tend to disappear. Indeed, if the indices of a colorless specimen and the surrounding medium are equal, the specimen will be practically invisible.

A difference in refractive index of ± 0.002 between the glass chip and the immersion liquid can be readily observed. With light of one wavelength (monochromatic light), temperature control, and sufficient practice, differences as small as ± 0.0001 may be detected. The refractive index of a substance varies considerably with different wavelengths of light. Normally, the value is determined in the presence of sodium light.

A common procedure for determining the refractive index of a glass chip is to immerse the chip in a liquid of about the same refractive index and then observe it through a microscope. The investigator may commence with a series of standardized immersion liquids, or he or she may mix two liquids until the refractive index of the mixture is the same as the glass sample and then determine the refractive index of the mixed liquids with a refractometer. To determine when the refractive index of the immersion liquid is equal to that of the glass chip, the investigator may observe the Becke line, using normal illumination with monochromatic light. If all of the glass chips examined show minimal contrast and no Becke lines in the same immersion liquid, it can be concluded that they all have comparable refractive indices.

An important advantage of the Becke line is not merely the fact that it indicates a difference between the indices of the glass and liquid, but that it indicates which possesses the higher value. Hence, the BECKE LINE MOVES TOWARD the medium of HIGHER refractive index if the focus of the microscope is RAISED and TOWARD the medium of LOWER refractive index if the focus is LOWERED. This observation allows an examiner to properly select a liquid that most closely matches the refractive index of glass. This is shown in Figure 5–1.

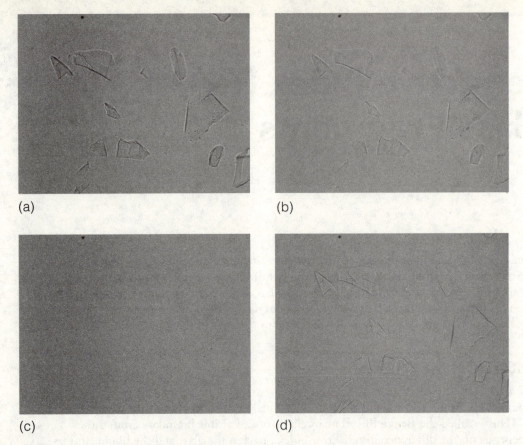

FIGURE 5-1 Determination of the refractive index of glass. (a) Glass particles are immersed in a liquid of a much higher refractive index at a temperature of 20°C. (b) At 68°C the liquid still has a higher refractive index than the glass. (c) The refractive index of the liquid is closest to that of the glass at 100°C, as shown by the disappearance of the glass and the Becke lines. (d) At the higher temperature of 160°C, the liquid has a much lower index than the glass, resulting in significant edge contrast. The reference glass fragment shown here has a refractive index of 1.529.

It is well known by people who use microscopes all of the time that when a colorless transparent object is being examined with a microscope by transmitted light, visibility of the object is enhanced as the condenser diaphragm is closed, although resolution is sacrificed. Furthermore, reducing the aperture of the optical system of the microscope enhances visibility by emphasizing the refractive index difference between the transparent object and the mounting medium. Therefore, in examining glass chips for refractive index, a minimum numerical aperture should be used.

STANDARD IMMERSION LIQUIDS

Standard immersion liquids may be prepared from two miscible liquids, one having a lower, and the other a higher refractive index than the refractive index of the glass samples. A series of mixtures is made to cover the expected range of glasses in steps of 0.001 or 0.002. Although the refractive indices of glasses may vary considerably (Table 5–1), the refractive indices of most glass samples encountered in practice lie between 1.51 and 1.52. Automobile headlight glass generally has a refractive index range of 1.47 to 1.49.

The liquids chosen should be of low volatility, chemically stable, and of congenial smell. Castor oil (1.48) and clove oil (1.54) serve as quite suitable liquids and are readily available. Mixtures of these two liquids are reasonably stable in refractive index. Several other liquids that can be used are shown in Table 5–2.

Many workers prefer to purchase their refractive index liquids. The refractive indices are adjusted to within ±0.0002 of the stated values, and each liquid is also labeled with its temperature coefficient and

TABLE 5-1	Indices of Refraction for Several Glasses
Glass	Index of Refraction
Headlight glass	1.47–1.49
Television glass	1.49–1.51
Window glass	1.51–1.52
Bottles	1.51–1.52
Ophthalmic lenses	1.52–1.53

TABLE 5-2	Liquids for Refractive Index Determination
Compound	$^nD^{20}$ °C
Methyl alcohol	1.3288
Water	1.3330
Ethyl acetate	1.3727
n-Butyl alcohol	1.4022
Olive oil	1.4667
Cyclohexanol	1.4678
Castor oil	1.4820
Benzene	1.5011
Chlorobenzene	1.5250
Clove oil	1.5430
Nitrobenzene	1.5526
Bromoform	1.5973
Iodobenzene	1.6200

dispersion. If you desire to prepare your own series, the adjustment of each mixture to its desired value is carried out with a refractometer, preferably the **Abbe refractometer**, which enables each mixture to be adjusted to the nearest ±0.0001. The standardized liquids are conveniently stored in 2- or 3-dram screw-capped vials in a rack. Thin glass rods may be used to transfer drops of liquid from the vials to the microscope slide.

EQUIPMENT

- 2 Cover slips (optional)
- 1 pk Filter paper
- 1 pr Goggles, safety
- 1 bx Kim wipes
- 4 Medicine droppers
- 2 Microscope slides (cavity works best)
- 1 Microscope (100 × is sufficient)
- 1 Mortar and pestle, small, to grind glass fragments
- 1 Refractometer, Abbe or equivalent
- 1 Sodium vapor lamp (preferably) or Ilford spectrum yellow filter
- 11 Stirring rods, glass, 3 mm × 10 cm
- 4 Vials, 3 dram, for glass fragments
- 11 Vials, glass, 3 dram with screw caps, for liquid samples

MATERIALS

Bromoform (R.I. = 1.59)
Castor oil (R.I. = 1.48)
Clove oil (R.I. = 1.54)
Ethanol, 95% (for cleaning)
Mixtures of olive oil and clove oil
  in 5:1, 4:2, 3:3, 2:4, and 1:5 ratios
Get headlight glass from an auto
  salvage yard
Olive oil (R.I. = 1.46)
Potassium chloride (KCl) crystals
Small chips of glass samples
Sodium chloride (NaCl) crystals

PART A: THE BECKE LINE CONCEPT

As an exercise in familiarizing yourself with the appearance of the Becke line, you will be asked to estimate the refractive indices of two solids: sodium chloride and potassium chloride. In order to accomplish this you will be supplied with the following three liquids: castor oil, clove oil, and bromoform.

1. Place a few crystals of sodium chloride on a microscope slide, add 1 drop of castor oil to the crystals, and cover them with a cover slip.

2. Turn on the sodium vapor lamp and adjust the microscope. If a sodium lamp is not available, an Ilford spectrum yellow filter, which has a maximum transmission of 590 nm, may be used to provide an appropriate equivalent of sodium light (589 nm). (Note: The nanometer is used as a measure of the wavelength of radiation. It is 1×10^{-9} m in length and is abbreviated nm.)

3. Most microscopes have a 16-mm (2/3-inch) objective that should be used to view the crystals. Bring the crystals into focus.

4. Observe the bright border or "halo" that surrounds one of the larger crystals. If the halo seems indistinct, it may be made more pronounced by closing down the condenser diaphragm.

5. Turning the coarse adjustment, slowly focus upward. Observe whether the bright line (Becke line) moves away from the crystal (toward the castor oil) or toward the crystal. Next, slowly lower the objective, and note the direction in which the Becke line moves. The Becke line moves toward the medium or lower refractive index if the focus is lowered. Does castor oil have a higher or lower refractive index than sodium chloride?

6. Repeat steps 1 through 5 for sodium chloride immersed in clove oil. Does sodium chloride have a lower or higher refractive index compared with clove oil?

7. Repeat steps 1 through 5 for sodium chloride immersed in bromoform. Does sodium chloride have a lower or higher refractive index compared to bromoform?

8. To which of the three liquids does sodium chloride's refractive index come the closest? Why?

9. Repeat steps 1 through 5 for each of the three liquids immersed in potassium chloride. Which liquid has the closest refractive index to potassium chloride?

PART B: REFRACTIVE INDEX OF AUTOMOBILE GLASS (ADVANCED)

CRIME SCENE

A hit-and-run accident has occurred. The officer at the scene recovers a few pieces of glass, which she believes came from the vehicle in question. The next morning, the police visit all the garages and service stations in town, and they find that eight headlights have been changed since the accident, three of which were broken at the time they were changed. The police recover these three headlights and send them to you. Your job is to measure the refractive index of the glass found at the scene and that of the three headlights to see if a match is possible.

METHOD

You will prepare a series of solutions ranging from either pure olive oil or castor oil to pure clove oil. The indices of refraction of the solutions composed of mixtures of the two liquids chosen are determined by use of the refractometer. Six or eight mixtures having refractive indices between 1.46 and 1.53 are usually sufficient and are easily made using medicine droppers. These solutions are then stored in properly labeled small screw-cap glass bottles. Proceed as follows.

1. Turn on the sodium vapor lamp and adjust the microscope.

2. The crime scene glass fragment is placed on a microscope slide in 1 drop of one of the standard liquids, and then covered with a small cover glass. The cover glass ensures that the chip is completely immersed and minimizes any spurious lens effects from the surface of the drop. As noted earlier, maximum sensitivity is obtained by having the minimum aperture in the optical system. Most microscopes have a 16-mm (2/3-inch) objective, which should be used with an eyepiece of $10\times$ magnification. Lower-powered objectives with stronger eyepieces may be preferred by some workers.

3. Observe the Becke line and then focus upward and downward to determine whether the glass fragment or the solution has the higher refractive index. When the refractive index of the glass and the immersion liquid are the same, the chip will become almost invisible, and it may be difficult to find and bring into focus the edges of the chip. If a white light is used, the glass chip may be found both by observing the color fringes—blue outside the chip and reddish on the inside—due to the dispersion difference between the glass and the liquid (Christiansen effect), and by noting the difference between the colorless glass chip and the (frequently) yellow immersion liquid. When the edge of the chip has been brought into focus, sodium light is substituted for the white light.

   By focusing up or down and following the Becke line (Figure 5–1), the investigator will be able to ascertain whether the refractive index of the fragment is the same as that of the liquid, or, if there is a difference, to make an approximate assessment by which the next immersion liquid may be selected.

4. The first liquid may be removed with filter paper and the next liquid flowed under the cover slip; any surplus can be absorbed by the filter paper. It is easier, however, to use a fresh chip, particularly if the larger of the two glass samples (scene or suspect) is examined first. With a little experience, the investigator should obtain the refractive index of the average glass sample after trying three or four immersion liquids.

5. Repeat this process until the refractive index of the glass is between the closest two immersion mixtures.

6. Record the refractive index range for this piece of glass.

7. Repeat the entire process for the remaining samples.

8. Turn off the sodium vapor lamp.

9. Clean out all of the vials.

10. Clean up the area.

SELECTED SOURCES FOR ADDITIONAL INFORMATION

Almirall, J. R., Cole, M. D., Gettingby, G., and Furton, K. G., "Discrimination of glass sources using elemental composition and refractive index: development of predictive models," *Sci. & Just.*, 38 (2), (1998), 93.

Evett, I. W., and Lambert, J. A., "Further observations on glass evidence interpretation," *Sci. & Just.*, 35 (4), (1995), 283.

Koons, R. D., and Buscaglia, J., "The forensic significance of glass composition and refractive index measurements," *J. Forens. Sci.*, 44 (3), (1999), 496.

Walsh, K. A. J., Buckleton, J. S., and Triggs, C. M., "A practical example of the interpretation of glass evidence," *Sci. & Just.*, 36 (4), (1996), 213.

EXPERIMENT 5 Name _____

DATA SHEET Date _____

REFRACTIVE INDEX OF GLASS FRAGMENTS

Part A: The Becke Line Concept

1. Sodium chloride crystals

    Observations:

    Castor oil   Clove oil   Bromoform

    Conclusions:

2. Potassium chloride crystals

    Observations:

    Castor oil   Clove oil   Bromoform

    Conclusions:

Experiment 5

Part B: Refractive Index of Automobile Glass (Advanced)

a. Index of refraction of standard solutions and proportions used in making the standards

Index of Refraction	Drops of Castor Oil	Drops of Clove Oil
1.		
2.		
3.		
4.		
5.		
6.		
7.		
8.		
9.		
10.		
11.		

b. Index of refraction of glass samples

A. Suspect 1: _____

B. Suspect 2: _____

C. Suspect 3: _____

D. Scene: _____

c. Matches of glass fragments based on the index of refraction.

How certain are you that the fragments you have matched do have a common origin? Give your reasons.

Powder Residues on Fabrics

EXPERIMENT 6

It is not uncommon for law enforcement officers to encounter the use of firearms in criminal investigations. Among other things, investigators often need to know the distance a firearm was held from the victim at the time of discharge. Determination of the distance from a target at which a weapon is fired can only be made by comparing the powder residue pattern around a bullet hole to patterns made by the suspect weapon fired at varying distances from a test target. If the suspect weapon is not available, the examiner will try to estimate the muzzle-to-target distance by examining the bullet hole(s) present on the target. Such factors as the presence of tearing, singeing, or melting of the fabric; the presence of carbonaceous smoke around the hole (unburned and partially burned gunpowder on the fabric); and the presence of metal particles are used in estimating the muzzle-to-target distance.

Smokeless powders are comprised of nitrocellulose obtained from cotton or wood fibers that have been treated with a mixture of concentrated nitric acid and sulfuric acid. Smokeless powder is therefore rich in what are chemically referred to as **nitrates**. When smokeless powder burns or partially burns, as when a cartridge is fired, it will decompose to form what are called **nitrites**.

The presence of nitrites on a fabric can be very helpful to a criminalist who is interested in determining whether a hole in question was made by the passage of a bullet through the fabric. By establishing the presence of nitrites on the fabric, the criminalist can chemically show that the hole was made by a bullet. Furthermore, if a suspect weapon is available, comparing the developed nitrite distribution pattern to patterns obtained from firing the weapon at known distances can be a useful technique for determining the shooting distance from the target. Such information will help investigators decide whether a shooting case was possibly homicide, suicide, or an accident. The technique discussed is of particular value when the cloth is colored or a mix of colors and the gray powder patterns are not visible.

In Part A of this experiment the firing of a bullet on a target will be simulated by placing the chemical sodium nitrite on a cloth or paper unless actual cloth with test firings has been prepared. The nitrite particles are then transferred from the surface onto a chemically treated photographic paper that contains a mixture of p-nitroaniline, 2-naphthol, and magnesium sulfate. In the presence of these chemicals, the nitrite particles will react to form a red-colored dye.

CRIME SCENE

A hunter has found the body of a deceased male in a wooded area. The first examination indicates that he probably died of a heart attack. However, the coroner notices a few small holes in the victim's shirt that could have been made by a small-caliber slug; or, the holes may be just circular tears from tree limbs punching through the material. The wound hole from a small-caliber weapon sometimes closes over, and unless extreme care is taken, it may well be overlooked. Your job is to determine if any of the holes in the shirt are bullet holes.

EQUIPMENT

2	Forceps		Photographic paper (glossy), 8 sheets
1	Funnel, short stem	1	Sprayer, aerosol
1 pr	Goggles, safety	2	Towels, cloth, about 45 cm × 45 cm
1	Iron, electric		Towels, paper
1	Pencil, grease	2	Trays, photographic

Cloths containing one bullet hole and one hole not made by a bullet. These should be about 30 cm × 30 cm squares of colored, striped, or multicolor fabric.

Cloths containing bullet holes at 1, 2, and 4 ft. These should be white cloth about 30 cm × 30 cm for the knowns so the student can see the powder pattern other than the nitrite particles.

Cloth containing a bullet hole made at an unknown distance (the instructor may wish to use cloths treated with sodium nitrite in place of actual bullet holes).

REAGENTS

Acetic acid, 10% (v/v)

Buffer (1.9 g of sodium bitartrate and 1.5 g of tartaric acid in 100 mL of H_2O, pH 2.8)

Hydrochloric acid (HCl), 5% (v/v)

Lead salt solution, 0.01% (w/v)

Photographic hypo ($Na_2S_2O_3 \cdot 5H_2O$) 227 g/L

Sodium hydroxide, 10% (v/v).

Sodium nitrite, (0.6 g in 100 mL of water)

Solution containing p-nitroaniline, 2-naphthol, and magnesium sulfate (0.25% each in 1:1 aqueous alcohol)

Sodium rhodizonate. A fresh, saturated, aqueous solution must be prepared daily.

METHOD

PART A: BULLET HOLES IN FABRIC[*]

1. Ordinary glossy photographic paper is completely desensitized by placing it in a hypo bath for 5 minutes (four sheets will be necessary).

2. Wash off the hypo and dry the paper by placing it between paper towels.

3. Soak the photographic paper in a solution containing p-nitroaniline, 2-naphthol, and magnesium sulfate.

4. Dry the paper.

5. Place a clean cloth towel on a flat surface.

6. Place the photographic paper on the cloth, emulsion side up.

7. Place the test fabric (face down) on this paper.

8. Place another towel, moistened with 10% acetic acid, on top of this.

9. Cover with a dry towel.

10. Press the entire pack for 5 to 10 minutes with a warm electric iron.

11. Repeat steps 1 through 10 for each test cloth.

---

[*] Based on material obtained from Maiti, 1973; see the selected sources at the end of this experiment.

The prepared photographic paper, when examined, is found to have a number of red spots, which correspond to the position of the partially burned powder grains (nitrites).

This test is sensitive to burned and partially burned black and smokeless powder. A permanent representation of the powder residue is produced without altering or destroying the fabric of the bullet hole. If the garment is bloodstained, the photographic paper should be moistened with 10% sodium hydroxide, using a cotton swab. The nitrite particles will now appear as blue spots on a pale yellow background and will not be mistaken for blood.

PART B: SODIUM RHODIZONATE TEST FOR LEAD RESIDUES

The firing of the weapon will not only propel gun powder residues toward the target, but primer residues also leave the muzzle as a cloud of finely dispersed particles. These primer residues generally contain lead, barium, and antimony. These particles are capable of traveling for long distances (up to 10 ft). When they strike the target, they may adhere, becoming part of the visible residue pattern, or they may bounce off, leaving behind an invisible trace of primer residues. In addition to the primer residues, lead and antimony removed from the bullet surface by the bore of the weapon may be deposited on the target. Lead and antimony may also originate from the base of the bullet when it is pushed toward the target by the expanding gases in the barrel.

The sodium rhodizonate test is a sensitive test for many types of metals. By spraying the sodium rhodizonate solution around the area of a suspect bullet hole, a firearms examiner can detect the presence or absence of lead. At the present time, firearms examiners are experimenting with the possibility of using lead distribution patterns around a bullet hole as a means of determining the distance from which the bullet was fired. The colors developed with sodium rhodizonate are entirely dependent upon the metal present and the degree of acidity. At a pH of 3, a pink color is obtained with lead. The test can be made more specific by spraying with 5% hydrochloric acid. The hydrochloric acid spray changes the color of the product of the reaction of sodium rhodizonate and lead (lead rhodizonate) to blue. Apparently, this blue color is caused by the formation of a complex between lead rhodizonate and hydrochloric acid.

CRIME SCENE

A man has been found shot to death, with a gun in his hand. He had talked about suicide for several weeks, but was also a feisty fellow known to have more than one enemy. If he committed suicide, the powder pattern should show a firing distance of less than 2 feet. A murder might also show a distance of less than 2 feet, but if it is more, suicide is ruled out. Your job is to test his shirt for the powder pattern.

You will be given three pieces of fabric with bullet holes on them from distances of 1, 2, and 4 feet. You are to determine their powder patterns, compare these with the suspect's shirt, and make your own conclusions.

METHOD

A number of the test materials used in the experiment described in Part A have either been treated with a lead-containing solution or are actual bullet holes in cloth.

1. Repeat steps 1 through 10 from Part A. Spray each of the cloth samples with sodium rhodizonate solution.

2. Overspray each target with the buffer. What color develops?

3. Overspray each target with 5% hydrochloric acid. What color develops?

SELECTED SOURCES FOR ADDITIONAL INFORMATION

Basu, S., Boone, C. E., Denio, D. J., and Miazaga, R. A., "Fundamental studies of gunshot residue deposition by glue-lift," *J. Forens. Sci.*, 42 (4), (1997), 571. (Na- rhodizonate)

Brazeau, J., and Wong, R., "Analysis of gunshot residues on human tissues and clothing by x-ray microfluorescence," *J. Forens. Sci.*, 42 (3), 1997, 424.

Glattstein, B., Vinokurov, A., Levin, N., and Zeichner, A., "Improved method for shooting estimation-part I: Bullet holes in clothing items," *J. Forens. Sci.*, 45 (4), (2000), 801.

Glattstein, B., Zeichner, A., Vinokurov, A., and Shoshani, E., "Improved method for shooting distance determination-part II: Bullet holes in objects that cannot be processed in the laboratory," *J. Forens. Sci.*, 45 (5), (2000), 1000.

Maiti, P. C., "Powder patterns around bullet holes in blood stained articles," *J. Forens. Sci. Soc.*, 13, 1973, 197.

Schwartz, R. H., and Zona, C. A., "A recovery method for airborne gunshot residue retained in human nasal mucus," *J. Forens. Sci.*, 49 (4), (1995), 659.

Singer, R. L., Davis, D., and Houck, M. M., "A survey of gunshot residue analysis methods," *J. Forens. Sci.*, 41 (2), (1996), 195.

EXPERIMENT 6 Name _____

DATA SHEET Date _____

POWDER RESIDUE ON FABRICS

Part A: Bullet Holes in Fabric

1. Attach your patterns to this sheet of paper.

2. What is your conclusion and what is your reasoning?

Part B: Sodium Rhodizonate Test for Lead Residues

1. Attach your patterns to this sheet of paper.

2. Based on your test patterns, what do you think the limits of such a test would be with respect to firing distance?

EXPERIMENT 7

Shooting Reconstruction by iPhone*

INTRODUCTION

The widespread use and popularity of "smartphones" and the numerous "apps" available have opened up a new avenue for crime-scene reconstruction documentation. Several apps are particularly pertinent to trajectory analysis and other aspects of shooting-incident reconstruction. These apps will be utilized in this exercise. Although it should never be presumed that these techniques are destined to replace the traditional techniques/hardware of the shooting incident reconstructionist, they certainly provide a viable backup as well as offer some unique added capabilities.

In this exercise you will learn to use the iPhone™ app Real Tools™ by Bahn Tech (see Figure 7–4) to determine trajectory angles. Additionally, you will measure the diameter of a fired bullet.

MATERIALS

Smartphone (iPhone™ or other)
Real Tools™ application
Zero base trajectory protractor
Trajectory rod
Centering cones
Double wall panel with through and through bullet holes
Plumb bob
Ruler graduated in mm
Magnetic compass

METHOD

CALIBRATION

Prior to using any new technology, it is essential that verification of that technology be carried out using known, proven technology. The use of the various tools available in the Real Tools™ app is no different. Calibration of each tool will be necessary. Calibration can usually be accomplished by comparing results obtained for a like measurement using a reliable similar device.

Plumb bob—calibration of the electronic plumb bob may be simply accomplished by holding the phone alongside a traditional plumb bob to ensure that there is consistency.

GPS—calibration of the GPS tool may be accomplished by comparing the results obtained with those obtained using a dedicated GPS unit. Repeating this for two additional positions is advisable.

---

* Courtesy: Edward E. Hueske, Forensic Training & Consulting, LCC, Palestine, TX 75803, www.edhueske.com.

FIGURE 7-1 Calibration of the electronic protractor using a zero base trajectory protractor. *Dr. Edward E. Hueske, Forensic Training & Consulting, LLC*

Compass—comparing the electronic compass reading to that of a magnetic compass will provide calibration.

Dial calipers—by setting the calipers to a given series of values, say 6, 9, and 12 mm, and by measuring with a ruler graduated in mm, calibration may be accomplished.

Protractor/angle gauge—by placing a trajectory rod through the entry and exit holes of a double wall fixture and simultaneously measuring the angle with the electronic device and a zero base protractor, calibration may be achieved (Figure 7–1).

TRAJECTORY ANGLE MEASUREMENT

A bullet passing through a double wall structure allows the insertion of a trajectory rod such that, barring highly distorted entry or exit holes, the trajectory of the responsible bullet may be directly measured.

1. Obtain a trajectory rod and insert it through both the entry and exit holes. If the holes are oversized relative to the rod diameter, centering cones may be placed onto the rod.

2. Using an imaginary x, y coordinate system on the face of the outer surface, use one of the angle gauges in Real Tools to determine the elevation (x angular coordinate) as illustrated in Figure 7–2, and record your result.

3. Following the same procedure, determine the horizontal or azimuth angle (y angular coordinate) and record that result.

FIGURE 7-2 Using the electronic protractor in Real Tools™ to establish the horizontal (x angle). *Dr. Edward E. Hueske, Forensic Training & Consulting, LLC*

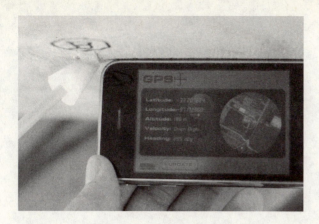

FIGURE 7–3 Using the GPS function to locate the bullet hole position. *Dr. Edward E. Hueske, Forensic Training & Consulting, LLC*

4. Using the GPS function, establish the location of the bullet hole you are working with (Figure 7–3).
5. Record the GPS coordinates for the location of the bullet hole.

EXPERIMENT 7   Name _____

DATA SHEET   Date _____

SHOOTING RECONSTRUCTION BY IPHONE

Part A: Trajectory Worksheet

Bullet hole identifier (number/letter) _____

x linear coordinate (inches) _____ y linear coordinate (inches) _____

x angular coordinate (degrees) _____ y angular coordinate (degrees) _____

GPS Latitude _____ GPS Longitude _____

Part B: Fired Bullet Measurement Worksheet

1. Obtain 2 fired bullet exemplars of different calibers.

2. Use the dial caliper function to measure the base diameters and record the results.

Bullet #1 cross-sectional diameter (mm) _____

Bullet #2 cross-sectional diameter (mm) _____

Questions

1. Why is calibration of the various tools necessary?

2. What advantages do you think the app tools offer for trajectory analysis?

Experiment 7

3. What disadvantages do you think may be involved in the use of app tools as opposed to traditional trajectory analysis tools?

4. What specific limitation is associated with using the GPS app at crime scenes?

5. What specific limitation(s) is/are associated with using the dial caliper app for measuring?

6. Which, if any, of the app tools would you say might actually replace traditional tools?

Instructor's Information

It is important to emphasize that the use of phone apps, for the most part, is not intended as a replacement for traditional equipment/methods of trajectory analysis. The intent is to make students aware of some useful adjuncts to more traditional equipment/methods.

Expected responses:

1. Without calibrating the various apps, there is no way to attest to their validity (i.e., precision and accuracy).
2. Apps offer ease of use due to compact size, availability, and low cost (Real Tools is $1.99; see Figure 7–4).
3. Apps present the difficulty of documentation (results obtained cannot be electronically stored, must be photographed/written down).

FIGURE 7-4 Overview of Real Tools™ appt. *Dr. Edward E. Hueske, Forensic Training & Consulting, LLC*

4. The GPS wind velocity reading obviously does not apply indoors.
5. The results are, at best, only an estimate due to the fact that visual positioning of the caliper is required rather than exact physical positioning.
6. The plumb bob app can be used to replace a traditional plumb bob.

EXPERIMENT 8

Satellite Imaging Lab*

INTRODUCTION

One of the most powerful and useful technologies available to the crime scene analyst and reconstructionist is satellite imaging. This allows ready access to aerial views as well as ground-level and 360-degree views. More important, this technology is available free online through MapQuest, Google Maps, and other sources.

In this exercise you will use Google Maps to locate two specific areas and demonstrate your proficiency with the technique by printing your results.

MATERIALS

Computer with Internet access
Printer

INSTRUCTIONS

1. Open Google Maps.
2. Click on the Pennsylvania map and go to East Pennsylvania, north of Philadelphia.
3. Type in "Dorney Park Road, Allentown, Pennsylvania".
4. Go northeast to the intersection of S Cedar Crest Boulevard and Hamilton Boulevard Bypass.
5. Click on "street view" and go north approximately 0.1 miles to locate the entrance to Cedar Crest College on the east side of Cedar Crest Boulevard.
6. Print the image of the west entrance to Cedar Crest College.
7. Now go back to the aerial map view and locate the intersection of Hamilton Boulevard and College Drive.
8. Click on "street view" and go northwest down College Drive approximately 500 feet to locate the entrance at South Quad Road.
9. Print the image of the South Quad Road entrance to Cedar Crest College.

---

* Courtesy: Edward E. Hueske, Forensic Training & Consulting, LCC, Palestine, TX 75803, www.edhueske.com.

QUESTIONS

1. What potential information does satellite imaging provide that could be useful in analyzing and reconstructing a crime?

2. What are some potential advantages of being able to access street views of scenes?

3. What are some potential disadvantages related to satellite imaging information as applied to crime-scene analysis and reconstruction?

4. Why is it essential to determine the date recorded for any images recovered for use in analyzing crime scenes?

5. Go online and look up "pictometry". What is pictometry?

6. What potential advantages do you think pictometry might have over the satellite imagery that is available at no cost (e.g., from Google, etc.)?

7. Can you think of any disadvantages of pictometry?

Attach the printouts of the two Cedar Crest College entrances to this sheet.

Instructor's Information

As an alternative to printing the results obtained, students may be instructed to sketch their results and turn the sketches in. By so doing, students without access to a printer are able to complete the exercise.

Expected responses:

The following responses to the questions posed would be expected. However, other responses may well be received and should be discussed as well.

1. Satellite imaging permits the analyst to see potential barriers and other obstacles that might limit view in some instances. Relative measurements are possible in spite of barriers.

2. It is not necessary to have to return to scenes in remote or dangerous locations when additional scene information is required.

60 Experiment 8

3. The images may not have been recorded at the same time of the year as the event under study (e.g. fall versus spring, etc.) resulting in differing visual conditions. The images cannot be magnified significantly without pixilation becoming a problem.

4. The date that a satellite image was recorded is pertinent to the authenticity of the scene conditions under study (i.e. when there is significant deviation in the date of a crime versus the date the scene image was recorded, the likelihood of changes having taken place increases).

5. Pictometry is a commercially available high resolution satellite imaging system that many large cities subscribe to for property tax evaluation purposes.

6. Pictometry, if available, allows for high magnification and subsequent high resolution detail views.

7. Pictometry is expensive and not available in all locales (particularly in small cities and towns).

EXPERIMENT 9

Blood Identification and Typing

Blood is a common form of physical evidence found at the scene of crimes involving physical violence. It may be present in pools, splatters, or stains. Blood should be looked for in burglaries as well. It is difficult for a burglar to break a window or force a door without getting scratched and thereby leaving a small amount of blood at the scene. The first analysis performed on this evidence is the determination of whether or not the stains are blood, and if so, whether they are of human origin. If blood is of nonhuman origin, it may be useful to know from what animal the blood originates. If the stains are of human origin, the analysis is then extended to the determination of blood group and other blood factors that can associate the blood with a particular person.

The fact that there is such a thing as a blood type was discovered in 1900 by Karl Landsteiner, who found that blood from one person would not always mix freely with blood from another person, but would sometimes clump or agglutinate.

He identified four types, which he named O, A, B, and AB. It has since been found that approximately 43 % of the population has O-type blood, 42% A, 12% B, and 3% AB. If a drop of blood is found at the scene of the crime, identification of its type may serve to screen out several suspects. Leone Lattes was the first to make use of blood groups in the courts of Italy in 1916. Blood typing was used in courts in England in 1922 and in the United States in the early 1930s.

In 1927 another system was discovered, the MN system. In this system approximately 30 % of the population is M, 22% N, and 48% MN.

In 1940 Alexander Weiner, working with rhesus monkeys, discovered a third system in which 85% of the population had a factor called Rh+; the 15% that did not have the factor were called Rh−. Since that time, other Rh factors have been discovered and divided into six groups: D, d, C, c, E, and e. This allows for a further 27 combinations. However, at the time of this writing, we do not yet have an antiserum for d, so there are only 18 usable combinations.

Many other substances have also been found in blood and are important for the discrimination of bloodstains; several of these are listed below.

1. Phosphoglucomutase (PGM): PGM-1, 58%; PGM-2, 6%; PGM 2-1, 36%

2. Adenylate kinase (AK): AK 1, 93%; AK 2-1, 7%

3. Adenosine deaminase (ADA): 1, 90%; 2-1, 10%; 2, 0.2%

4. Glucose-6-phosphate dehydrogenase (G-6-PD): B, 62%; BA, 25%; A, 12%

5. 6-Phosphogluconate dehydrogenase (6-PGD): A, 92%; AC, 8%; C, 0.2%

6. Erythrocyte acid phosphate (EAP): A, 13%; B, 35%; C, 0.2%; BA, 43%; CA, 3%

7. Esterase D (EsD): 1, 79%; 2-1, 19%; 2, 2%

8. Polymorphic proteins—Group Specific Component (Gc) and haptoglobins (Hp): Hp1, 14%; Hp2-1, 53%; Hp2, 32%

Let us see what value these factors can have for the forensic chemist. Before 1900, blood was just that—blood—and other than the fact that you could tell from an analysis of the blood spatter design that the attacker was wounded and perhaps where, blood could not be used to narrow the list of suspects. That has now changed dramatically.

Suppose that a bloodstain was found to be A, N, Hp-1, Rh−, PGM-2, and EAP-BA. What are the chances that a suspect would have this type?

$$1 \text{ per} \left(\frac{100}{42} \times \frac{100}{22} \times \frac{100}{14} \times \frac{100}{15} \times \frac{100}{6} \times \frac{100}{43} \right) = 1 \text{ per } 19,975$$

This can free a lot of innocent people and corroborate the guilt of a suspect.

If a few drops of fresh blood are available along with the apparatus and expertise to test the blood for all of the systems now known, it is possible to narrow the list of suspects to about 1 in 7,000,000. With the more recently discovered DNA probe technique (discussed in part in a later experiment), it is possible, at least theoretically, to identify 1 out of 10,000,000,000 people. Because there are only about 6,800,000,000 in the world, this makes modern blood typing an individual technique.

As noted, many systems of blood grouping can be used, but the one that we shall use in this exercise is the ABO system, and possibly the Rh system. Our purpose will be to determine whether a particular stain is blood or not, and if so, to type that blood by the ABO system. (The Rh factor will be determined at the option of the instructor.)

This exercise is performed on liquid blood, as the volume of sample will make it easier for you to do the determination. A later experiment deals with stains and will be easier to do after having gained experience from this one.

The determination of blood is best made by means of a preliminary color test. The most common test used for this purpose is the chemical phenolphthalein. This test is also known as the Kastle-Meyer color test. The Kastle-Meyer color test is based on the observation that blood hemoglobin possesses peroxidase-like activity. Peroxidases are enzymes that accelerate the oxidation of several classes of organic compounds by peroxides. When a bloodstain, phenolphthalein reagent, and hydrogen peroxide are mixed together, the blood's hemoglobin will cause the formation of a deep pink color. Field investigators have found Hemastix® strips to be a useful presumptive field test for blood. Like the Kastle-Meyer test, Hemastix® strips will react with peroxidases. Designed as a urine dipstick test for blood, the strip can be moistened with distilled water and placed in contact with a suspect bloodstain. The appearance of a green color is indicative of blood. Another approach is a Hematest tablet.

PART A: IS IT REALLY BLOOD?

Materials

> Bleach such as Clorox®
>
> Distilled water
>
> Denatured alcohol
>
> Hematest tablets (from any drug store)

Note: To be on the safe side, please wear disposable gloves when working with blood samples and place them in a biohazard bag for proper disposal when the lab is over. Everyone worries about AIDS, but hepatitis B is far more communicable.

To identify a stain as blood, we must know what kind of reaction is to be expected in a positive test. We do this by means of a Hematest tablet. Hemoglobin catalytically decomposes hydrogen peroxide or sodium peroxide with the liberation of oxygen. In an acid solution, oxygen acts on the o-tolidine found in a Hematest tablet to turn it into a blue-colored derivative. The reagents are all contained within the test tablet, except for the hemoglobin that catalyzes the reaction. This is contained within the bloodstain.

1. Place 1 drop of blood on a piece of filter paper and allow it to dry.

2. Obtain a Hematest tablet and break it up into four more or less equal parts.

3. Place one portion of the tablet in the center of the bloodstain. Put 1 drop of distilled water on the tablet, wait a few seconds, and place another drop of distilled water on the tablet, being certain that

the water flows down the sides of the tablet and onto the stain. Within a few seconds you will see a blue-green ring spreading out on the filter paper around the base of the tablet. This is a positive test that the stain is indeed blood. There are some other types of stains that will interfere and produce the same color as will blood, such as dry bleach residues and some plastics; therefore, the test is only presumptive, and a second test should always be made on an adjacent, unstained area to check for background interferences. This concept is called running a blank and, as a general rule in criminalistics, should always be done.

4. Now obtain four pieces of cloth that have stains on them and repeat this test for each. The scraps of cloth are numbered. If the test is positive, identify the stain on the cloth as blood, and include the number of the scrap on the data sheet. If the test is negative, record the stain as being of an origin other than blood, along with its identification number. Be sure to run a blank. Repeat this test for each of the other samples of stain on the cloth. Record all identification numbers and results on the data sheet. This test is often done at the crime scene to determine whether a stain is blood and therefore evidence to be collected.

PART B: PRESUMPTIVE TESTING WITH KASTLE-MEYER REAGENT

Safety

Clothing protection, eye protection, chemicals

Supplies

(3) 25-mL beakers or other small vessel

Chicken blood or liver homogenate (1:3, in sterile water)

Single-ended cotton swabs

A piece of Styrofoam, to use as a swab stand

Sterile water in a dropper bottle

Phenolphthalein solution in a dropper bottle (Premixed solution available from www.Forensicssource.com)

Hydrogen peroxide solution (3%) in a dropper bottle

"Evidence"—stains on fabric or paper, provided by your instructor (substances like liver homogenate, ketchup, shoe polish, lipstick). Those stains not visible when dry should be circled in pencil.

Preparing Your Reagents

To 200 mL distilled water, add 4 g phenolphthalein, 40 g potassium hydroxide, and 20 g zinc dust. Boil the mixture until the pink coloration has almost completely disappeared. Cool to room temperature and store this solution in a dark amber bottle with some zinc powder added (to keep the solution in the reduced form) and store in a refrigerator. This can keep for over a year. Test the working solution with a known blood sample prior to reusing the stock solution. Store at 4°C. Before use, dilute an aliquot of stock solution with an equal volume of ethyl alcohol.

Working Solution

Phenolphthalein stock solution	10 ml
Ethanol	40 ml

Pour this solution into small amber bottles for student use.

Alternately, commercially prepared presumptive blood testing reagents and kits can be purchased from www.Forensicssource.com.

Procedure

NOTE: When applying a drop of any reagent to the cotton tip of a swab, NEVER TOUCH THE DROPPER TO THE SWAB! Physical contact between the swab and the dropper will cause contamination. This will contaminate the reagent itself when you reinsert the dropper into the bottle.

TESTING YOUR REAGENTS

1. Place two swabs on your swab stand by poking the free end of the swab down into the foam block. Place them approximately 3 inches apart
2. Apply 1 drop of liver homogenate to swab #1. This is your positive control.
3. Apply 1 drop sterile water to swab #2. This is your negative control.
4. Apply 1 drop hydrogen peroxide to each swab.
5. Apply 1 drop phenolphthalein solution to each swab.
6. Your positive control should turn pink. Any future analysis that displays this result is considered to be a positive presumptive identification of blood.
7. Your negative control should not show ANY change. Any future analysis that displays this result is considered to be a negative test for blood. If your negative control turns pink, even a little, alert your instructor and/or ask for new reagents and swabs.
8. Good practice dictates that a negative control should be included with every test batch.

TESTING YOUR EVIDENCE

1. Label the "evidence" you have been assigned. Each item should receive a number.
2. Work with only one item at a time. Do not allow the items to touch one another. Also, do not stand or lean over a piece of evidence while you are working. Reagents can drip onto it and compromise your analysis!
3. Prepare two swabs by moistening the tip of each with one drop of sterile water.
4. Set one swab aside as your negative control.
5. Roll the other swab over the stain. If you have an item with a circle marked on it, you should swab the center of the circle.
6. Apply a drop of hydrogen peroxide to each swab. Do you see a color change?
7. Apply a drop of phenolphthalein to each swab. Do you see a color change?
8. Record your findings in your notebook.
9. Repeat this process for each piece of "evidence."

PART C: PRESUMPTIVE TESTING WITH HEMASTIX®

Safety

Clothing protection

Supplies

Hemastix®, available from local pharmacy
Plain wood toothpicks (not dyed)
Sterile water in a dropper bottle

Chicken blood or liver homogenate (1:3, in sterile water)

"Evidence"—stains on fabric or paper, provided by your instructor (substances like liver homogenate, ketchup, shoe polish, and lipstick). Those stains not visible when dry should be circled in pencil.

Procedure
TESTING YOUR REAGENTS

1. Remove two Hemastix® test strips from the container without touching the spongy pad on the end. Place them on your bench with the pad facing up.
2. Apply 1 drop of sterile water to the pad of each strip. Note: The end of the dropper should not make contact with the test strip! The test pad should remain yellow in color.
3. Set aside one of the two strips. This is your negative control.
4. Your negative control should not show ANY change. Any future analysis that displays this result is considered to be a negative test for blood. (If your negative control turns greenish, even a little, alert your instructor and/or ask for new supplies.)
5. Apply 1 drop liver homogenate to the second strip. This is your positive control.
6. The spongy pad on your positive control should turn green. Any future analysis that displays this result is considered to be a positive presumptive identification of blood. Remember, these test strips produce this same response to any sample containing peroxidase, for example, potato juice and horseradish, so a green color change is NOT definitive proof of the presence of blood!
7. Good practice dictates that a negative control should be included with every test batch.

TESTING YOUR EVIDENCE

1. Label the "evidence" you have been assigned. Each item should receive a number.
2. Work with only one item at a time. Do not allow the items to touch one another.
3. Prepare two test strips by moistening the pad on each with one drop of sterile water.
4. Set one strip aside as your negative control.
5. Scratch the end of a clean toothpick over the stain. If you have an item with a circle marked on it, you should take a sample from the center of the circle.
6. Touch the tip of the toothpick to the pad of the second test strip. Do you see a color change?
7. Record your findings in your notebook.
8. Repeat this process for each piece of "evidence."

PART D: CONFIRMATION FOR BLOOD

Blood contains hemoglobin. Forensic scientists have utilized a microscopic crystal with Takayma reagent to confirm the presence of hemoglobin upon completion of a presumptive test for blood.

Equipment

    White lab paper
    Gloves
    One known blood control (positive control)

A bloodstained swatch
Forceps
Glass slides
Glass cover slips
Microscope
Small electric hot plate

Chemicals

Takayama Reagent

Sodium hydroxide (10% v/v)	5 ml
Pyridine	5 ml
Glucose (5 gm/50 ml distilled water)	5 ml
Distilled water	16 ml

Procedure

1. Set the hot plate to the lowest setting
2. Place one bloodstained fiber on a microscope slide and add a cover slip.
3. Let 2 drops of the reagent flow under the cover slip and come into contact with the fiber. Avoid air bubbles.
4. Set the slide on the hot plate; gently heat the slide until bubbles begin to form under the cover slip. Do not overheat. Remove the slide carefully so as not to burn your fingers.
5. Microscopic examination will reveal hematin crystals if positive for blood.
6. Place the slide on the microscope stage and use the lowest objective lens to focus on the slide. When a reddish area is seen, increase the magnification to the next highest lens.
7. Look for dark red/brown coarse feather crystals. The presence of these confirms that blood is present.
8. Record your results.

PART E: INCOMPATIBILITY RELATIONSHIPS IN THE ABO SYSTEM

Equipment

1 pr Gloves, rubber or plastic
1 pr Goggles, safety
    Microlance, sterile, disposable
    (buy individually prepackaged)
1 Brush, test tube
2 Bulbs for disposable pipets
    Cover glasses
    Filter paper squares, 2 × 2 cm
1 Rack, test tube, for 10-cm test tubes
    Wood splints (toothpicks serve well)
1 Microscope (100×)
    Microscope slides
1 Pencil, grease
    Pipets, disposable

Unknown blood samples (from students or from a hospital blood bank)

Known A, B, O, and AB blood samples (get outdated blood either from a hospital or the closest Red Cross blood bank; keep refrigerated)

Pieces of cloth stained with various red to brown materials (e.g., paint, shoe polish, ketchup)

Anti-A antiserum (get outdated material from a hospital)

Anti-B antiserum (get outdated material from a hospital)

Anti-D antiserum, for Rh+ or Rh− (get outdated material from a hospital)

Definitions

Agglutination—the clumping together of blood cells.

Agglutinin—an antibody in plasma that promotes agglutination.

Agglutinogen—a substance in red blood cells that acts as an antigen and incites the production of agglutinin.

Antibody—a substance in blood that reacts with a specific antigen, causing blood cells to clump together.

Antigen—a substance that incites the formation of antibodies.

Hemoglobin—the oxygen-carrying coloring matter of red blood cells.

Plasma—the colorless fluid of the blood.

Serum—the clear yellowish liquid part of blood after the fibrin and corpuscles have been removed.

Table 9–1 shows the relationship between different blood groups in the ABO system. Whole blood can be separated into serum and red blood cells. Mixing serum or whole blood from donors of one blood type with red blood cells or whole blood from an individual of a different type may result in an incompatibility reaction. For instance, when serum or whole blood from a type A individual is mixed with red blood cells or whole blood cells from a type B individual, the red blood cells clump together, or agglutinate. This reaction occurs because type A blood contains anti-B antibodies. These antibodies combine with B antigens on the red blood cells to cause agglutination. This is shown in Figure 9–1.

The agglutination takes place because the type-A serum contains substances known as anti-B antibodies, which react with materials called type-B antigens present on the surface of type-B blood cells. This reaction between antigen and antibody causes the red blood cells to stick to each other, as shown in Figure 9–1. Determinations of blood groups of the ABO system are rapid and simple. The type is readily determined by adding a known commercial antiserum (antibodies) to the blood and looking for the presence or absence of agglutination.

This section deals with the typing of blood by use of the ABO system.

TABLE 9–1	General Summary of Incompatibility Relationships for the Blood Group	
Blood Groups	**Antigens on Red Blood Cells**	**Antibodies in Serums**
A	A	Anti-B
B	B	Anti-A
AB	A and B	Neither anti-A or anti-B
O	Neither A nor B	Anti-A and anti-B

FIGURE 9–1 Schematic diagram of agglutination.

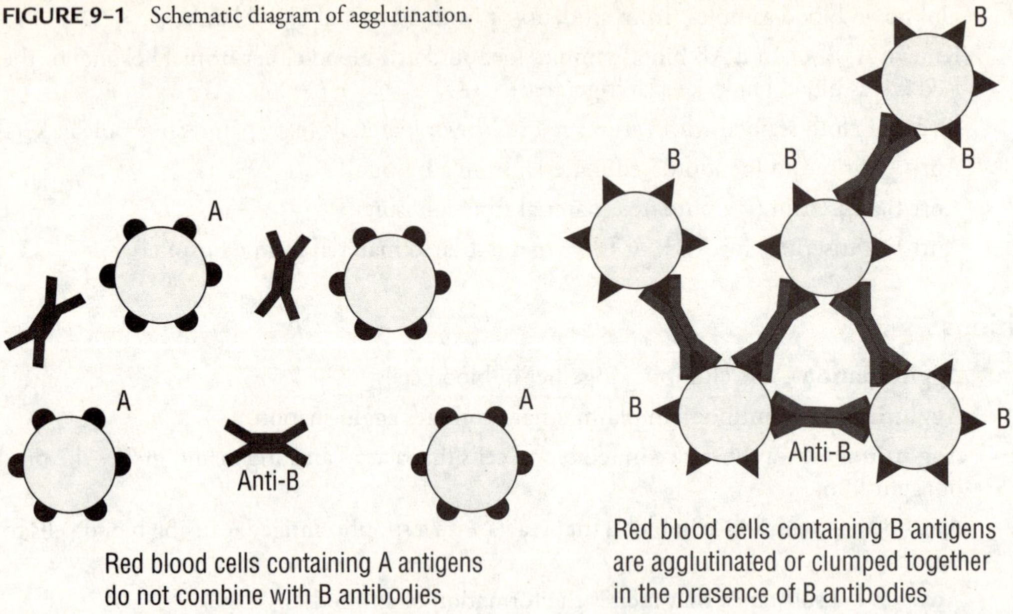

Red blood cells containing A antigens do not combine with B antibodies

Red blood cells containing B antigens are agglutinated or clumped together in the presence of B antibodies

Procedure

1. Obtain a glass microscope slide and a grease pencil.
2. Mark off the slide into three equal parts, as shown in Figure 9–2.
3. Label the three sections A, B, and D, respectively, from left to right (D is for Rh+ or Rh−).
4. Obtain a test tube with a labeled blood sample in it, and record the number of the sample on the data sheet.
5. Place 1 small drop of the blood sample on each of the three sections of the slide using a disposable pipet.
6. Dispose of the pipet in a waste container filled with 10% bleach solution.
7. Spread out the drop with a wooden splint or toothpick.
8. Take the small bottles of antisera and add 1 drop of antiserum A to the drop of blood in the section of the slide labeled A, 1 drop of antiserum B to the section B drop of blood, and 1 drop of antiserum D to the section D drop of blood.
9. Use a small wood splint to stir and mix the drops, being careful to avoid contaminating one section with the next. Use a clean wood splint for each section.
10. After mixing, look at the drops. If agglutination has occurred, you will see small specks or dots in the drop. If not, it will be clear.
11. Place the slide on the stage of a microscope, and examine each drop for agglutination.
12. Sketch the appearance of agglutinated red blood cells and non-agglutinated red blood cells in the spaces labeled on the data sheet. It is possible that the blood sample you have selected does not show one or the other of these states. If it does not, complete the sketching when you have observed a drop that does show the other state.
13. Repeat step 12 with three other labeled blood samples, recording all results on the data sheet.
14. Repeat the typing procedure for at least two unknown samples of blood. Be sure to record the identification number for each sample of blood that you work with.

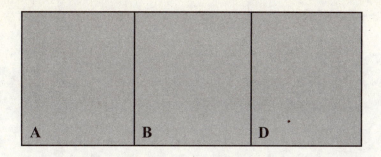

FIGURE 9–2 Preparation for A and B blood typing.

15. Optional: Type your own blood. With a sterile hemostat, puncture the tip of your middle finger. (Caution: Always cleanse the tip of your finger with 70% alcohol before and after making the puncture.) Place a drop of blood in each of three sections of a fresh slide. Immediately cover the puncture with a bandage and put on disposable gloves.

16. Perform steps 7 through 11.

17. If you have had your blood typed before, how do your results compare?

18. When you have finished typing the blood samples, record the results and return the tubes, uncontaminated, so that someone else may use them.

    NOTE: When you clean up the area, rinse with bleach anything that you are going to save that has come in contact with blood. Hepatitis is more communicable than AIDS, so we are taking no chances in either case.

19. Clean all of the slides you have used, first with denatured alcohol, next with soap and water, then bleach, and, finally, rinse them with distilled water, wipe them dry, and return them to the box.

20. If syringes were used, rinse them with bleach and then with distilled water.

21. Be certain to return all other materials that you have used, and clean up your bench area.

22. Complete the data sheet, answer all questions, and hand in to your instructor.

SELECTED SOURCES FOR ADDITIONAL INFORMATION

Espinoza, E.O., Kirms, M.A., and Filipek, M.S., "Identification and quantitation of sources from hemoglobin of blood and blood mixtures by HPLC," *J. Forens. Sci.*, 41 (5), (1996), 804.

Hulse-Smith, L., Mehdizadeh, N.Z., and Chandra, S., "Deducing drop size and impact velocity from circular bloodstains," *J. Forens. Sci.*, 50 (1), (2005), 54.

Liechti-Galliti, S., and Neeser, D., "Efficient and reliable PCR-based detection of the ABO blood group alleles: Genotyping on stamps and other biological evidence samples," *J. Forens. Sci.*, 41 (4), (1996), 653.

Mizuno, Natsuko, Ohmori, T., Sekiguchi, K., Kato, T., Fujii, T., Fujii, K., Shiraishi, T., Kasai, K., and Sato, H., "Alleles responsible for ABO phenotype-genotype discrepancy and alleles in individuals with a weak expression of A or B antigens," *J. Forens. Sci.*, 49 (1), (2004), 21.

Noda, H., Yokota, M., Tatsumi, S., and Sugiyama, S., "Determination of ABO blood grouping from human oral squamus epithelium by the highly sensitive immune histochemical staining method ENVISION+," *J. Forens. Sci.*, 47 (2), (2002), 350.

Raymond, M.A., Smith, E.R., and Liesegang, J., "The physical properties of blood: Forensic considerations," *Sci. & Just.*, 36 (3), (1996), 153.

Roy, R., "Concentration of urine samples by three different procedures: ABO typing from the concentrated urine samples," *J. Forens. Sci.*, 35 (5), (1990), 1133.

EXPERIMENT 9 Name _____

DATA SHEET Date _____

BLOOD IDENTIFICATION AND TYPING

1. Make a sketch of the bloodstained filter paper with a positive reaction to the Hematest tablet.

2. Identification of stains as blood (positive or negative).

   Cloth sample ID   **Test Result**

   _____   _____

   _____   _____

   _____   _____

   _____   _____

3. Blood typing (known samples): + indicates agglutination; − indicates no agglutination.

Blood type	Antiserum A	Antiserum B	Antiserum D
_____	_____	_____	_____
_____	_____	_____	_____

Experiment 9

4. Appearance of agglutinated and non-agglutinated red blood cells.

Agglutinated	Non-agglutinated

5. Blood typing (unknown samples)

Sample No.	Antiserum A	Antiserum B	Antiserum D	Blood type
_____	_____	_____	_____	_____
_____	_____	_____	_____	_____
_____	_____	_____	_____	_____

Questions

1. The ABO blood typing was quite easily performed on the volume of blood used in this exercise. Do you feel that it could be done as easily on a very small volume by use of a microscope? What difficulties can you foresee?

2. How do you suppose one would go about typing a dried bloodstain?

3. (One to think about.) Do animals have different blood types within a certain species (other than humans, who are also of the animal kingdom)?

EXPERIMENT 10

Fingerprinting

Fingerprints are a very common form of physical evidence. It requires considerable expertise in the area of fingerprinting to be able to accurately classify prints and match prints with each other. If a suspect's fingerprints match those found at a crime scene, this is highly conclusive proof of a link between the two.

In this experiment you will not attempt to classify fingerprints. Rather, you will investigate the methods used in developing and lifting latent fingerprints from a number of objects made of a variety of materials. You will also try to match the prints with inked prints. Chemical methods used to make fingerprints visible will be covered in Experiment 11.

Latent prints are those invisible prints left on an object by a person. These must be developed through the use of dusting powder or a chemical solution. **Inked prints** are those taken directly from a person's fingers through the use of an ink pad or block.

The origin of the use of fingerprints is lost in history, although it is known that the Chinese knew of and used fingerprints before the birth of Christ. In 1886, a Scottish physician, Henry Fauld, first published the view that fingerprints could be used for identifying individuals. We owe the beginnings of our present system to Sir Francis Galton in the 1880s. Sir Edward Richard Henry developed a simplified system for classifying fingerprints, which was adopted by Scotland Yard in 1901.

There are a number of basic fingerprint patterns (arches, loops, whorls). The fingers on a person's hand may contain a number of patterns. These patterns are shown in Figure 10–1. You should make yourself familiar with the characteristic appearance of each of the patterns, as you will be making comparisons with these patterns later in this exercise.

The tips of a person's fingers have small **friction ridges** on them. Along the ridges are small pores that secrete salt (NaCl), water, and proteins. It is these substances, along with oil, that may be picked up by touching the hairy portions of the body and that will be deposited on objects that come in contact with the surface of our fingers.

Usually, burglaries and other crimes are committed during times when a building or room is dark. In feeling his or her way around an unfamiliar setting, the person committing the crime may touch several objects. Clear, latent prints are then left in many places. It requires some time to dust and lift these prints. An experienced person is required for this task, as a very good print may be ruined by a poor dusting technique.

There are a variety of fingerprint dusting powders. The choice of powder color depends to a large extent on the color of the object being investigated for prints. We will make use of two colors of dusting powder: gray for use on dark-colored objects and black for use on light-colored objects, as well as anthracene for multicolored objects.

One formula for black powder is 88% MnO_2, 14.75% graphite, and 0.2% aluminum. Aluminum is a good sticking agent. Instructions for the use of these powders will be given later.

FIGURE 10–1 Fingerprint patterns.

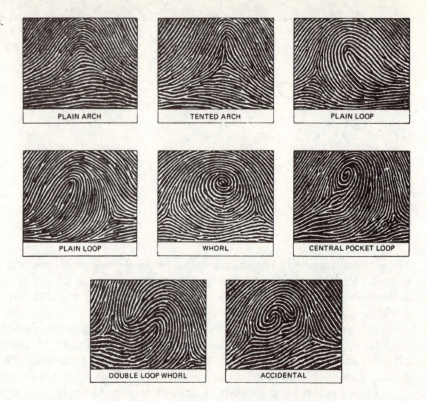

Latent prints are developed by powders and lifted from the object by use of transparent tape, hinged lifters, rubber lifters, and KromeKote paper. Lifters are available with black, white, or transparent backgrounds. One uses black lifters with gray powder and white lifters with black powder. Rubber lifters produce a negative print; that is, the print is the reverse of an inked print from a person's finger. The print on the lifter is photographed, the negative reversed, and a positive print made from it. KromeKote paper has been found useful to lift fingerprints from sweaty or oily surfaces such as skin.

The transparent tape is basically a wide, clear adhesive tape. When pressed against the powder, the print is transferred to the adhesive surface of the tape. The tape is now placed on a paper whose color will provide a suitable contrast with the print. The transparent tape also provides an immediate positive print. You will use both transparent tape and hinge lifters in this experiment.

The hinged lifter consists of a plastic, adhesive-backed sheet attached to a colored cardboard. When the examiner is ready to lift the print, a black or white lifter is selected. (This will be determined by the color of the powder used.) The backing is removed from the plastic sheet, exposing the adhesive. The plastic sheet is now pressed against the developed print, allowing the print to be picked off of the surface. The plastic sheet is then pressed against the colored cardboard. Unlike with the rubber lifter, a positive print is immediately obtained.

You may not be able to obtain really clear latent-print development in this exercise, and perhaps this will serve to illustrate to you the importance of technique in this operation. Practice is very important.

You will develop a few of your own latent prints in the beginning of this exercise. If you should find that your skin is quite dry and does not deposit prints very well, this can be remedied. Handling paper dries the skin very quickly. If this is the case, rub your fingers along the side of your nose to pick up some skin oil, or run your fingers through your hair, which will accomplish the same purpose. Good prints will usually result if this is done.

We will not use a crime scene in this experiment. Instead, you will use your own fingerprints in the first portion of your work, and those of other members of the class in the second portion.

Fingerprinting

EQUIPMENT

- Black backing cards (smooth)
- 4 Brushes, fingerprint
- Dark-colored glass or ceramic tiles
- Fingerprint cards, FBI type
- 1 Forceps
- 1 pr Goggles, safety
- 1 Hand magnifying lens (10 × or stronger)
- Lifters, hinged, 1½ × 2 inches, black, white, and transparent
- Light-colored glass or ceramic tiles
- 1 Plate, glass, 15 × 15 × 0.5 cm
- 1 Roller, 1.5 cm dia × 10 cm long
- 1 pr Scissors
- 2 Towels, cloth
- Transparent bookbinding tape in a dispenser
- UV (ultraviolet) lamp (Mineralite works well)
- White backing cards (smooth)

MATERIALS

- Anthracene, powdered
- Black fingerprint dusting powder
- Gray fingerprint dusting powder
- Ink, black, paste, water soluble
- Methanol

METHOD

PART A: MAKING A LATENT FINGERPRINT VISIBLE

1. Pick out some glass, metal, or plastic object in the laboratory that has a hard, smooth surface and is not multicolored.

2. Place one of your fingers firmly on the object. If your finger is dry, rub it along the side of your nose or run your fingers through your hair to pick up some oil.

3. Choose a fingerprint dusting powder of contrasting color.

4. Obtain the brush that is used for that color of powder. (Do not interchange the brushes, as you will obtain poorly developed latent prints owing to the mixture of dusting powers.)

5. Tap the handle of the brush or twirl the brush between the fingers to remove excess powder from the bristles from previous use.

6. Place some of the dusting powder in the lid or on a piece of paper, and dip the tip of the bristles of the brush in the dusting powder. **It is poor technique to have the powder up in the center of the bristles**, as one is unable to control the amount of powder deposited on the surface to be dusted and can easily ruin very clearly defined latent prints.

7. Using a circular, sweeping motion, and just grazing the surface, brush across the surface until you see the print beginning to appear. Concentrate your brushing on the exposed fingerprint, taking care to continue to brush lightly. If necessary, pick up additional dusting powder, using the same steps as you did before. Once the ridges appear, the motion of the brush should follow the direction of the ridge flow. When the print is clearly developed, stop brushing. Further development may easily destroy the print.

8. Carefully remove any excess powder with a clean brush.

PART B: LIFTING A LATENT PRINT

Two different methods will be done: transparent tape and hinged lifters.

Transparent Tape

1. Pick up the roll of transparent bookbinding tape and with a smooth motion pull off approximately 6–7 cm from the roll. Do not cut the tape from the roll yet.

2. Place the free end of the tape about 6 cm from the top of the developed print. Cover the print with the tape by smoothing the tape over the print with your finger, beginning from the free end and working slowly over the print. **Do not simply lay the tape over the print!** Air bubbles under the tape will partially ruin the lifted fingerprint—hence the necessity for slow, careful smoothing of the tape over the print.

3. After the tape completely covers the print, and extends approximately 1 cm past it, use the roll of tape as a handle, and lift the tape with the developed print smoothly from the surface in one continuous, unbroken motion. This will prevent distortion of the print.

4. Place the free end of the tape on a backing card of contrasting color to the dusting powder used. Repeat the laying-down, smoothing operation to eliminate any air bubbles, as you did previously, until the print is taped to the backing card.

5. Cut the tape from the roll, trim any excess tape from the card, and label it for future use. Paste the card onto the data sheet.

6. Record the object from which the print was taken, your initials, and the date on the backing card.

Hinged Lifters

The directions that follow are from the Sirchie Laboratories.

7. Repeat the developing and lifting of prints from one of the objects on the lab bench that has a different color than the one you just did. Make use of the opposite-colored dusting powder. Use a hinged lifter to remove the print from the surface.

8. Open the hinged lifter so that the arrow points to the upper right. The arrow and printing are on the plastic cover.

9. Using your thumb and forefinger, peel off the transparent cover, starting at the upper-right corner to where the arrow points. The plastic cover with printing and the arrow is then thrown away. The adhesive sheet is now exposed.

10. The tacky side of the lifter is then carefully placed over the latent powdered image or prints. Rub the plastic sheet lightly, and then lift off the powdered print. Note that the A is facing you when lifting the latent print.

11. The lifted print is then covered with the hinged cover, and is thus protected from scratches or dirt.

    The best way to cover a latent print after being lifted is to place the lifter on its back (with the adhesive side facing up), then form a curl in the hinged cover and roll on the cover.

12. The lifted print is now permanently sealed. Keep the star facing you or facing up, and the latent print is in its positive position, just as it was found on a surface.

    Keep in mind that the fingerprint obtained will be the mirror image of the standard inked fingerprint impression on file cards. The mirror image can be reversed by photographing the print and using appropriate darkroom techniques. If the print is sent to an outside agency for comparison without reversing the image, an explanation should accompany the print to prevent a technician who is unaware of the circumstances from having difficulty identifying the print.

PART C: FLUORESCENT DUSTING POWDER (ADVANCED)

There are times when you suspect the presence of a print on a multicolored object and the question arises as to what type of dusting powder to use. One approach is to use a fluorescent compound such as anthracene. The latent print is dusted the same as before, but it is observed under ultraviolet radiation, which causes the print to produce a purple fluorescence.

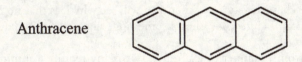

1. Place a fingerprint on a multicolored object so that the print covers at least two colors.
2. Dust the print with fine anthracene powder. If the powder does not stick well, it may be mixed with 1% Aluminum dust. The powder should go through a 100-mesh screen.
3. Go into a darkroom and expose the print to UV radiation from a Mineral light or other UV source. The print should glow purple.
4. Place a small amount of the anthracene powder on your fingers and look at them under the UV lamp.
5. Wash your hands and repeat the process.
6. What did you observe?

PART D: OBTAINING AN INKED PRINT

You will now obtain inked prints from the hand of another person. Always stand at the subject's left, whether you are rolling the left- or the right-hand fingers. The subject should stand at forearm's length from the edge of the bench and should be slightly behind you. In rolling the fingers of the right hand, the right thumb should be rolled inward, from right to left and the other four fingers rolled outward, from left to right. This procedure is reversed for the left hand.

1. Obtain a tube of black paste ink, a flat glass plate, an ink roller, fingerprint card, and a classmate. If a fingerprint card is not available use the data sheet.
2. Place about a 1-cm strip of ink in the center of the glass plate. Roll smooth and even with the roller. **Remember, more prints are ruined from too much ink than from too little.**
3. Lay the fingerprint card so that you can easily transfer a print to it.
4. Hold the subject's hand in your left hand, with all of the subject's fingers curled except the one you are inking and recording on the card. Grasp the extended finger of the subject with your right thumb and index finger. Roll the subject's finger on the inked surface, from nail to nail, keeping the finger flat on the plate from the first joint to the tip.
5. Roll the inked finger on the card as previously instructed. Use gentle pressure in rolling the finger to avoid smearing the ink.
6. Roll the ink on the glass again, or place the next finger on an unused spot.
7. Repeat this procedure for all of the subject's fingers on both hands. At the end of a roll, lift the finger upward to prevent smudging of the edge of the print.
8. Have the subject whom you used record the inked prints of your fingers.
9. Clean your fingers by wiping them with a towel moistened with methanol.
10. Referring to Figure 10–1, assign fingerprint patterns to each of your inked prints.

PART E: MATCHING PRINTS

In this exercise you will attempt to match the prints on an object with the prints of a member of the class. There are several glass, metal, and plastic objects on the lab bench. Each is mounted on a piece of Masonite or plywood and held in place by a piece of masking tape over the top. This is the way an object should be transported to the laboratory. It allows you to pick up the object without adding additional prints, and the tape over the top touches very little of the object.

What really makes one fingerprint different from another? You must look closely for the fine structure of the ridges or their ridge characteristics and then you will see why it is that no two fingerprints have ever been found that are identical. Figure 10–2 shows some ridge characteristics that you should look for in a fingerprint.

Requirements vary from examiner to examiner, but many require a minimum of 8 to 10 points of similarity between two prints before they will testify that the prints are identical.

In this part of the experiment you will try to match a print with three others. (It would require a great deal of time to match the prints on an object with those of a class member if you had to work with the class as a group.) Your laboratory instructor has collected fingerprints on various objects from members of the chemistry department or this class; these have been divided into groups of three. You will work with the inked prints of the three members of the group to which you are assigned.

1. Develop and lift the fingerprints from the object with dusting powder and transparent tape.

2. Fix the tape with the lifted print to the contrasting-color backing card.

3. Use a magnifying hand lens to examine the prints carefully, and record any identifying characteristics you may find.

4. Examine the inked prints, and match the sample prints with one of them if you possibly can.

5. Record your results on the data sheet.

   Do you now see why a classification system is necessary? The FBI has about 700,000,000 prints, and the new computer-enhanced pattern recognition programs can narrow these down to just a few in less than 15 minutes. You will learn the rudiments of the classification system in your lecture.

6. Referring to the fingerprint pattern chart (Figure 10–1), determine the various patterns of your own prints.

7. Record this information on the data sheet.

8. Look for identifying characteristics common to your own inked prints and the latent prints you have developed from your own fingers.

9. Record these characteristics also.

10. Complete all recorded information required on the data sheet and tape your developed latent prints and inked prints in the proper spaces. After answering all the questions, give this material to your laboratory instructor.

11. You are finished with the laboratory portion of this exercise. Clean and put away all materials used.

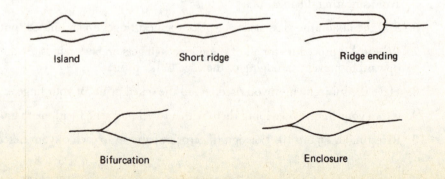

FIGURE 10–2 Five structure characteristics of ridges.

SELECTED SOURCES FOR ADDITIONAL INFORMATION

Allred, C.E., Lin, T., and Menzel, E.R., "Lipid specific latent fingerprint detection: fingerprints on currency," *J. Forens. Sci.*, 42 (6), (1997), 997.

Asano, K.G., Bayne, C.K., Horseman, K.M., and Buckhanan, M.V., "Chemical composition of fingerprints for gender determination," *J. Forens. Sci.*, 47 (4), (2002), 374.

Azoury, M., Cohen, D., Himberg, K., Qvintus-Leino, P., Saari, T., and Almog, J., "Fingerprint detection on counterfeit US$ banknotes: The importance of preliminary paper examination," *J. Forens. Sci.*, 49 (5), (2004), 1015.

Bentson, R.K., Brown, J.K., Dinsmore, A., Harvey, K.K., and Kee, T.G., "Post firing visualization of fingerprints on spent cartridge cases," *Science and Justice*, 36 (1), (1996), 3.

Dixon, K., Wu, J., Brennan, R.W., and Goldsmith, P., "Development of a finger printing device for use on a mobile robot," *J. Forens. Sci.*, 49 (2), (2004), 290.

Geller, B., Almog, J., Margot, P., and Springer, E., "A chronological review of fingerprint forgery," *J. Forens. Sci.*, 44 (5), (1999), 963.

Geller, B., Almog, J., and Margot, P., "Fingerprint forgery: A survey," *J. Forens. Sci.*, 46 (3), 2001, 731.

Kahana, T., Grande, A., Tancredi, D.M., Penaluev, J., and Hiss, J., "Fingerprinting the deceased: traditional and new techniques," *J. Forens. Sci.*, 46 (4), (2001), 908.

Knowles, R., "The new (non-numeric) fingerprint evidence standard," *Sci. & Just.*, 40 (2), (2000), 120.

Laporte, Gerald M., and Ramotowski, R.S., "The effects of latent print processing on questioned documents produced by office machine systems utilizing inkjet technology and toner," *J. Forens. Sci.*, 48 (3), (2003), 658.

Migron, Y., Hocherman, G., Springer, E., Almog, J., and Mandler, D., "Visualization of sebaceous fingerprints on fired cartridge cases: a laboratory study," *J. Forens. Sci.*, 43 (3), (1998), 543.

Schmidt, C.W., Nawrocki, S.P., Williamson, M.A., and Marlin, D.C., "Obtaining fingerprints from mummified fingers: A method for tissue rehydration adopted from the archeological literature," *J. Forens. Sci.*, 45 (4), (2000), 874.

Schwartz, L., and Frerichs, I., "Advanced solvent-free application of Ninhydrin for detection of latent fingerprints on thermal paper and other surfaces," *J. Forens. Sci.*, 47 (6), (2002), 1274.

Steele, C.A., and Ball, M.S., "Enhancing contrast of fingerprints on plastic tape," *J. Forens. Sci.*, 48 (6), (2003), 1314.

Stucker, M., Geil, M., Kyeck, S., Hoffman, K., Rochling, A., Memmel, U., and Altmeyer, P., "Interpapillary lines: The variable part of the human fingerprint," *J. Forens. Sci.*, 46 (4), (2001), 857.

Wen, Che-yen, and Yu, C., "Fingerprint pattern restoration by digital image processing techniques," *J. Forens. Sci.*, 48 (5), (2003), 973.

EXPERIMENT 10　　　　　　　　　　　　　　Name _____

DATA SHEET　　　　　　　　　　　　　　　Date _____

FINGERPRINTING

Part A: Visualizing Fingerprints

1. Describe the surface you used and the results you had.

Part B: Lifting Fingerprints

1. Latent prints lifted with transparent tape.

2. Latent prints lifted with the hinged lifter.

Part C: Fluorescent Dusting Powder

1. Describe what you saw when you irradiated the print dusted with anthracene with UV radiation.

Experiment 10

2. What was the effect on the fluorescence after you washed your hands?

Part D: Obtaining Inked Fingerprints

Fingerprint patterns of inked prints—attach the FBI card to this report. Place your fingerprints in the spaces below. Below each print, label it with its general pattern.

1. R. thumb   R. index   R. middle   R. ring   R. little

    L. thumb   L. index   L. middle   L. ring   L. little

2. List the identifying characteristics of your fingerprints.

Federal Bureau of Investigation, United States Department of Justice
Washington, D.C. 20537

Experiment 10

FEDERAL BUREAU OF INVESTIGATION
UNITED STATES DEPARTMENT OF JUSTICE
CJIS DIVISION/CLARKSBURG, WV 26306

APPLICANT

1110-0046 3/21/2010

1. LOOP

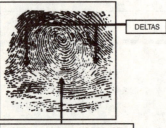

- CENTER OF LOOP
- DELTA

THE LINES BETWEEN CENTER OF LOOP AND DELTA MUST SHOW

2. WHORL

- DELTAS

THESE LINES RUNNING BETWEEN DELTAS MUST BE CLEAR

3. ARCH

ARCHES HAVE NO DELTAS

FD-258 (REV. 12-10-07)

THIS CARD FOR USE BY:

1. LAW ENFORCEMENT AGENCIES IN FINGERPRINTING APPLICANTS FOR LAW ENFORCEMENT POSITIONS.*
2. OFFICIALS OF STATE AND LOCAL GOVERNMENTS FOR PURPOSES OF EMPLOYMENT, LICENSING, AND PERMITS, AS AUTHORIZED BY STATE STATUTES AND APPROVED BY THE ATTORNEY GENERAL OF THE UNITED STSTES. LOCAL AND COUNTY ORDINANCES, UNLESS SPECIFICALLY BASED ON APPLICABLE STATE STATUTES DO NOT SATISFY THIS REQUIREMENT.*
3. U.S. GOVERNMENT AGENCIES AND OTHER ENTITIES REQUIRED BY FEDERAL LAW.**
4. OFFICIALS OF FEDERALLY CHARTERED OR INSURED BANKING INSTITUTIONS TO PROMOTE OR MAINTAIN THE SECURITY OF THOSE INSTITUTIONS.

Please review this helpful information to aid in the successful processing of hard copy criminal and civil fingerprint submissions in order to prevent delays or rejections. Hard copy fingerprint submissions must meet specific criteria for processing by the Federal Bureau of Investigation.

- Ensure all information is typed or legibly printed using blue or black ink.
- Enter data within the boundaries of the designated field or block.
- Complete all required fields. (If a required field is left blank, the fingerprint card may be immediately rejected without further processing.) The required fields for hard copy fingerprint cards are: originating agency identifier number - date of birth - place of birth - name - sex fingerprint impressions - any applicable state stamp - Other (race, height, weight, eye color, hair color)
  - * criminal fingerprint cards also require an arrest charge and date of arrest.
  - * civil fingerprint cards also require a reason fingerprinted and date fingerprinted

- Do not use highlighters on fingerprint cards.
- Do not enter data or labels within 'Leave Blank' areas.
- Ensure the 'Reply Desired' field is checked when applicable (criminal only).
- Ensure fingerprint impressions are rolled completely from nail to nail.
- Ensure fingerprint impressions are in the correct sequence.
- Ensure notations are made for any missing fingerprint impression (i.e. amputation).
- Do not use more than two retabs per fingerprint impression block.
- Ensure no stray marks are within the fingerprint impression blocks.

Training aids can be ordered online via the Internet by accessing the FBI's website at: fbi.gov, click on 'Fingerprints', then click on 'Ordering Fingerprint Cards & Training Aids'. Direct questions to the Identification and Investigative Services Section's Customer Service Group at (304) 625-5590 or by e-mail at <cjiaison@leo.gov>.

PRIVACY ACT STATEMENT

Authority: The FBI's acquisition, preservation, and exchange of information requested by this form is generally authorized under 28 U.S.C. 534. Depending on the nature of your application, supplemental authorities include numerous Federal statutes, hundreds of State statutes pursuant to Pub.L. 92-544, Presidential executive orders, regulations and/or orders of the Attorney General of the United States, or other authorized authorities. Examples include, but are not limited to: 5 U.S.C. 9101; Pub.L. 94-29; Pub.L. 101-604; and Executive Orders 10450 and 12968. Providing the requested information is voluntary; however, failure to furnish the information may affect timely completion or approval of your application.

Social Security Account Number (SSAN). Your SSAN is needed to keep records accurate because other people may have the same name and birth date. Pursuant to the Federal Privacy Act of 1974 (5 USC 552a), the requesting agency is responsible for informing you whether disclosure is mandatory or voluntary, by what statutory or other authority your SSAN is solicited, and what uses will be made of it. Executive Order 9397 also asks Federal agencies to use this number to help identify individuals in agency records.

Principal Purpose: Certain determinations, such as employment, security, licensing, and adoption, may be predicated on fingerprint-based checks. Your fingerprints and other information contained on (and along with) this form may be submitted to the requesting agency, the agency conducting the application investigation, and/or FBI for the purpose of comparing the submitted information to available records in order to identify other information that may be pertinent to the application. During the processing of this application, and for as long hereafter as may be relevant to the activity for which this application is being submitted, the FBI may disclose any potentially pertinent information to the requesting agency and/or to the agency conducting the investigation. The FBI may also retain the submitted information in the FBI's permanent collection of fingerprints and related information, where it will be subject to comparisons against other submissions received by the FBI. Depending on the nature of your application, the requesting agency and/or the agency conducting the application investigation may also retain the fingerprints and other submitted information for other authorized purposes of such agency(ies).

Routine Uses: The fingerprints and information reported on this form may be disclosed pursuant to your consent, and may also be disclosed by the FBI without your consent as permitted by the Federal Privacy Act of 1974 (5 USC 552a(b)) and all applicable routine uses as may be published at any time in the Federal Register, including the routine uses for the FBI Fingerprint Identification Records System (Justice/FBI-009) and the FBI's Blanket Routine Uses (Justice/FBI-BRU). Routine uses include, but are not limited to, disclosures to: appropriate governmental authorities responsible for civil or criminal law enforcement, counterintelligence, national security or public safety matters to which the information may be relevant; to State and local governmental agencies and nongovernmental entities for application processing as authorized by Federal and State legislation, executive order, or regulation, including employment, security, licensing, and adoption checks; and as otherwise authorized by law, treaty, executive order, regulation, or other lawful authority. If other agencies are involved in processing this application, they may have additional routine uses.

Additional Information: The requesting agency and/or the agency conducting the application-investigation will provide you additional information pertinent to the specific circumstances of this application, which may include identification of other authorities, purposes, uses, and consequences of not providing requested information. In addition, any such agency in the Federal Executive Branch has also published notice in the Federal Register describing any system(s) of records in which that agency may also maintain your records, including the authorities, purposes, and routine uses for the system(s).

INSTRUCTIONS:

* 1. PRINTS MUST GENERALLY BE CHECKED THROUGH THE APPROPRIATE STATE IDENTIFICATION BUREAU, AND ONLY THOSE FINGERPRINTS FOR WHICH NO DISQUALIFYING RECORD HAS BEEN FOUND LOCALLY SHOULD BE SUBMITTED FOR FBI SEARCH.
2. IDENTITY OF PRIVATE CONTRACTORS SHOULD BE SHOWN IN SPACE "EMPLOYER AND ADDRESS". THE CONTRIBUTOR IS THE NAME OF THE AGENCY SUBMITTING THE FINGERPRINT CARD TO THE FBI.
3. FBI NUMBER, IF KNOWN, SHOULD ALWAYS BE FURNISHED IN THE APPROPRIATE SPACE.

** MISCELLANEOUS NO. - RECORD: OTHER ARMED FORCES NO. PASSPORT NO. [FP]. ALIEN REGISTRATION NO. (AR), PORT SECURITY CARD NO. (PS), SELECTIVE SERVICE NO. (SS) VETERANS' ADMINISTRATION CLAIM NO. (VA).

Part E: Matching Prints

1. Identify the object you examined and the procedure you used.

2. Suspect print number _____

   Identity of the suspect to whom the print belongs _____

EXPERIMENT 11

Fingerprinting (Advanced)

This experiment is divided into four parts: the use of ninhydrin, silver nitrate, and Super Glue® to obtain fingerprints, and a fluorescent enhancement of the Super Glue prints.

Your fingers are continually in contact with sweat and body oil. Below is a summary of the components of a fingerprint:

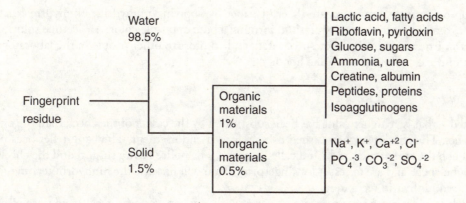

EQUIPMENT

- Aluminum foil (tank liner)
- 1 Bag, plastic, large, zip-top (alternate)
- 1 Beaker, 50 mL
- 1 Beaker, 250 mL
- 1 Beaker, 1,000 mL
- Blank paper checks
- 2 Brushes, dusting
- 1 Can, beer, EMPTY
- Cotton balls (alternate method)
- Dusting powder, black
- 1 Forceps
- 1 Funnel, powder, 65 mm
- 1 pr Gloves, disposable
- 1 pr Goggles, safety
- 1 Iron, steam
- 1 Paper, black, 8½ × 11 inches
- 2 Racks, wire test tube
- 2 Sprayers, aerosol
- 1 Tank, 5-gallon (fish tank will do, but with a glass, plastic, or metal cover)
- 2 Trays, photographic developing
- 2 Towels, cloth
- Towels, paper
- 1 UV (ultraviolet) lamp (Mineralite works well)

87

MATERIALS

Acetone

Fluorescent dye, 5% in methanol

Methanol silver nitrate,
2% in distilled water

Ninhydrin solution, 5% in acetone

Zinc chloride solution:
    Ethyl alcohol, 25 mL
    Acetic acid, 5 mL
    Zinc chloride, 3g

Super glue

Sodium hydroxide, 5% (alternate method)

Sodium thiosulfate (Hypo), 200 g + 140 g
of sodium bisulfate/L of water

Super Glue

Freon TF, 70 mL (also called Fluorisol,
Freon 113, Fluorocarbon solvent 113,
or 1,1,2-trichloro-1,2,2 trifluoroethane)

    Mix the EtOH and HOAc and dissolve the zinc. Then add the Freon. If two layers form, add 1–2 mL of isopropyl alcohol.

METHODS

PART A: OBTAINING FINGERPRINTS FROM PAPER BY MEANS OF NINHYDRIN

You will now develop fingerprints on a separate sheet of paper by applying ninhydrin. Ninhydrin reacts with the amino acids from the proteins of perspiration, forming a blue to purple color. An acetone solution is used. Ninhydrin is an irritant, so in the interests of safety and comfort to other people in the laboratory, perform this portion of the experiment in a fume hood.

Crime Scene

A check has been **kited**—that is, a higher value has been substituted by the casher of the check than the one signed for by the owner. The check was then cashed using a forged endorsement. The bank teller became suspicious, did not touch the face of the check, and called security. The police have a suspect and the check. You have been given the check and are to test it for fingerprints. You will first use the ninhydrin technique, then the metal-enhanced ninhydrin technique.

    NOTE: Ninhydrin will react with any protein, particularly any **on your fingers**. If you are at all sloppy, you will have purple fingers for over a week. We suggest you wear disposable plastic gloves when doing this experiment.

    If you have a thief in the dorm, place a little ninhydrin on a dollar bill or some other object that the thief likes. After the item is taken, look for the person with the purple fingers.

1. Plug in and turn on the steam iron.
2. Touch one or more fingers of one hand to each end of a check.
3. Pour a few milliliters of the ninhydrin solution into a spray bottle and screw the bottle into an aerosol can.
4. Under a hood, lightly spray the paper with ninhydrin solution.
5. Place the sheet of paper in a folded cloth towel.
6. Dry the paper for 3 to 4 minutes, and then cover the paper with a second cloth towel.
7. Iron the upper cloth towel. This will heat the paper without scorching it. Apply heat to the upper towel for a few minutes, then remove the upper towel and observe the developed latent fingerprints. They will be colored a light blue or blue violet.
8. Cover one end of the check with a piece of paper and spray the other end with 3% zinc chloride. The print should change to orange, which may make it stand out better on some objects. If nickel

nitrate is used, the print will turn red. Notice any areas that are not well developed and circle them with pencil.

9. Take the check to a darkroom and examine it under UV radiation from a Mineralite. (An argon laser is usually used for this and works much better, because nickel will not fluoresce.) Compare those places on the original fingerprints that you circled and determine if the fluorescence has improved the detection level.

10. Attach this check to the data sheet.

PART B: THE SILVER NITRATE METHOD

One of the components secreted by the pores on the fingertips is sodium chloride (NaCl). Sometimes it is possible to bring out fingerprints on paper by adding a solution of silver nitrate ($AgNO_3$). This solution slowly reacts with the chloride to form silver chloride. Upon exposure to UV radiation, the effect is like that of a photographic film; silver is formed and the ridges turn black on a brown background. Once the print has been developed and photographed, the silver can be removed by either a mercuric nitrate solution or "Hypo."

This technique is sometimes the only one that will work with really old prints because the salt is all that remains. Care must be taken because the black ridges fade away and the brown background gets quite dark. This coloration can be removed by dipping the paper in a 2% solution of mercuric nitrate (CAUTION: this solution is toxic). Silver nitrate stains may be removed with 5 g of mercuric chloride and 5 g of ammonium chloride in 100 mL of distilled water. A newer technique to remove background coloration and stains is to use a mixture of 200 g of sodium thiosulfate and 140 g of sodium bisulfate/liter of water. It takes 10–15 minutes to be effective.

Crime Scene

It is suspected that an employee is going through desks that he has no business looking through. The manager noticed some checks had been rearranged on his desk. It is desirable to detect the suspect's fingerprints on the checks without leaving any trace so the suspect won't get suspicious. You have been given one of the checks and are to use the silver nitrate method to develop any fingerprints on it. You are to then treat it with a hyposulfate solution to remove the silver so the check can be returned to its original place and as close to its original condition as possible.

1. Place your fingerprints on a check as you did in the ninhydrin experiment.

2. Pour sufficient silver nitrate solution in a tray to cover the paper. Wear disposable gloves. **Do not get silver nitrate solution on your skin**. It will turn black when exposed to sunlight and will take days to wear off.

3. With the aid of forceps, immerse the paper in the silver nitrate solution, making certain it is covered completely. Allow it to remain in the solution for 4–5 minutes.

4. Use the forceps to remove and drain it.

5. Transfer the paper to a folded towel.

6. Allow the paper to dry in a darkened area. Do not expose the paper to direct sunlight.

7. Develop the print by directing the radiation from a UV lamp on the paper. Do this carefully, as too much exposure will cause the prints to form and fade very fast. The paper will turn brown, with the print becoming visible as a black or very dark brown color.

8. Dip HALF of the paper (so you can compare to the other half) into a tray containing the hypo and sodium bisulfate and let it stay there until the color fades (from 10 to 15 minutes).

9. Remove the paper with a forceps, allow the excess liquid to drip away, and then place it between the folds of a cloth towel to damp dry.

10. Fold your print (if you get one) in black paper and attach it to your report.

PART C: THE USE OF SUPER GLUE

In 1976 in Saga prefecture in Japan, Masao Soba was working with Aron-Alfa, the Japanese version of Super Glue, which is in a double container. He noticed white fingerprints on the outside of the inner container and decided to determine how they were formed. In 1978 Noboyuki Otsubo showed Ed German and Paul Norkus of the U.S. Army Crime Lab what the technique was. They brought it to this country and taught it to Frank Kendall. Frank Kendall did experiments to improve the technique and in 1980 published the first English-language version of the technique. Since that time, the use of Super Glue to detect fingerprints has become one of the more useful techniques.

Essentially all you need to do is to place the object to be examined in an enclosed chamber (covered fish tank), add a small amount of Super Glue in a small container (bottle cap), and warm it (coffee cup warmer) until it begins to fume. It is thought by many that the fumes are attracted to the fingerprints because the prints are of opposite charge to the fumes. A white image is formed. It is suspected that the process involves the salt on the print because the technique works well with old prints that would most likely have lost their oils. If the print is faint, it may be enhanced by dusting it with dusting powder, or it may be sprayed lightly with a fluorescent solution and then examined under UV radiation.

Super Glue is a mixture of 98–99% of either methyl-, ethyl-, or butyl-2-cyanoacrylate and 1–2% of an inhibitor. The polymerization is easily catalyzed by a base, water being sufficiently basic. The trace moisture on your fingers is the cause of Super Glue sticking your fingers together so quickly.

The moisture in the air is sufficient to initiate polymerization once a drop of the glue is placed on an object. This produces a few long and very strong polymer chains, as you have seen demonstrated in TV commercials. If too much moisture is present, a large number of reactions will be started and only weaker short chains will form. Whereas this is poor for glue, it works better for fingerprint detection, and many investigators place a small container of water in the developing chamber. Without heat, it takes several hours to form a clear print. With gentle warming, good prints can be obtained in 10–15 minutes.

If sodium hydroxide, a strong base, is used, no heating is necessary to develop fingerprints. A cotton ball is soaked in 0.5 M NaOH solution and dried. This cotton ball is placed in the fuming chamber, and when a few drops of Super Glue are added, fumes will form within a few seconds.

This is an excellent method to examine large areas without having to meticulously dust them. For example, the entire inside of a car can be examined in 10–15 minutes.

There are some problems. Fingerprints developed with Super Glue are hard to remove, requiring a mild abrasive and much rubbing, which can ruin the surface. And although acetone can be used to dissolve the print, it also dissolves paint and may ruin that surface. Therefore, you should not fingerprint an object that may be used again unless you are fairly certain it contains a print. If you fingerprint the inside of a car, the white prints are probably there to stay. Other solvents are nitromethane, dimethylsulfoxide, dimethylformamide, and methylethyl ketone.

The Super Glue technique works well on glass, metal, and plastic. If the item is to be examined for blood, saliva, seminal fluid, fibers, hairs, or anything else, this should be done before fuming with Super Glue because the fuming will usually ruin the examination of other substances. If you are going to do a gun, cork the end of the barrel first.

Super Glue fumes are not particularly toxic, but they will make your nose burn and tears may form at higher concentrations. You will smell it long before these things happen. Nonetheless, it is recommended that the developing chamber be placed in a hood or that you have an exhaust system of some type present.

Crime Scene

An empty beer can was found under the seat of an abandoned vehicle suspected of being used in a kidnapping. The owner of the car says that he never drinks that brand of beer. Your job is to determine if there are any prints on this can that do not match the owner's (to check out his story) and to possibly determine those of the kidnapper.

1. Obtain a developing chamber (probably a fish tank, as in the example in Figure 11–1), Super Glue and a sheet of aluminum foil long enough to cover all but about 10 cm of the inside of the tank.

   In an educational laboratory, a good, inexpensive container is a large plastic container with a sealable cover, easily obtained and inexpensive to replace if necessary. The disadvantage of such a container is the inability to observe the development of prints on the object.

FIGURE 11-1 A typical Super Glue fuming cabinet. Courtesy *Sirchie Fingerprint Laboratories, Youngsville, NC, www.sirchie.com.*

2. Remove any objects from the inside of the developing chamber. Steps 3 through 5 may be omitted at the discretion of your instructor.
3. If the chamber is glass, wipe off the walls with a cloth dampened with acetone. Do not use acetone on plastic; it will fog up immediately. Use dimethylformamide or one of the other solvents discussed earlier.
4. Place the aluminum foil around the inside of the chamber so that a small opening is located so you can see your object when it is placed on the rack.
5. Place a small amount of rubber cement along the top of the chamber to hold the foil in place. Over a period of time, the walls will become coated with Super Glue polymer, eventually making direct observation impossible.
6. Place a small hot plate inside the chamber and off to one side. A single coffee cup warmer is preferred for this as it produces the right temperature and provides constant heat.
7. Place a support rack inside of the chamber. A wire test tube rack is preferred because it is open and lets the fumes penetrate the object from all directions.
8. Your object will be an empty can of beer. For this experiment, wipe the can clean of prints, and then place several prints on it at various places and over different colors of paint. Now put on plastic gloves on one hand, handle the can, and place it on the rack. Remove the glove (leave it inside out) and place it next to the beer can.
9. Place a **small** metal cup (bottle cap or specimen can) on the hot plate and then add 8–10 drops of Super Glue to it.
10. Place a small beaker of water in the chamber.

92   Experiment 11

11. Place the cover on the chamber and turn on the heater. It normally takes about 2 minutes for the glue to fume. You will be able to smell it. Watch the area of the beer can where you know there is a print, as well as the finger tips of the glove. It will usually take about 5 minutes before a clearly visible print is obtained. Let the reaction continue for about 10–12 minutes.

12. Turn off the heater, and, wearing gloves, remove the can. Examine it carefully and write down your observations on the data sheet. Do the same thing with the plastic glove.

13. Proceed to Part D.

PART D: ENHANCEMENT OF SUPER GLUE FINGERPRINTS BY DUSTING AND FLUORESCENCE (ADVANCED)

Comparisons of various enhancement techniques will be done in this part. You will dust some prints, you will spray some prints, and you will dip some prints. You will do your best to compare the results so that you will know what can be done. There are two schools of thought on the use of fluorescent dyes to enhance the Super Glue imprint. One is to lightly spray the print with a diluted solution of the dye and examine it under UV radiation. The other is to dip the object in a more concentrated solution, leave it there for 1–2 seconds, rinse it off with ethanol, and then examine it with UV radiation. We will let you try both methods.

Please be careful on those steps that involve the use of fluorescent materials. KEEP EVERY ITEM USED WITH FLUORESCENT MATERIALS IN A SEPARATE CONTAINER (A ZIP-TOP BAG WORKS WELL) AND USE A SEPARATE LAB BENCH FOR THIS WORK. DO NOT ALLOW ANY ITEM THAT HAS COME IN CONTACT WITH THESE DYES TO BE USED ON ANYTHING ELSE. Even a small drop will contaminate a bench top, and it takes days of washing to completely remove it. Please be careful.

Several fluorescent dyes are commercially available. Rhodamine 6G was made especially to fluoresce at 515 nm so that an argon laser could be used.

1. Locate a poorly developed fingerprint near the end on one side of the can. This will be used for the dipping experiment. Locate two poorly developed fingerprints on the opposite end of the can, one on each side. One will be used for dusting and the other for spraying. Do the same with the glove; only one finger at a time will be used.

   NOTE: Repeat each step with a fingerprint on the plastic glove.

2. Decide which print you want to try to enhance by dusting and examine it closely to see where parts are missing. Carefully dust it with black dusting powder, using the same dusting technique you learned in Part A of Experiment 8. Describe on the data sheet any differences you found.

   NOTE: This fingerprint can now be lifted by any of the techniques described earlier.

3. Wrap a paper towel around the end of the can you are going to dip so that spray won't get on the print. Fasten it with tape.

4. Place a few milliliters of the fluorescent dye in the sprayer and lightly spray (in a hood or spraying chamber) the print you have selected.

5. Allow the dye to thoroughly dry, and then view it in a darkened room with a Mineralite (either long or short wavelength). An argon laser may be used if one is available.

6. Place about 100 mL of the dye solution in a 250-mL beaker.

7. Remove the paper towel and dip the end of the can into the dye solution until the print is completely submerged. Let it stay there for 1–2 seconds, and then let it drip dry for 10–15 seconds.

8. Hold the can over a 1,000-mL beaker and rinse the surface with a stream of ethanol from a wash bottle.

9. Allow the dye to thoroughly dry, and then view it in a darkened room with a UV lamp (either long or short wavelength). An argon laser may be used if one is available.
10. Write your observations and conclusions on the data sheet.

SELECTED SOURCES FOR ADDITIONAL INFORMATION

Almog, J., Springer, E., Wieser, S., Frank, A., Khodzhaeu, O., Lidor, R., Bahar, E., Varkony, H., Dayans, S., and Rozen, S., "Latent fingerprint visualization by 1,2-indanedione and related compounds: Preliminary results," *J. Forens. Sci.*, 44 (1), (1999), 114.

Azoury, Myriam, Gabbay, R., Cohen, D., and Almog, J., "ESDA processing and latent fingerprint development: The humidity effect," *J. Forens. Sci.*, 48 (3), (2003), 564.

Bersellini, C., Garofano, L., Giannetto, M., Lusardi, F., and Mori, G., "Development of latent fingerprints on metallic surfaces using electropolymerization processes," *J. Forens. Sci.*, 46 (4), (2001), 871.

Bramble, S.K., "Separation of latent fingerprint residues by thin layer chromatography," *J. Forens. Sci.*, 40 (6), (1995), 969.

Bramble, S.K., "Fluorescence spectroscopy as an aid to imaging latent fingerprints in the ultraviolet," *J. Forens. Sci.*, 41 (6), (1996), 1038.

Caldwell, J.P., Henderson, W., and Kim, N.D., "ABTS: a safe alternative to DAB for the enhancement of blood fingerprints," *J. Forens. Sci.*, 45 (4), (2000), 785.

Caldwell, J.P., Henderson, W., and Kim, N.D., "Luminescent visualization of latent fingerprints by direct reaction with a lanthanide shift reagent," *J. Forens. Sci.*, 46 (6), (2001), 1303.

Caldwell, J.P., and Kim, N.D., "Extension of the color suite available for chemical enhancement of fingerprints in blood," *J. Forens. Sci.*, 47 (2), (2002), 332.

Davies, P.J., Kobus, H.J., Taylor, M.R., and Wainwright, K.P., "Synthesis and structure of the zinc (II) and cadmium (II) complexes produced in the photoluminescent enhancement of ninhydrin developed fingerprints using group 12 metal salts," *J. Forens. Sci.*, 40 (4), (1995), 565.

Elber, R., Frank, A., and Almog, J., "Chemical development of latent fingerprints: computational design of ninhydrin analogues," *J. Forens. Sci.*, 45 (4), (2000), 757.

Flynn, Katherine, Maynard, P., Du Pasquier, D., Lennard, C., Stoilovic, M., and Roux, C., "Evaluation of iodine-benzoflavone and ruthenium tetroxide spray reagents for the detection of latent fingermarks at the crime scene," *J. Forens. Sci.*, 49 (4), (2004), 707.

Gardner, Sarah, J., and Hewlett, D.F., "Optimization and initial evaluation of 1,2-indandjone as a reagent for fingerprint detection," *J. Forens. Sci.*, 48 (6), (2003), 1288.

Halahmi, E., Levi, O., Kronik, L., and Boxman, R.L., "Development of latent fingerprints using a corona discharge," *J. Forens. Sci.*, 42 (50), (1997), 833.

Hauze, D.B., Petrovskia, O., Taylor, B., Joullie, M.M., Ramotowski, B., and Cantu, A.A., "1,2 indanediones: New reagents for visualizating the amino acid components of latent prints," *J. Forens. Sci.*, 43 (4), (1998), 744.

Hewlett, D.F., Winfield, P.G.R., and Clifford, A.A., "The ninhydrin process in supercritical CO^2," *J. Forens. Sci.*, 41 (3), (1996), 487.

Jones, N.E., Davies, L.M., Brennan, J.S. and Bramble, S.K., "Separation of visibly-excited fluorescent components in fingerprint components in fingerprint residue by thin layer chromatography," *J. Forens. Sci.*, 45 (6), (2000), 1286.

Lewis, L.A., Smithwick, R.W., Devault, G.L., Bolinger, B., and Lewis, S.A., "Processes involved in the development of latent fingerprints using the cyanoacrylate fuming method," *J. Forens. Sci..*, 46 (2), (2001), 241.

Lock, E.R.A., Mazzella, W.D., and Margot, P., "A new europium chelate as a fluorescent dye for cyanoacrylate pretreated fingerprints—EuTTAPhen: Europium thenoyltrifluoro acetone ortho phenanthroline," *J. Forens. Sci.*, 40 (4), (1995), 654.

Migron, Y., and Mandler, D., " Development of latent fingerprints on unfired cartridges by palladium deposition: A surface study," *J. Forens. Sci.*, 42 (6), (1997), 986.

Ramminger, U., Nickel, U., and Geide, B., "Enhancement of an insufficient dye-formation in the ninhydrin reaction by a suitable post treatment process," *J. Forens. Sci.*, 46 (2), (2001), 288.

Roux, C., Jones, N., Lennard, C., and Stoilovic, M., "Evaluation of 1,2-indanedione and 5,6-dimethyl-1,2-indanedione for the detection of latent fingerprints on porous surfaces," *J. Forens. Sci.*, 45 (4), (2000), 761.

Schwartz, L., and Frerichs, I., "Advanced solvent free application of ninhydrin for detection of latent fingerprints on thermal paper and other surfaces," *J. Forens. Sci.*, 47 (6), (2002), 1274.

Tissier, P., Didierjean, J.C., Prudhomme, C., Pichard, J., and Crispino, F., "A "cyanoacrylate case' for developing fingerprints in cars," *Sci. & Just.*, 39 (3), (1999), 163.

Wiesner, S., Springer, E., Sasson, Y., and Almog, J., "Chemical development of latent fingerprints: 1,2-indanedione has come of age," *J. Forens. Sci.*, 46 (5), (2001), 1082.

EXPERIMENT 11 Name _____

DATA SHEET Date _____

FINGERPRINTING (ADVANCED)

Part A: Ninhydrin

1. Attach your developed prints to this sheet.

2. Do you think the zinc metal treatment was of any value? Explain.

Part B: The Silver Nitrate Technique

1. Attach your developed prints to this sheet.

2. Do you think the clearing solution was effective? Explain.

Part C: Super Glue

1. About how long did it take before you were able to observe some prints?

2. Describe several of the prints that you obtained on the various paint colors.

3. How good were the prints on the glove?

Part D: Fluorescent Enhancement: Techniques (Advanced)

1. Describe the differences you observed between a regular Super Glue print and one that has been dusted.

2. Describe the differences you observed between a regular Super Glue print and one that has been sprayed with a fluorescent solution.

3. Describe the differences you observed between a regular Super Glue print and one that has been dipped into a fluorescent solution.

Comparison of Tool Marks and Casting

EXPERIMENT 12

In crimes that involve breaking and entering, as well as in safe burglaries, tools are used to affect entry or to open a locked safe. These tools are pointed or have sharp edges that leave identifying marks on the objects upon which they are used.

There are two types of characteristics that relate the tool to the mark it makes on an object: (1) class characteristics, which include such factors as size and general configuration of tools, and (2) individual characteristics, which include structural anomalies that are unique to and distinctive of one specific tool. Individual characteristics are random in nature and result from wear devices used in the manufacture of the tool, from grinding, sharpening, or other finishing procedures, and also from use of the tool.

Examination of a tool mark requires a detailed study of the specific tool and a mapping of its surface structure. A definite distinction must be made between class and individual characteristics in each tool examined. New tools present a problem in this procedure, whereas worn tools are a much simpler case.

NOTE: The terms *mold* and *cast* are often used incorrectly. If you pour Plaster of Paris onto a tire track or footprint, that is called a **cast**. The tire track or footprint indentation acts as the **mold**. If you now use the cast to make a copy in order to obtain something that looks like the original, that is also a cast, because now the first cast becomes the mold for the second one! It is easy to see why the terms get confused. Suppose you place Plaster of Paris over your face and let it harden. Your face is the mold. When you remove the plaster, you have a cast of your face. If you now fill that cast (which now becomes the mold) with molten bronze and let the bronze harden, when you chip away the plaster, you now have a cast (exact likeness) of your handsome features. Centuries ago, when transportation was slow and embalming techniques not well established, a death mask was made of the deceased's face from wax so that relatives could identify the body at a later date. This was called a **moulage**.

CRIME SCENE

A rear door of a commercial building has been "jimmied." Following the breaking open of the door, the burglar entered the building and removed a large number of items. Investigating officers have made casts of the tool marks on the doorjamb, a footprint outside a window, and a tire print in a patch of dirt in the alley. These have been properly marked and sent to the area forensic laboratory. These pieces of physical evidence, along with others, have led to the apprehension of two suspects. Both suspects carry tools in their cars. Screwdrivers and pry bars have been taken from the tools in both cars and sent to the laboratory for comparison with the casts taken at the scene of the crime. You will examine three screwdrivers, catalog the class characteristics and individual characteristics of each, and attempt to match one of the three screwdrivers with the cast of the tool marks left at the scene.

Experiment 12

EQUIPMENT

- 2 Aluminum strips, approx. 5 × 10 cm
- 1 Beaker, 150 mL
- 1 Beaker, 1,000 mL
- 4 Cardboard, strips, approx. 2 × 30 cm
- 1 Casserole
- 1 Emery paper
- 1 Forceps
- 1 pr Goggles, safety
- 1 Hand lens, 10×
- 1 Lead strip, approx. 5 × 10 cm
- 1 Microscope, stereoscope
- 1 Ruler, metric scale
- 1 Spatula
- 1 Stirring rod, large
- 1 Tongue depressor or spoon
- 3 Toothpicks or wood splints
- 1 Wood block to make tool marks on
- 1 Wood or cardboard box, about 10 cm deep and large enough for a footprint, filled with moist dirt so that you can make molds and casts inside in rainy weather

MATERIALS

Spray can, lacquer
Plaster of Paris
Molds of tool marks from scene
Impression plastic (such as Citricon bulk putty base) or liquid silicone rubber compound, or modeling clay
Screwdrivers (samples), 5 of different head types
WD-40 or similar light lubricant

METHOD

PART A: MAKING A CAST OF A TOOL IMPRINT

Current casting techniques for tool marks use fast-setting silicone plastics such as those used by a dentist to make tooth impressions. Silicone plastic sets quickly, is easy to handle, does not break as easily as other plastics, and gives good impressions of fine detail. Modeling clay can also be used, but be sure it is soft.

You will be given a piece of wood from a window frame that has been pried open. You will make a cast of the pry mark, and determine which of the prying tools on the table was used to open the window.

Whether you use the Citricon putty or the liquid silicone rubber, the technique is the same. The impression material is prepared in about the same way as you make epoxy glue—a catalyst is added and worked in, then the material is applied to the mark, allowed to set, and removed.

1. Take one scoop of the silicone-base material (about the size of a ping-pong ball), and add 6 drops of the catalyst from the tube.

2. Work in the catalyst for about 2 minutes, and no longer than 3 minutes, by squeezing the base between your fingers.

3. Press a spatula on one side of the ball to press out any fingerprints, and place this side down on the tool mark.

4. Press the impression material firmly into the tool mark, and allow it to set a few minutes until it hardens.

5. Remove the impression, look at it with the magnifying glass and then with the stereoscopic microscope if one is available, and record any identifying marks.

6. Determine which tool made the mark, and record your observations.

PART B: INDIVIDUAL CHARACTERISTICS OF TOOL MARKS

1. Obtain one of the suspect screwdrivers and record the identifying letter on the data sheet.

2. Place a small strip of either lead or aluminum on a flat surface, and use a piece of emery paper to clean and shine the surface (only if needed). Be sure the piece of metal is flat. If it isn't, place a block of wood on it and hit the wood a few times with a hammer to flatten the metal.

3. Hold the sharpened edge of the screwdriver at an angle of 45° to the surface of the lead strip. Exert pressure and draw the blade edge of the screwdriver across the lead strip in one continuous motion. This will leave marks on the plate that are characteristic of that screwdriver and that you will compare with those on your cast. These marks are called **individual** characteristics.

4. Repeat this process a second time, alongside the first trial.

5. Turn the blade of the screwdriver over and repeat the operation to obtain two samples of the scratch marks from this side of the blade. Label this strip of lead with the letter of the screwdriver used to make the marks.

6. Do this for each of the screwdrivers. Be sure to label each mark.

7. Use a hand lens to examine the surface of both sides and edges of the screwdriver blade. A lower-power microscope can also be used.

8. Record all characteristics as class or individual, to the best of your ability. Pay particular attention to the small nicks and wear markings on the blade, as these are the most useful data for comparison with the cast.

9. Repeat the previous steps for the second and third suspect screwdrivers.

10. Be certain that all of the lead or aluminum strips are well labeled for identification.

11. Compare the marks made by the "jimmy" tool that you see in the cast with the marks you have obtained on the lead strip. Also look for nicks and other marks that may be used for comparison.

12. Based on the results of your observations, try to match the suspect tool with the tool marks left at the scene of the crime.

13. Record your result.

This exercise illustrates the difficulty of working with and comparing tool marks as physical evidence in the investigation of crime scenes. In actual laboratory practice, a follow-up of what you have just done is made with a comparison microscope. Its use requires experience and very careful observation. It requires the ability to distinguish between class and individual characteristics of the tool. Although class characteristics are not going to do much in the way of relating a tool mark to a single tool, their value lies in ascertaining the type of tool used and, in some instances, in eliminating certain suspect tools from involvement in a crime. For example, in one year in a Scandinavian country, there were 100,000 burglaries. For these cases, 10,000 tool casts were made, of which 200 led to convictions.

PART C: PLASTER OF PARIS CASTS OF FOOTPRINTS AND TIRE TREADS

Plaster of Paris (calcium sulfate, $CaSO_4$) is a favorite for making casts because it is inexpensive and readily available. Using it correctly is not as easy as you might expect, because it is heavy and tends to crumble the fine structure of the print unless it is poured carefully.

1. Find either a footprint or a tire mark that you want to cast.

2. Carefully surround the impression with a metal or wood strip of not less than 2 cm in height. This will prevent the plaster from flowing beyond the impression area and will allow the rest to be built up to the desired thickness.

3. To help maintain the fine structure, spray the print with lacquer from a spray can. This will hold the particles in place while the Plaster of Paris is poured in. Do not spray directly onto the impression, as you may disturb its fine details.

4. The Plaster of Paris is poured in two steps. First, add enough plaster (7 parts) to water (4 parts) to make an initial pouring 1 cm thick. The mixture should be the consistency of pancake batter. Mix thoroughly, making sure that all the lumps are removed.

5. To prevent any disruption of the impression, the slurry should not be poured directly onto the surface. Instead, the mixture must be poured slowly onto a spoon or tongue depressor held over the impression. Cover the entire impression with approximately 1 cm of Plaster of Paris.

6. Carefully add a few small sticks (tongue depressors) or wire mesh to the surface of the plaster in order to reinforce the cast.

7. Add enough plaster to water to make a second pouring 1 cm thick.

8. Allow the plaster to harden. You can inscribe identifying information on the cast's surface while it is drying. Use straight lines for the lettering.

9. Once you are sure that the cast is firm, clean off the surface by gently brushing away any adhering soil.

10. Carefully examine the cast for any telltale identification marks such as cuts, torn-out places, or imbedded materials.

11. If it is a shoe print, make measurements and compare it with your own shoe. Estimate the shoe size using your shoe as a reference.

12. Label the cast and show it to your instructor.

13. Clean up your area.

PART D: MAKING A CAST FROM A MOLD (ADVANCED)

In Part A you made a cast (negative) of a tool mark impression. We will now use that as a mold to make another cast, but one that is a (positive) of the original impression.

1. Use a dental-plastic, silicone-rubber, or modeling-clay cast of the impression as the mold for this part.

2. Place ball of moist modeling clay about 2–3 cm in diameter in the bottom of a casserole dish and flatten it out.

3. Place your impression of the tool mark into the clay and carefully press it down so that the impression rises up and there are no holes under it. This is your mold for the next step, so inspect it carefully to ensure that there are no cracks, rough spots, or other places where the casting material might stick and prevent you from removing it later.

4. Prepare a mixture of Plaster of Paris and water (tap water is fine). Add the plaster to approximately 20 mL of water in a 150 mL beaker. Stir to remove all lumps. The consistency of the mixture should resemble pancake batter. Add water or plaster to make it that consistency.

5. If you want to have a better chance of removing the mold from the cast without breaking it, spray the mold lightly with WD-40 or some other light oil. Too much oil will run into the small indentations and ruin the fine detail.

6. Pour the plaster into or over the mold. Place a piece of wood splint (or a few toothpicks) into the plaster and press them down below the surface. This will add strength to the cast.

7. Allow it to harden. Then tip the casserole dish upside down and, with gentle tapping, remove the cast from the mold (no swearing now).

SELECTED SOURCES FOR ADDITIONAL INFORMATION

Berx, V., and De Kinder, J., "3D measurements on extrusion marks in plastic bags," *J. Forens. Sci.*, 47 (5), (2002), 976.

Brown, S., Klein, A., and Chaikovsky, A., "Deciphering indented impressions on plastic," *J. Forens. Sci.*, 48 (4), (2003), 869.

DeForest, P.R., "A review of tire imprint evidence," *J. Forens. Sci.*, 37 (2), (1992), 663.

DeGruchy, S., and Rogers, T.L., "Identifying chop marks on cremated bones," *J. Forens. Sci.*, 47 (5), (2002), 933.

Glattstein, B., Shor, N., Levins, N., and Zeichner, A., "pH indicators as chemical reagents for the enhancement of footwear marks," *J. Forens. Sci.*, 41 (1), (1996), 23.

Nichols, R.G., "Firearm and toolmark identification criteria: A review of the literature, Part II," *J. Forens. Sci.*, 48 (2), (2003), 318.

Novoselsky, Y., Glattstein, B., Volkov, N., and Zeichner, A., "Microchemical spot tests in toolmark examination," *J. Forens. Sci.*, 40 (5), (1995), 865.

Quatrehomme, G., Garidel, Y., Grevin, G., Liao, Z., Boublenza, A., and Ollier, A., " Facial casting as a method to help identify severely disfigured corpses," *J. Forens. Sci.*, 41 (3), (1996), 518.

Shor, Y., Tsach, T., Vinokurov, A., Glattstein, B., Landau, E., and Levin, N., "Lifting shoe prints using gelatin lifters and a hydraulic press," *J. Forens. Sci.*, 48 (2), (2003), 368.

Springer, E., "Toolmark examinations: A review of its development in the literature," *J. Forens. Sci.*, 40 (5), (1995), 885.

Zugibe, F.T., Costello, J., and Breithaupt, M., "Identification of a killer by a definitive sneaker pattern and his beating instruments by their distinctive patterns," *J. Forens. Sci.*, 41 (2), (1996), 310.

EXPERIMENT 12   Name _____

DATA SHEET   Date _____

COMPARISON OF TOOL MARKS AND CASTING

Part A: Making a Cast of a Tool Imprint

1. Sketch any identifying marks that you see on the impression.

2. Label your cast and turn it in with this data sheet.

3. What would you do differently if you did it again?

Part B: Individual Characteristics of Tool Marks

Suspect screwdriver _____

1. Sketch what you believe are the marks that make a comparison possible.

2. List some characteristics of the screwdrivers below.

   Suspect screwdriver _____

   Class characteristics   Individual characteristics

Suspect screwdriver _____

Class characteristics   Individual characteristics

Cast from tool mark at scene of crime

Class characteristics   Individual characteristics

Results: Which, if any, of the suspect screwdrivers match the tool marks left at the scene of the burglary?

Part C: Plaster of Paris Casts of Footprints and Tire Treads

1. Record any measurements and identifying marks of the footprint.

2. Record any measurements and identifying marks of the tire print.

3. Mark your cast(s) and turn them in with this data sheet.

Part D: Making a Second Cast from a Mold (First Cast) (Advanced)

1. Sketch any identifying marks that you see on this impression that you did not see on the first cast.

2. Label your cast and turn it in with this data sheet.

3. What would you do differently if you did it again?

Questions

1. Based upon your knowledge of the techniques used, is it possible to determine, with any degree of certainty, the class characteristics of a tool from the tool marks left at the scene of a crime?

2. What would be the greatest aid to tool mark comparisons?

3. Would drill bits leave identifying tool marks?

4. Do you believe that the sprayed-on lacquer was of any benefit?

EXPERIMENT 13

Reproducing Bite Marks

A type of physical evidence that may be encountered in some crime situations is bite marks. These marks may be left on someone's person, as the result of an assault or sexual attack, on a discarded piece of fruit the perpetrator was eating prior to the criminal act, or on a variety of other items or surfaces. Sometimes the pattern of these bite marks could be very useful in assisting to make an identification. If the bite marks are found on someone's skin, photography is likely the best method of preservation. If on a surface that will degrade quite quickly, it may be best to make a cast of the surface, from which a mold is made as a permanent replication of the teeth pattern. If a suspect is found who has the same bite pattern, it could be valuable evidence serving to place that person at the scene of the crime.

EQUIPMENT

1 Electric hot plate, any model, 120 volt
1 Double boiler kettle, 2-quart size is convenient

REAGENTS

FLEXWAX 120® or a similar substance
(NOTE: FLEXWAX 120 is obtainable from AMACO INC, phone 1-800-374-1600. It melts to a clear liquid at 120°F. If maintained at that temperature it will not cause burns to human skin.)

Small soft bristle brushes   Plaster of Paris
Water   Cup, foam

METHOD

1. Cut out the bottom of a foam cup. Cut the cutout circle in half. Place the two halves one over the other.

2. Open your mouth as wide as possible and insert the foam half in your mouth. Bite down firmly, but do not bite so hard that your teeth go through the plate.

3. Use a soft bristled brush to dip into the melted FLEXWAX and apply a thin coat of wax to the bite mark portion of your foam cup. Let it cool briefly and then apply a second coat of wax. Repeat this procedure until you have a sturdy coating of wax on your foam cup, covering the bite mark portion and extending around the foam cup for a short distance in each direction.

4. Cool the wax thoroughly. This step can be accelerated by holding the wax-covered portion of your foam cup under cold running water over the sink.

5. This step requires some care! Remove the wax cast from the foam, being very careful not to distort the impression of the teeth marks you have made. The foam should come out of the cast quite easily.

6. Support your wax cast in such a way that you can fill it with Plaster of Paris, which you will now prepare.

7. Place about 100 mL of tap water in a 250-mL beaker. Add Plaster of Paris until you have a mixture with a medium batter consistency. Remember that when Plaster of Paris is added to water, hydration takes place and heat is produced that will cause the plaster to "set" quite rapidly. Stir your plaster and water mixture thoroughly and move rapidly through the pouring step. It is necessary to obtain fine detail in your cast in order for it to be forensically useful.

8. Pour the plaster mixture into your mold and agitate it slightly to make certain that it fills all of the impression detail. This will also help to remove air bubbles that sometimes become trapped in the plaster as it hardens.

9. Let the plaster-filled mold rest until the plaster has hardened. If your mixture was prepared properly this will not take more than 15 minutes or so.

10. Take the mold containing the plaster cast to the kettle of melted FLEXWAX. Peel the wax from the plaster and put it back into the kettle. Be careful not to waste the wax, as it is reusable many times.

11. Compare the cast of your teeth marks with the casts of others in the class.

12. Label your cast with your name and section number, complete the data sheet and questions, and be ready to hand them in for grading at the designated time. Be sure to clean up your bench area.

SELECTED SOURCES FOR ADDITIONAL INFORMATION

Bernitz, H., Van Heerden, W.F.P., Solheim, T., and Owen, J.H., "Technique to capture, analyze, and quantify anterior teeth rotation for application in court cases involving tooth marks," *J. Forens. Sci.*, 51 (3), (2006), 624.

James, H., and Cirillo, G., "Bite mark or bottle top?," *J. Forens. Sci.*, 49 (1), (2004), 119.

Kennedy, R.B., Chen, S., Pressman, I.S., Yarmashita, A.B., and Pressman, A.E., "A large scale statistical analysis of barefoot impressions," *J. Forens. Sci.*, 50 (5), (2005), 1071.

Kennedy, R.B., Pressman, I.S., Chen, S., Peterson, P.H., and Pressman, A.E., "Statistical analysis of barefoot impressions.," *J. Forens. Sci.*, 48 (1), (2003), 55.

Kouble, R.F., and Craig, G.T., "A comparison between direct and indirect methods available for human bite mark analysis," *J. Forens. Sci.*, 49 (1), (2004), 111.

McKinstry, R.E., "Resin dental casts as an aid in bite mark identification," *J. Forens. Sci.*, 40 (2), (1995), 300.

EXPERIMENT 13 Name _____

DATA SHEET Date _____

REPRODUCING BITE MARKS

Questions

1. Identify the object upon which you found the bite marks.

2. Were the bite marks plainly visible on the object?

3. Could you see enough detail in the bite marks to allow you to make a visual comparison with someone's teeth?

4. Was greater detail in the bite marks visible in the plaster cast you made? Explain.

5. Did you notice distinct differences between your teeth pattern and those of others in the class with whom you compared casts? If so, would these differences be specific enough to allow you to be identified by the bite pattern of your teeth, given expertise and experience in the use of this method?

Experiment 13

6. Describe another crime situation in which this type of reproduction could be useful. (Other than comparison of bite marks.)

If you are interested in further work with FLEXWAX 120, perhaps your instructor will suggest an optional exercise that you could complete.

EXPERIMENT 14

Restoring Serial Numbers on Metals

Most items of commerce are marked in some manner by the manufacturer to identify them. As the value of the items increases, more permanent identifying marks are used. In addition, with items of higher value, there is a need to give each item its own identifying mark.

Marking is most easily done by stamping a code or serial number on the item in question. When a serial number is stamped into a piece of wood, such as on good-quality furniture, the wood fibers are ruptured to a considerable depth below the visible stamp. If a thief sands off the serial number, it is possible in many cases to treat the surface with dilute sodium hydroxide, which will react faster with broken fibers than with unbroken ones. The serial number will then reappear to some extent, perhaps enough for identification. Trichloroethylene is used in the same way with plastics and hard rubber, and several solutions can be used with the metals. In all cases, the basis of serial-number restoration is that the molecules or crystals under the stamped number are under strain compared with surrounding areas, so that when a reagent is applied, it will react faster with one area than the other. A great deal of patience is required, and a camera should be handy to record the results, as they sometimes fade quickly. If a camera is not available, sketch the lines on a piece of paper as they appear.

Many etching solutions contain acid and metallic ions such as copper. Apparently, when iron is under stress, it is more susceptible to electrochemical reaction with copper and hence will dissolve at a faster rate as compared with the surrounding areas of metal. This chemical reaction is as follows:

$$Cu^{+2} + Fe = Cu + Fe^{+2}$$

The copper deposits where the iron has dissolved, thus enhancing the color difference, which is the basis for using etching agents to restore obliterated serial numbers.

Experience indicates that a trained person has a reasonably good chance to restore serial numbers on metals, a fair chance on wood and plastic, and a very poor chance on leather goods, although it can and has been done.

The basic technique is as follows:

1. Clean the surface.

2. Smooth the surface with fine emery cloth.

3. Build a dam around the area with clay if irregularly shaped; otherwise, simply swab the area.

4. Add a reagent and watch.

5. Apply a fresh reagent to the dam every 15 to 20 minutes, or swab at 2- to 3-minute intervals.

6. If nothing happens after 1 to 2 hours, change reagents.

7. Be patient and have a camera ready. You may not get a second chance.

Experiment 14

CRIME SCENE

After much diligent detective work, the police have located the hideaway of a gang of household thieves. The thieves know something about criminalistics and have removed the serial numbers from everything: typewriters, jewelry, guns, car batteries, bicycles, and other items. What is needed is to positively identify whether any article of this material is from a list of goods previously reported as stolen. Your job is to see if you can restore a serial number on any one of the articles before you.

EQUIPMENT

1 Beaker, 100 mL
1 Block of wood, to wrap emery cloth around
1 Camera
  Cotton swabs (such as Q-tips®)
1 Emery cloth
1 pr Goggles, safety
1 Medicine dropper

Unknowns: small pieces of different types of metal and wood that have had names or numbers stamped on them and then removed with a grindstone. (Do not grind or sand the numbers or letters too deeply, only until they disappear.)

MATERIALS

Acetone, in a wash bottle   Modeling clay

Below is a list of metals and solutions that have been found to work well for each.

Mild steel: rolled hot, with a black film of slag on it from oxidation. Prepare a solution of 90 g of $CuCl_2$ + 120 mL of HCl + 100 mL of water.

Stainless steel: rolled cold, therefore having a shiny appearance. Use 90 g of $CuCl_2$ + 120 mL of HCl + 100 mL of water.

Cast iron: brittle, with a definite graininess on the surface as well as the interior. Use 90 g of $CuCl_2$ + 120 mL of HCl + 100 mL of water.

Brass and copper: Use 25 g of $FeCl_3$ + 25 mL of HCl + 100 mL of water.

Aluminum: Use 25 g of $FeCl_3$ + 25 mL of HCl + 100 mL of water.

Lead: Use a 10% $AgNO_3$ solution; will turn your skin black when exposed to sunlight wherever it touches you unless washed off immediately.

Silver (jewelry): Use 32 mL of HNO_3 plus 290 mL of distilled water. This will turn your skin yellow wherever it touches you unless washed off immediately.

Tin: Use a 10% HCl solution.

METHOD

1. Carefully clean the surface (if a metal) with acetone to dissolve any grease.
2. Normally the area would be photographed. You may do it in this case if you are set up for it.
3. Place a piece of fine emery cloth around a small block of wood and polish the surface (do not use a circular motion) so that it shines and the rough grinding or filing marks disappear. This is done to remove deep scratches that would hold excess solution and to remove the oxide coating on a metal's surface.
4. Again clean the surface with acetone and be careful to avoid getting fingerprints on the surface.
5. If the plate is curved, build a small clay dam around the area to hold the reagent. Be careful to keep the area itself clean.
6. Decide what type of metal you have and get the proper reagent.

7. Pour 30–40 mL of the reagent into a 100-mL beaker.

8. If a clay dam is necessary, use a medicine dropper to add the reagent to the metal surface until it is covered, and observe the surface. If no clay dam is used, a cotton swab can be used to apply reagent to the surface. The swab should be moved slowly back and forth over the suspect area.

9. Watch the surface carefully. If numbers or letters begin to appear, sketch them on a piece of paper because some may appear while others disappear.

10. If nothing happens, continue swabbing the suspect area at 2- to 3-minute intervals for at least 30 minutes before quitting.

11. If a good set of numbers appears, photograph them immediately.

12. Clean up the area and turn in your plate to the instructor, along with any sketches you made of partial numbers.

SELECTED SOURCES FOR ADDITIONAL INFORMATION

Mongan, A.L., "Visualization of a restored serial number using scanning electron microscopy (S.E.M.)," *J. Forens. Sci.*, 41 (6), (1996), 1074.

Randich, E., Fickies, T.E., Tulleners, F.A., Andresen, B.D., and Grant, P.M., "Restoration tactics for seriously corroded Cu and Cu-alloy firearms evidence," *J. Forens. Sci.*, 45 (6), (2000), 1316.

Srinivasan, G.J., and Thirvnavukkarasu, G., "Decipherment of an obliterated vehicle identification number," *J. Forens. Sci.*, 41 (1), (1996), 163.

Thirvnavukarasu, G., Hemalatha, M., and Kuppuswamy, R., "Restoration of obliterated paint registration number on vehicle," *J. Forens. Sci.*, 47 (2), (2002), 374.

EXPERIMENT 14 Name _____

DATA SHEET Date _____

RESTORING SERIAL NUMBERS ON METALS

1. State the type of object to be tested.

2. Name the solution used and discuss why you chose it.

3. Record what was observed, with the approximate times involved.

Restoring Bloody Shoe Prints

EXPERIMENT 15

Processing surfaces that have been contaminated with blood presents problems in the detection of friction ridge skin impressions because the blood prints have different properties than those of latent print deposits that are made with sweat, fats, or oils. Blood prints on nonporous surfaces can be processed with Coomassie Brilliant Blue or Leucocrystal Violet to detect the faint deposits of friction ridge skin impressions. Coomassie Brilliant Blue and Leucocrystal Violet are dyes that stain proteins present in blood to give a blue-black or bright blue product. The reagents will not detect the normal constituents of latent fingerprints and must therefore be used in sequence with other techniques when blood-contaminated latent prints are examined.

At the scene of a violent crime, there are often blood spots on the floor. If the assailant happens to walk on this blood, it gets on the soles of his or her shoes and can leave partial prints for several steps. After a few steps, the visible portion of the bloody print is gone but faint traces of the shoe print still remain. By properly applying these dyes to the suspect area, it is possible to make an invisible print visible.

The Leucocrystal Violet requires only one reagent, but the Coomassie Blue is the least expensive method for beginners to use. This technique works very well with some pieces of evidence. Although it will not provide sufficient ridge detail to identify a fingerprint, if done properly, it is possible to make visible shoe sole prints that are normally invisible on hard to semi-hard surfaces such as paper, cardboard, floor tile, and wood flooring. In favorable cases, they can even be made visible on carpeting.

The solutions needed for Coomassie Brilliant Blue and Leucocrystal Violet processing have an indefinite shelf life and may be reused at the forensic scientist's discretion. Storage of the solutions should be in appropriately labeled glass bottles.

After mixing, the reagents should be tested by application of the reagent to a prepared latent print that is made with blood or a blood portion. After testing, the reagents can be stored until needed and may be tested prior to use.

ADVANTAGES

Coomassie Brilliant Blue and Leucocrystal Violet are simple, inexpensive processes that may be best for detecting faint, blood-contaminated friction ridge skin impressions on nonporous surfaces.

Leucocrystal Violet may well be the reagent of choice, because it is a one-step process that fixes and stains the suspected bloodstains. Leucocrystal Violet has very little background staining and should be the reagent of choice for use on any porous or semi-smooth surfaces such as walls.

DISADVANTAGES

Coomassie Brilliant Blue and Leucocrystal Violet will interfere with forensic examinations for body fluids, fibers, hairs, paint, and most other examinations. Care should be taken during the evaluation process so that the impact on other types of examinations is minimized.

Coomassie Brilliant Blue and Leucocrystal Violet will only stain traces of blood present and will not detect the friction ridge skin impressions composed of normal latent print constituents.

PART A: COOMASSIE BLUE PROCESSING

CRIME SCENE

Crime scene investigators were called to the scene of a homicide. The victim was lying in a small pool of blood. It appeared that the assailant stepped in the edge of the pool. A few visible but smudgy prints were observed leaving the scene and the trail led over a crushed cardboard box and onto a tile floor. Your job is to attempt to develop any residual sole prints on the piece of cardboard box.

EQUIPMENT

2	Atomizer bottles (like those for thin layer chromatography)	1 pr	Goggles, safety
1	Balance, ±0.01 g	1	Graduated cylinder, 100 mL
2	Beakers, 1,500 mL	1	Magnetic stirrer and stir bar
1	Bottle, wash, per 4 students, 250 mL	2	Storage bottles, clear or dark

MATERIALS

Coomassie Brilliant Blue (also known as Acid Blue 83)

Glacial acetic acid

Methanol

Developer solution:

1. Place a 1,500-mL beaker on the magnetic stirrer.
2. Measure out 0.96 grams of Coomassie Brilliant Blue, 84 mL of glacial acetic acid, 410 mL of methanol, and 410 mL of distilled water.
3. Combine the premeasured ingredients in the beaker and stir for approximately 30 minutes or until all of the Coomassie Brilliant Blue is dissolved.
4. Decant the reagent into an appropriately sized storage bottle or rinse bottle and store until needed.

Rinse solution:

1. Place a 1,500-mL beaker on the magnetic stirrer.
2. Measure out 100 mL of glacial acetic acid, 450 mL of methanol, and 450 mL of distilled water.
3. Mix the solution for about 30 seconds and decant into an appropriately sized storage bottle or rinse bottle and store until needed.

Final bath: a water rinse. Distilled water is preferred, but tap water will work if necessary.

METHOD

1. Spray the suspect area with methanol to help fix the print.
2. Spray the fixed suspect area liberally with the Coomassie Brilliant Blue.
3. Allow the developer to remain for 30–90 seconds as needed to make the print visible.
4. Using a wash bottle, hold the cardboard over the sink and rinse off the developer.
5. The developer and rinse may be applied again and again if necessary until the desired contrast is achieved.
6. When you are satisfied with the development, use a final rinse with distilled water to minimize background staining and improve the contrast.
7. Optional: You may photograph the developed print.
8. Compare your print with those of the suspects.

PART B: LEUCOCRYSTAL VIOLET PROCESSING

This is simpler than Coomassie Blue processing, in that it is a one-step process, but the reagent is not as common.

CRIME SCENE

Refer to the crime scene in Part A. This is an alternate method to do the same detection.

EQUIPMENT

1 Beaker, 500 mL
Magnetic stirrer
1 Spray or wash bottle

MATERIALS

Developer solution:

1. Combine in a 500-mL beaker in the following order:

    (1) 5-Sulfosalicylic acid, 10 g
    (2) Sodium acetate, 3.7 g
    (3) Leucocrystal Violet, 1
    (4) Hydrogen peroxide, 3%, 500 mL

2. Test the reagent by preparing a series of blood prints on a non-porous surface and processing by applying the reagent. Note the development of color and intensity.
3. Decant the reagent into an appropriately sized dark storage bottle or rinse bottle and store until needed.

METHOD

When making examinations for latent prints in suspected blood on surfaces, the precautions taken for serological examinations are the same as given previously for Coomassie Blue, although suspected bloodstains revealed with Leucocrystal Violet may be further examined serologically with the PCR technique.

Dilute bloodstains can be developed with Leucocrystal Violet, as the reagent seems to work well up to a dilution of 1:100.

Leucocrystal Violet uses a one-step application of the reagent onto the suspected blood-bearing surface. The reagent is used as follows:

1. The Leucocrystal reagent is used by spraying or rinsing the suspected blood-bearing surface. Any bloodstains will be colored a purplish blue.

2. The developed impressions need to be photographed as soon as possible, as exposure to light will cause background staining and possible degradation of the developed image.

    NOTE: A third reagent, Amido Black, can also be used. It is much more involved than the previous methods, but it works very well on painted surfaces. The interested investigator may refer to the literature cited below for details.

SELECTED SOURCES FOR ADDITIONAL INFORMATION

Ashe, R., Griffin, R.M.E., and Bradford, B., "The enhancement of latent footwear marks present in grease or oil residues on plastic bags," *Sci. & Just.*, 40 (3), (2000), 183.

Davis, R.J., and Keeley, A., "Feathering of footwear," *Sci. & Just.*, 40 (4), (2000), 273.

Evett, I.W., Lambert, J.A., and Buckleton, J.S., "A Bayesian approach to interpreting footwear marks in forensic casework," *Sci. & Just.*, 38 (4), (1998), 241.

FBI LFPS Research Team, Federal Bureau of Investigation LFPS Research Memo, 1990.

Fischer, J., Orange County Sheriff's Department Research Memo, 1995.

Fruchtenicht, T.L., Herzig, W.P., and Blackledge, R.D., "The discrimination of two-dimensional military boot impressions based on wear patterns," *Sci. & Just.*, 42 (2), (2002), 97.

Hoogstrate, A.J., Van Den Heuvel, H., and Huyben, E., "Ear identification based on surveillance camera images," *Sci. & Just.*, 41 (3), (2001), 167.

Napler, T.J., "Scene linking using footwear mark databases," *Sci. & Just.*, 42 (1), (2002), 39.

Shor, Y., Vinokurov, A., and Glattstein, B., "The use of an adhesive lifter and pH indicator for the removal and enhancement of shoeprints in dust," *J. Forens. Sci.*, 43 (1), (1998), 182.

EXPERIMENT 15 Name _____

DATA SHEET Date _____

RESTORING BLOODY SHOE PRINTS

Part A: Coomassie Blue

1. Attach your developed shoe print to this data sheet.

2. Identify the suspect whose inked shoe print matches your developed bloodstain shoe print.

Part B: Leucocrystal Violet (Optional)

1. Attach your developed shoe print to this data sheet.

2. Identify the suspect whose inked shoe print matches your developed bloodstain shoe print.

Questions

1. Did this method of shoe print development provide good detail?

2. Is this an absolute or comparative analysis?

3. Do you suppose that this method could be used to develop bloody shoe prints on carpeting or upholstered surfaces? If you are interested, ask your instructor to let you try it. (You provide the scrap of carpeting).

EXPERIMENT 16

Examination of Hair and Textile Fibers by Microscopy

Hair is a very common form of evidence in many cases of homicide, as well as in crimes of sexual assault. It also enters into many cases of burglary. Some of the points that may be proven by the use of hair as physical evidence are as follows:

1. It can link a suspect to the scene of the crime.
2. It can indicate the entrance or exit route of the criminal.
3. It can show contact with the victim.
4. It can serve to identify clothes or shoes abandoned, or denied, by the suspect.
5. It can indicate the contact of a victim in a hit-and-run accident with the car of the suspect. Sometimes the contact itself is not in doubt, but the exact part of the car where the victim was hit plays an important role in the evaluation of the dynamic features of the case.

Hair is only one of many fibers that are analyzed and compared as physical evidence. Fibers from textiles and woolen materials are just as important. The first part of this exercise will be concerned with hair and the second section will show you a simple technique for looking at cross sections of fibers.

Hair from any part of the body exhibits a range of characteristics, such as color, length, and diameter. Even hair from different parts of the same area—the crown, sides, and rear of the head, for example—will differ somewhat. It is therefore necessary for the forensic examiner to keep this in mind when collecting reference hairs and to obtain an adequate supply to compare with the suspect's hair. Usually, the collection of several dozen hairs from relevant parts of the body will suffice.

The parts of a hair that are easily seen by use of a microscope under magnification are the **medulla**, the **cortex**, and the **cuticle**, as shown in Figure 16–1. Many animal hairs are easily distinguished from human hairs by the size and shape of their medullae and the patterns of their cuticle or scale structure. Synthetic fibers have no medulla or scale pattern and are therefore readily distinguishable from animal hair. Figure 16–2 shows several scale patterns.

Definition of Terms Describing Scale Patterns

Coronal—scale structure characteristic of hairs of very fine diameter resembling a stack of paper cups. These scales are commonly encountered on small rodents and bats and only rarely in human hair.

Imbricate—overlapping scales with narrow margins. These scales are found on the hairs of humans and often of animals.

Spinous—triangular-shaped scales that frequently protrude from the hair shaft. These scales are never found in human hairs.

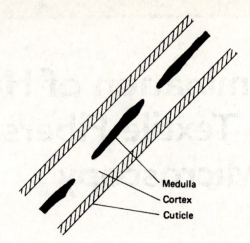

FIGURE 16–1 Structure of hair.

CRIME SCENE

Two persons are in an automobile involved in a one-car accident. Some property damage is sustained, and the car is badly damaged. This accident takes place in the evening with no witnesses present. The two persons in the automobile are only slightly bruised, neither sustaining any serious injury. Both do, however, suffer bumps on their heads, with some laceration of the skin and resultant bleeding. One person's head has come in contact with the windshield of the automobile, as evidenced by the cracked windshield, a small amount of blood, and a few strands of hair stuck to the glass at the place of impact. This was on the passenger side of the automobile. Both persons are suspected of having been under the influence of alcohol, and each maintains that the other was driving the automobile at the time of the accident. The officers at the scene, in attempting to determine the identity of the driver, collected the blood and hairs from the impact point of the windshield. They have obtained sample hairs from the head of each of the two persons involved and have transferred all of these materials to a forensic laboratory.

The hair samples comprise the physical evidence that you will work with in this exercise. Be certain that you properly label your samples so that you do not lose their identity. You will find the gross samples labeled "Person A," "Person B," and "Scene."

Attempt to identify the scene samples as either person A or person B. Note that hair should not be cleaned before it is examined. The adhering dust and impurities are sometimes of more evidential value than the hair itself.

EQUIPMENT

- 1 Beaker, 50 mL
- 1 Blade, razor, single edge
- 24 Bottles, screw cap, 6 dram, for samples
- 1 Compound microscope (100× is a good magnification)
- 3 Cover glass
- 1 pr Forceps
- 1 pr Goggles, safety
- 1 Medicine dropper
- 3 Microscope slides
- 1 Needle
- 1 Needle, dissecting
- 1 pr Scissors
- Tissue paper (facial tissues or similar material)

MATERIALS

Alcohol (ethyl or isopropyl)

Clear nail polish

Canada balsam

Glycerin

Rubber cement

Hair samples from various sources, labeled Scene, Person A, and Person B; also animal hairs and synthetic fibers.

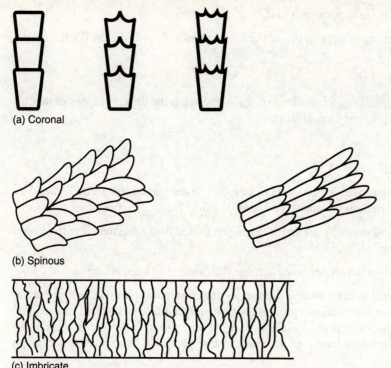

FIGURE 16-2 Scale patterns of several types of hair.

METHOD

PART A: GENERAL INTERNAL CHARACTERISTICS

This is a qualitative exercise in which you will try to determine characteristics of hair samples and attempt to match these hair samples with others.

1. Obtain a strand of human hair labeled **Scene** and place it on a glass microscopic slide.

2. Place a drop or two of glycerin on the hair in order to hold it in place, and put a cover slip over the hair. This is known as a **wet mount**.

3. Place the slide on the stage of the compound microscope, and adjust the magnification to 100×.

4. Locate the root end of the hair, if it has one. If the hair has been forcibly pulled out, you will see a bulb-shaped enlargement (pull out one of yours and examine it). This is the hair root, and adhering to it you will see particles of matter composed of small pieces of flesh and tissue that surround the hair root.

5. Make a sketch of what you see in the proper place on the data sheet.

6. Scan along the length of the hair body. Note any foreign particles clinging to the hair. Is the medulla fragmental (that is, present in isolated spots), interrupted (long columns with open spaces now and then), or continuous (unbroken column)? Is it entirely absent?

7. Note the color, relative diameter, and pigment distribution of the hair. You may want to increase the magnification of your microscope to make these observations. Your instructor will explain how you can compare relative diameters of the hair samples.

8. Make a sketch of each type of medulla you observe as you examine different hair samples. At a magnification of 300× or greater, some hairs may show irregularly shaped air spaces, known as **cortical fusi**, dispersed throughout the cortex. When present in abundant numbers, their size and distribution should be noted.

9. Examine the tip of the hair. This end can be determined by the gradual tapering of the hair. If the hair has been cut recently, you will see a square appearance at the end. Normally, hair tapers to a fine point as it grows. If hair has split ends, it is normally due to artificial waving, bleaching, or dyeing, although repeated brushing may also produce this effect.

10. Repeat Part A for the hair samples from persons A and B.
11. Record any differences you detect in the appearance of the Scene, Person A, and Person B hairs on the data sheet.
12. Does A or B compare to the scene hair?
13. Repeat the previous steps for hairs obtained from known animals. Sketch the different types of medullae you observe as you examine different animal hairs.

PART B: SCALE PATTERNS

Scale patterns are of little value in human hair comparisons but can aid in distinguishing animal hairs. You will now attempt to examine the scale pattern of human and animal hairs.

1. Clean the strand of hair you intend to use by pulling it through a folded tissue moistened with alcohol to remove grease and oil from the hair surface.
2. Examine the hair briefly under the microscope to determine if cleaning has been effective.

    The pattern of cuticle scale is useful in determining the species origin of hair. In human hair, the scales overlap smoothly, whereas in other mammalian species they protrude in a rough, serrated form. Some examiners use a scale count per given distance to aid in making a comparison. It is difficult to examine the scales directly, so what is most often done is to prepare a cast of the scales. Proceed as described in the steps that follow.

3. Smear a glass slide with a thin layer of clear nail polish.
4. Before the clear nail polish dries, which takes place very quickly, place a strand of hair on the surface of the polish.
5. Before the polish has thoroughly dried, but after the surface becomes partially solidified, lift the strand of hair off of the slide. You should now see an imprint of the hair in the polish.
6. Place the slide on the stage of the microscope, focus, and observe the scale pattern of the hair.
7. Now try observing the scale pattern on a strand of hair placed on a slide. Which is more easily seen?
8. Record your observations on the data sheet.
9. Repeat the above, only use rubber cement and then Canada balsam instead of nail polish.
10. Record your observations on the data sheet and tell which you like best.
11. Repeat this procedure for a hair from one of the samples obtained from an animal.
12. Make sketches of the scale patterns of the two different hairs you have used in this exercise.

PART C: HAIR COLOR

1. Try to obtain various colors of hair from other persons in the class: red, blonde, black, brown, etc.
2. Try to obtain an example of gray hair. If you are able to obtain this for examination, what do you notice that is different with respect to the other colors of hair you have examined?
3. Complete the data sheet and return all materials (cleaned) and the microscopes to the area designated by your laboratory instructor.

PART D: MAKING CROSS SECTIONS OF FIBERS (ADVANCED)

Hair and fibers are not all round as they appear to the naked eye; rather, most have unique shapes when viewed in cross section. This characteristic can be used in many cases to aid the criminalist in the identification of a particular type of hair or fiber. Figure 16–3 shows the cross sections of several synthetic fibers.

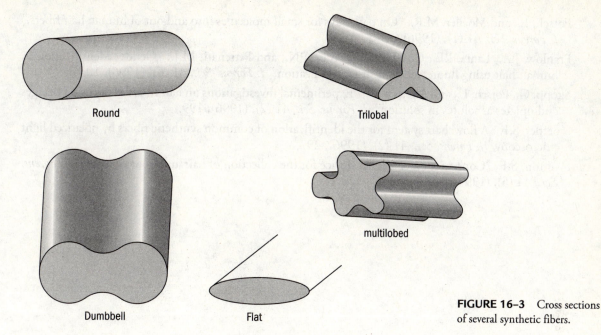

FIGURE 16-3 Cross sections of several synthetic fibers.

For the best results, several fibers should be used, and they should be thinly sliced so light from the microscope can be transmitted through them and should be evenly cut so several can be in focus at the same time. Reflected light can be used, but it is not preferred. If, as in many criminal cases, only one or a few fibers are available, then they may be packed in the holder with several known fibers. There are several sectioning techniques described in the literature, but only two of the easier methods will be described here.

Thread the yarn or fiber bundle through a cork, which will hold the fibers intact through frictional forces. Cut a very thin slice to ensure that you have evenly cut fibers of the same length. Next, view the section using transmitted or reflected light depending upon how thin the section was cut. This is a simple method, but cork is not always easy to cut smoothly.

An alternative to a cork is a potato. The potato is very easy to cut into thin slices; however, the moisture from the potato can, with time, obscure the cross-section shape. Additionally, this method is not practical for long-term preservation of the thinly sliced cross section.

SELECTED SOURCES FOR ADDITIONAL INFORMATION

Benner, B.A., Goodpasture, J.V., Degrasse, J.A., Tully, L.A., and Levin, B.C., "Characterization of surface organic components of human hair by on-line supercritical fluid extraction-gas chromatography/mass spectrometry: A feasibility study and comparison with human identification using mitochondrial DNA sequences," *J. Forens. Sci.*, 48 (3), (2003), 554.

Bisbing, R.E., *The Forensic Identification and Association of Human Hair in Forensic Science Handbook*, 2nd Edition, Volume I, R. Saferstein, ed., Upper Saddle River, NJ: Pearson Education, 2002.

Goodpasture, J.V., Drumheller, B.C., and Benner Jr., B.A., "Evaluation of extraction techniques for the forensic analysis of human scalp hair using gas chromatography/mass spectrometry (GC/MS)," *J. Forens. Sci.*, 48 (2), (2003), 299.

Grieve, M.C., "New man-made fibres under the microscope—Lyocell fibres and Nylon 6 block co-polymers," *Sci. & Just.*, 36 (2), (1996), 71.

Grieve, M.C., and Deck, S., "A new mounting medium for the forensic microscopy of textile fibres," *J. Forens. Sci. Soc.*, 35 (2), (1995), 109.

Houck, M.M., and Buidowle, B., "Correlation of microscopic and mitochondrial DNA hair comparisons," *J. Forens. Sci.*, 47 (5), (2002), 964.

Kempson, I.M., Skinner, W.M., and Kirkbride, P.K., "A method for the longitudinal sectioning of single hair samples," *J. Forens. Sci.*, 47 (4), (2002), 889.

Potsch, L., and Moeller, M.R., "On pathways for small molecules into and out of human hair fibers," *J. Forens. Sci.*, 41 (1), (1996), 121.

Prahlow, J.A., Lantz, P.E., Cox-Jones, K., Rao, P.N., and Pettenati, M.J., "Gender identification in human hair using fluorescence in situ hybridization," *J. Forens. Sci.*, 41 (6), (1996), 1035.

Skopp, G., Potsch, L., and Aderjan, R., "Experimental investigations on hair fibers as diffusion bridges and opiates as solutes in solution," *J. Forens. Sci.*, 41 (2), (1996), 199.

Stoeffler, S.F., "A flowchart system for the identification of common synthetic fibers by polarized light microscopy," *J. Forens. Sci.*, 41 (2), (1996), 297.

Swinton, S.F., "Construction of a roller device for the collection of hair and fiber evidence," *J. Forens. Sci.*, 44 (5), (1999), 1089.

EXPERIMENT 16   Name _____

DATA SHEET   Date _____

EXAMINATION OF HAIR AND TEXTILE FIBERS BY MICROSCOPY

Part A: General Internal Characteristics

1. Observations from the examination of hair

    a. Root

    b. External end

    c. Sketch of root and external end of hair

2. Observations Note the color, relative diameter, and pigment distribution in the hairs examined.

    a. Scene

    b. Person A

    c. Person B

3. Sketch various forms of the medulla (label each with the form it represents).

130   Experiment 16

4. Can you make a positive match, based on these notes, as to which person, A or B, was the driver of the automobile? Based upon your observations, which person, A or B, was the driver?

5. Sketch several animal hairs and synthetic fibers (label each).

Part B: Scale Patterns

1. Draw a scale pattern of human hair obtained with fingernail polish.

2. Draw scale patterns of the same hair obtained with rubber cement and/or Canada balsam.

3. Draw a scale pattern of hair from an animal (label).

Part C: Hair Color

1. List the similarities and differences between different colors of hair samples.

   Red

   Brown

Black

Blonde

Gray

Part D: Making Cross Sections of Fibers (Advanced)

1. Sketch the cross section of the sample fibers.

2. Sketch the cross sections of at least three known fibers.

3. Does the sample match any of the standards? If so, which ones?

Drug Analysis: Microchemical Spot Tests for General Classes*

When a sample suspected of being a drug is brought into the laboratory, a series of microchemical color spot tests are first made to see if the sample does indeed contain a drug, and, if so, what general class is involved. These color tests are quick screening tests for a variety of drugs. If a drug is present and a definite identification is desired, then a thin-layer chromatographic (TLC) separation may be performed, and this may be followed by a confirmatory test such as obtaining an infrared spectrum or analyzing the sample by gas chromatography/mass spectrometry (GC/MS). The spot tests most commonly done are:

1. Marquis reagent—usually turns violet in the presence of the opium alkaloids, such as heroin, morphine, and codeine. The amphetamines, or "uppers," such as dextro-amphetamine and methamphetamine turn Marquis reagent orange → red-brown.

2. Cobalt thiocyanate—for the coca alkaloids, cocaine (HCl) in particular, a blue, flakey precipitate is formed.

3. p-Dimethylaminobenzaldehyde (p-DMAB) (Ehrlich's reagent)—forms a blue color with LSD.

4. Duquenois test—forms a purple color with marijuana. This test is used for the detection of marijuana. We will not do this test here.

5. Dille-Koppanyi test—cobalt acetate and isopropylamine for the barbiturates. A red-violet color is formed by barbituric acid or its derivatives. These are the "downers." Examples are phenobarbital, secobarbital, amobarbital, and pentobarbital.

6. Mecke's reagent—selenous acid in sulfuric acid; an alternative test for the opium alkaloids that gives a distinct color-change sequence for each alkaloid, such as green for codeine.

EQUIPMENT

1 Beaker, 50 mL
1 Beaker, 250 mL
8 Bottles, dropping
1 pr Goggles, safety
    Disposable gloves
1 Mortar and pestle, small
1 Rack, dropping bottle
6 Rods, glass stirring, 10 cm
3 Spatulas
4 Spot plates, 3 × 4 wells

---

* The instructor must have the proper Drug Enforcement Administration registration, as well as state, local, and institutional authorization, to conduct this experiment; however, synthetic samples, which do not require such a license, can also be used.

MATERIALS

Alcoholic KOH: 5 g KOH in 100 mL EtOH

Chloroform

Cobalt acetate: 0.1 g Co(OAc)$_2$·4H$_2$O in 100 mL dry methanol plus 0.2 mL glacial acetic acid

Cobalt thiocyanate: 2 g per 100 mL H$_2$O

p-Dimethylaminobenzaldehyde: 2 g in 50 mL 95% ethanol and 50 mL concentrated hydrochloric acid

Drug standards

Isopropylamine: 5 mL plus 95 mL dry methanol

Marquis reagent: 8–10 drops of 40% formaldehyde added to 10 mL H$_2$SO$_4$; decays with age

Mecke's reagent: 0.25 g H$_2$SeO$_3$ in 25 mL H$_2$SO$_4$

Stannous chloride: 5 g SnCl$_2$ in 10 mL HCl, diluted to 100 mL with H$_2$O

CRIME SCENE

Acting on the complaint of a neighbor, two police officers arrive at a house to quiet a disturbance. What they observe makes them suspect that drugs are being used. They obtain several samples from a "punch bowl" on a table in the room and bring them to the lab. Your job is to determine if these are drugs and, if so, what kind.

You will first run a set of knowns, and then do as many unknowns as your instructor gives you.

METHOD

Laboratory Safety: Gloves and goggles should be worn routinely as good laboratory practice.

Several habit-forming drugs can be obtained in doses too small to be harmful, yet strong enough to give a positive test. The samples given to you may be prepared from one of these drugs, or they may be actual street drugs. Your unknown may contain any of the drugs shown in Table 17-1. First, you will go through all of the tests with each drug listed; then you will do one or more unknowns.

1. Obtain one or more spot plates, and arrange them so that you can make the tests shown in Figure 17-1. You will need a total of 30 holes in a 6 × 5 arrangement.

2. Obtain knowns from your instructor, such as:

   Opium alkaloids—Codeine   Coca alkaloids—Cocaine   LSD—if available

   Barbiturates—Nembutol   Amphetamines—Dexadrine

3. For each sample, place a few crystals or drops of the drug into each of the five holes across the spot plate (holes 1 to 5: opium alkaloids; 6 to 10: coca alkaloids; 11 to 15: LSD; and so on), as shown in Figure 17-1.

4. Add a few drops of Marquis reagent to the first spot in each row (wells 1, 6, 11, 16, 21, and 26). Stir, and observe the results. Record these on your data sheet. A violet color is considered a positive test for natural opium alkaloids.

5. To the second spot in each row (wells 2, 7, 12, 17, 22, and 27), add 3 drops of cobalt thiocyanate, and wait a few minutes. If a blue precipitate forms, add 3 drops of SnCl$_2$ and stir. This is a test for cocaine-type drugs. Record your results. Cocaine will form a precipitate not soluble in SnCl$_2$, whereas novocaine is soluble.

6. To the third spot (wells 3, 8, 13, 18, 23, and 28), add 15 to 20 drops of H$_2$O if the sample is a solid. Add 10 drops of the p-DMAB solution. Formation of a blue color after 10 to 20 minutes is a positive test for LSD. Record your results.

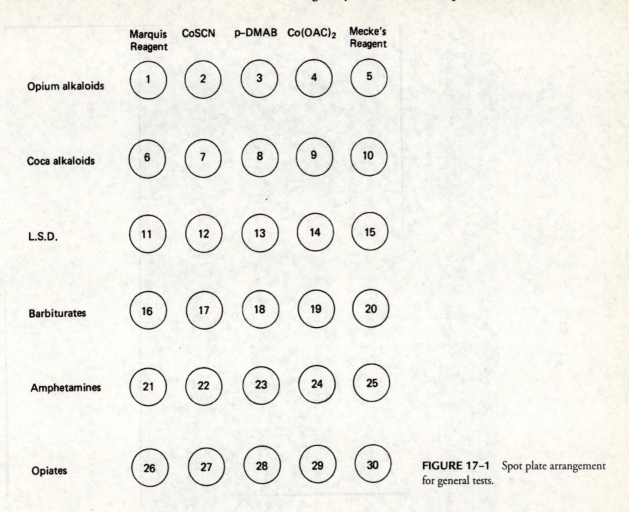

FIGURE 17-1 Spot plate arrangement for general tests.

7. To the fourth spot (wells 4, 9, 14, 19, 24, and 29), add 20 drops of cobalt acetate solution and mix. Then add 10 drops of isopropylamine solution and mix. A red color is characteristic of barbiturates.

8. To the fifth spot (wells 5, 10, 15, 20, 25, and 30), add 10 drops of Mecke's reagent. This reagent produces different colors with each drug, and usually the colors change two, three, and even four times during the test. Watch carefully, and record all changes. Refer to Table 17–1.

9. Repeat steps 4–8 on your unknown drug samples. Make your decision and record your data.

10. Clean up the equipment and return it to its proper place.

SELECTED SOURCES FOR ADDITIONAL INFORMATION

Anastos, N., McIntyre, I.M., Lynch, M.J., and Drummer, O.H., "Postmortem concentrations of citalopram," *J. Forens. Sci.*, 47 (4), (2002), 882.

Avelia, J., and Lehrer, M., "Fatality due to methyl acetylene-propadiene (MAPP) inhalation," *J. Forens. Sci.*, 49 (6), (2004), 1361.

Bravo, D.T., Harris, D.O., and Parsons, S.M., "Reliable, sensitive, rapid and quantitative enzyme-based assay for Gamma-hydroxybutyric acid (GHB)," *J. Forens. Sci.*, 49 (2), (2004), 379.

Burrows, D.L., Hagardorn, A.N., Harlan, G.C., Wallen, E.D., and Ferslew, K.E., "A fatal drug interaction between oxycodone and clonazepan," *J. Forens. Sci.*, 48 (3), (2003), 683.

TABLE 17-1 Color Tests for Screening Selected Drugs

Drug	Marquis Reagent	Cobalt Thiocyanate	Cobalt Acetate Isopropylamine	Selenious Acid	p-DMAB
Morphine	Violet				
Codeine	Red violet to blue violet			Green to blue-green	
Dihydrocodeine	Yellow to orange to brown to violet			Yellow to green	
Narcotine	Violet that fades				
Papaverine	Pink to blue			Green to blue	
Heroin	Violet				
Cocaine		Blue precipitate insoluble in $SnCl_2$			
Novocaine		Blue precipitate soluble in $SnCl_2$			
Demerol	Yellow to dark green				
Methadone	No color	Blue precipitate			
LSD				Pink	Blue
Nembutal			Red-violet		
Phenobarbital			Red-violet		
Sodium seconal			Red-violet		
D-amphetamine-SO_4	Red orange to brown				
Acetylsalicylic acid	Red in 15 minutes				

Color Test Reagents/Kits for Preliminary Identification of Drugs of Abuse, National Institute of Justice Law Enforcement and Corrections Standards and Testing Program, NIJ Standard 0604.01, 2000.

Couper, F.S., McIntyre, I.M., and Drummer, D.H., "Extraction of psychotropic drugs from human scalp hair," *J. Forens. Sci.*, 40 (1), (1995), 83.

Dasenbrock, C.O., Ciolino, L.A., Hatfield, C.L., and Jackson, D.S., "The determination of nicotine and sulfate in supermarket ground beef adulterated with Black Leaf 40," *J. Forens. Sci.*, 50 (5), (2005), 1134.

Defrancesco, J.V., Witkowski, M.R., and Ciolino, L.A., "GHB free acid: 1. Solution formation studies and spectroscopic characterization by HNMR and FT-IR," *J. Forens. Sci.*, 51 (2), (2006), 321.

Kalasinsky, K.S., Hugel, J., and Kish, S.J., "Use of MDA (the "love drug") and methamphetamine in Toronto by unsuspecting users of Ecstasy (MDMA)," *J. Forens. Sci.*, 49 (5), (2004), 1106.

Kugelberg, F.C., Holmgran, P., and Druid, H., "Codeine and morphine blood concentrations increase during blood loss," *J. Forens. Sci.*, 48 (3), (2003), 664.

McDermott, S.D., and Power, J.D., "Drug smuggling using clothing impregnated with cocaine," *J. Forens. Sci.*, 50 (6), (2005), 1423.

McKibben, T., "Simple and rapid color screening tests for flunitrazepam (Rohypnol)," (Date rape drug. 3 methods, purple color) *J. Forens. Sci.*, 44 (2), (1999), 496.

Wilson, W. L., "The identification and analysis of Canadian designer drugs," *J. Forens. Sci. Soc.*, 31 (2), (1991), 233.

Witkowski, M.R., Ciolino, L.A., and Defrancesco, J.V., "GHB free acid: II. Isolation and spectroscopic characterization for forensic analysis," *J. Forens. Sci.*, 51 (2), (2006), 330.

Wolf, B.C., Lavezzi, W.A., Sullivan, L.M., and Flannagan, L.M., "One hundred seventy two deaths involving the use of oxycodone in Palm Beach County," *J. Forens. Sci.*, 50 (1), (2005), 192.

EXPERIMENT 17　　　　　　　　　　　　　　　　　Name _____

DATA SHEET　　　　　　　　　　　　　　　　　　Date _____

DRUG ANALYSIS—SPOT TESTS FOR GENERAL CLASSES

Part A: General Internal Characteristics

1. Opium alkaloid known　　　　　　　　　　　　　　　　　　Observations

    Spot 1

    Spot 2

    Spot 3

    Spot 4

    Spot 5

    Test tube

2. Coca alkaloid known　　　　　　　　　　　　　　　　　　Observations

    Spot 6

    Spot 7

    Spot 8

    Spot 9

    Spot 10

    Test tube

Experiment 17

   3. LSD known   Observations

        Spot 11

        Spot 12

        Spot 13

        Spot 14

        Spot 15

        Test tube

   4. Barbiturate known   Observations

        Spot 16

        Spot 17

        Spot 18

        Spot 19

        Spot 20

   5. Amphetamine known   Observations

        Spot 21

        Spot 22

        Spot 23

        Spot 24

        Spot 25

6. Opiate (synthetic opiums) known   Observations

  Spot 26

  Spot 27

  Spot 28

  Spot 29

  Spot 30

7. Unknown 1   Unknown 2

Drug Analysis: Microcrystalline Tests*

When a sample suspected of being a drug is brought into the laboratory, microcrystalline tests are often performed following the presumptive microchemical color spot tests, to aid in the identification of a drug. These microcrystalline tests are quick tests to further identify a variety of drugs. Microcrystalline tests are primarily chemical-precipitation tests in which a light microscope is used to observe and distinguish the different types of crystals formed. These tests require skill and expertise on the part of the analyst, which can be gained adequately only through appropriate training and experience. Microcrystalline tests allow very small samples of drugs and other substances to be analyzed using a light microscope. The ability to manipulate small quantities of material can be very important in forensic science where the amounts of samples received as evidence are often limited. Historically, microcrystalline tests have been used to identify illicit drugs. Once the microcrystalline tests are completed, a confirmatory test is done to identify the drug. The confirmation of the substance can be performed by GC/MS, LC/MS, infrared spectrophotometry, or Raman microspectrophotometry. Some commonly performed microcrystalline tests are:

1. 5% Gold chloride in 10% HCl—widely utilized for more than 100 years by forensic scientists in the general scheme of analysis for cocaine. It can also be used for the analysis of phencyclidine, methamphetamine, and amphetamine.

2. 5% Platinum chloride—for the analysis of cocaine, methamphetamine, and amphetamine.

3. 2% Potassium permanganate (acidified)—for the analysis of phencyclidine.

EQUIPMENT

- 10 Microscope slides
- 1 pr Goggles, safety
- Disposable gloves
- 5 Bottles, dropping
- 4 Spatulas

Standard light microscope, with adjustable magnification including 100×.

MATERIALS

Acetic acid, 10% (v/v)
Gold chloride ($HAuCl_4$), 5% (w/v), in reagent-grade water
Hydrochloric acid, 10% (v/v)
Platinum chloride (H_2PtCl_6), 5% (w/v), in reagent-grade water

---

* Requires the same Drug Enforcement Administration license as Experiment 17; however, synthetic samples or drug standards can also be used.

Potassium permanganate, 2% (w/v), in 0.5% (v/v) phosphoric acid

Phosphoric acid, concentrated

Sodium hydroxide, 1.0 N to 10.0 N

Knowns: drug standards

Unknown: Sample (1) of an unknown drug

CRIME SCENE

An undercover police officer purchased a drug sample from a suspect and brings it to the lab. Your job is to use microcrystalline tests to determine if the sample contains a drug(s) and, if so, what kind.

METHOD

Laboratory Safety: Gloves and goggles should be worn routinely as good laboratory practice.

You are to perform the microcrystalline tests as described below on the standard drug samples given to you by your instructor. You will then perform the same tests on your unknown(s). Document your observations of the microcrystals through the microscope by drawing the crystals you observe on the data sheet.

PART A: TESTING OF KNOWN SAMPLES

1. Obtain 10 or more microscope slides.

2. Obtain knowns from your instructor, such as:

   Coca alkaloids (cocaine)

   Phencyclidine, if available

   Amphetamines (methamphetamine and amphetamine)

3. Use a small sample—a few crystals or drops of the drug—for each test.

4. Complete each microcrystalline test using the steps outlined in the Procedures section.

5. Record your results.

Procedures

Helpful Hints: Formation of crystals corresponding to those obtained with authenticated standards indicates presence of the drug. The shape of these crystals may vary slightly depending on the concentration of the drug in the acid solution.

If a dense cloud of precipitate is formed upon the addition of the precipitating agent, the crystals may not be readily visible. It may be necessary to repeat the test with a reduction of the concentration of suspected drug in the acid solution. This reduction is done by either decreasing the sample size or increasing the volume of solvent.

Acetic acid may be substituted for hydrochloric acid when testing for cocaine.

Phosphoric acid may be substituted for hydrochloric acid and acetic acid when testing for amphetamines. The crystals tend to precipitate faster from the phosphoric acid. There also tends to be less interference when using the concentrated phosphoric acid.

Gold Chloride

1. Place a small sample, a few particles of powder, on a microscope slide.
2. Dissolve the sample in a few small drops of 10% (v/v) hydrochloric acid or 10% (v/v) acetic acid.
3. Add a few drops of 5% (v/v) gold chloride to the edge of the acid solution on the microscope slide.
4. Observe the formation of the crystals using a light microscope.

Platinic Chloride

1. Place a small sample, a few particles of powder, on a microscope slide.
2. Dissolve the sample in a few small drops of 10% (v/v) hydrochloric acid.
3. Add a few drops of 5% (v/v) platinic chloride to the edge of the acid solution on the microscope slide.
4. Observe the formation of the crystals using a light microscope.

Potassium Permanganate

1. Place a small sample, a few particles of powder, on a microscope slide.
2. Dissolve the sample in a few small drops of 10% (v/v) hydrochloric acid or 10% (v/v) acetic acid.
3. Add a few drops of 2% (v/v) acidified potassium permanganate to the edge of the acid solution on the microscope slide.
4. Observe the formation of the crystals using a light microscope.

PART B: TESTING OF UNKNOWN SAMPLES

1. Obtain microscope slides and unknown samples.
2. Repeat all of the microcrystalline tests described in the Procedures section on your unknown drug samples.
3. Document your observations and record your data.
4. Clean up the equipment and return it to its proper place.

SELECTED SOURCES FOR ADDITIONAL INFORMATION

Evans, H.K., "Drug and microcrystal tests for forensic drug identification," *Microscope*, 47 (3), (1999), 147.

McKibben, T., Chappell, J.S., Evans, H.K., and Mauslof, N., "Analyses of inorganic components found in clandestine drug laboratory evidence," *J. Clandestine Lab. Investigating Chem. Assoc.*, 5 (4), (1995), 19–33.

Standard Guide for Microcrystal Testing in the Forensic Analysis of Cocaine, E1968-98, *Annual Book of ASTM Standards*, Vol. 14.02, Conshohocken, PA: ASTM Int., (2003), 679–681.

Standard Guide for Microcrystal Testing in the Forensic Analysis of Methamphetamine and Amphetamine, E1969-01, *Annual Book of ASTM Standards*, Vol. 14.02, Conshohocken, PA: ASTM Int., (2003), 682–684.

Standard Guide for Microcrystal Testing in the Forensic Analysis of Phencyclidine and Its Analogues, E2125-01, *Annual Book of ASTM Standards*, Vol. 14.02, Conshohocken, PA: ASTM Int., (2003), 868–870.

EXPERIMENT 18 Name _____

DATA SHEET Date _____

DRUG ANALYSIS: MICROCRYSTALLINE TESTS

Part A: General Internal Characteristics

1. 5% Gold Chloride in 10% HCl   Observations

   Cocaine

   Methamphetamine

   Amphetamine

   Unknown

2. 5% Platinum Chloride   Observations

   Cocaine

   Methamphetamine

   Amphetamine

   Unknown

3. 2% Potassium Permanganate (acidified)   Observations

   Phencyclidine

   Unknown

Separation of Drugs Using Thin-Layer Chromatography*

This experiment will demonstrate a technique that forensic scientists use to screen for controlled substances (drugs) in both solid-dosage evidential samples and biological fluids. Forensic chemists and toxicologists use a scheme of analysis that typically involves screening an unknown drug sample by using presumptive tests followed by a confirmatory test. The Scientific Working Group for the Analysis of Seized Drugs (SWGDRUG) has published guidelines for the screening and confirmation of controlled substances (www.swgdrug.org). Thin-layer chromatography (TLC) is one of the techniques used by forensic scientists to screen for illicit drugs.

TLC utilizes a thin film of silica gel or alumina coated onto a glass or plastic strip. As in paper chromatography, this thin film is called the **stationary phase**. A mixture of the compounds to be separated is placed in a small spot at one end of a strip, and a liquid organic solvent (**mobile phase**) is passed over the spot. As the solvent moves up the strip, it carries with it the various components in the spot. Because each compound present has a different size, shape, and distribution of electrical field, each compound will adhere to the stationary phase and dissolve in the solvent to a different extent. Thus, if two compounds are started at the same place and solvent is passed over them, one compound will move along the strip more quickly than the other. After a period of time, the flow of the mobile phase is stopped; the strip is dried and then sprayed with a reagent that will produce colored spots, if the compounds are not colored. The distance the compound moves relative to the distance the mobile phase moves is a characteristic of that compound and is known as the **retardation factor** or more commonly referred to as the R_f value.

$$R_f = \frac{\text{distance of sample band front from application}}{\text{distance of solvent front from application point}}$$

---

* The instructor must have the proper Drug Enforcement Administration registration, as well as state and local authorization, to conduct this experiment. It requires a Class I drug license to be in possession of the controlled substances mentioned. Permission can sometimes be obtained to have someone in the area that has a Class I license oversee this experiment. Law enforcement officers do not need a license, physicians and pharmacists usually only have Class II licenses. However, synthetic samples can be prepared by applying a few drops of the liquids obtained from the Gelman drug kits (600 Wagner Road, Ann Arbor, Mich.), which do not require a license. Drug standards exempt from Drug Enforcement Administration licensing requirements can also be obtained from Analabs, Inc. (North Haven, Conn.), Sigma Chemical Co. (St. Louis, Mo.), and Applied Science (State College, Pa.). Also, non-controlled drugs may also be substituted for the drugs listed in the procedure. The instructor should test the samples chosen to ensure success prior to conducting the experiment with the students.

Drugs can be tentatively identified by comparing R_f values with standards analyzed on the same TLC plate and system. Standard mixtures of drugs may be prepared and spotted on plates to screen for multiple drugs at the same time. Therefore several drugs can be identified in a single specimen.

The chromatography sheets or plates that may be used come in a variety of types. Silica gel plates are the most commonly used plates for separation of drugs.

CRIME SCENE

Several weeks of surveillance of a home suggested that the occupants were heavily involved in drug dealing. After documenting frequent visits from several known suspected drug users, a police raid was conducted on the residence. A number of items were discovered and documented in crime scene photographs. These items were sent to the crime laboratory for analysis. The analysis you will perform will be TLC of a sample(s) from this seizure.

PROCEDURE

Analyze your unknown sample on the same thin-layer chromatographic plates as the following standards. Prepare a 5-mg/mL solution of your unknown(s) in methanol. Spot each unknown on two plates (one for each thin-layer chromatographic mobile phase system). Also spot the known standards in the following list. It is best practice to bracket your samples with standards. In other words, spot three of the standards in columns 1, 2, and 3; then spot your unknowns; then spot the other three standards in the last three columns. If you have room on the thin-layer chromatographic plate it is good to spot your unknowns lightly and also in another column heavily. Performing analysis in this manner may detect a trace amount of drug that might go undetected otherwise.

SAFETY

For all laboratory work, follow the safety procedures that have been outlined for your institution. If you are unsure how to handle a particular chemical, consult the Material Safety Data Sheet (MSDS) information or ask your instructor for assistance. **All thin-layer chromatographic analyses including development must be performed in a fume hood.**

REAGENTS

1. Fluram (fluorescamine) 0.100 g in 500 mL acetone

2. Iodoplatinate solution
   a. 1 g platinic chloride in 10 mL dH_2O
   b. 60 g KI in 200 mL dH_2O
   Mix a and b and dilute to 500 mL dH_2O.

CHEMICALS

- Methanol
- Acetone
- Ethyl acetate
- Ammonium hydroxide
- Toluene
- Dioxane
- Ethanol

All reagents and chemicals should be ACS reagent grade or better.

STANDARDS

For each of the following, use 3 mg/mL in methanol.

- Amphetamine
- Methamphetamine
- Cocaine
- Heroin
- Ketamine
- Quinine
- Caffeine

MATERIALS AND SUPPLIES

- TLC plates: Merck Silica Gel #5763   0.250 mm w/o fluorescent indicator
- TLC spotting capillaries
- TLC development tanks, 2
- Blotter paper for TLC tanks
- TLC reagent spray bottles
- Fume hood
- UV light viewing box
- Hand blow dryer
- Pencil
- Ruler

TLC SOLVENT SYSTEMS

Tank #1	Tank #2
85 mL ethyl acetate	50 mL toluene
10 mL methanol	40 mL dioxane
5 mL NH_4OH	5 mL ethanol
	5 mL NH_4OH

METHOD

1. Obtain an unknown drug sample (from crime scene seizure).
2. Transfer approximately 10 mg of your unknown powder to a 10-cm test tube.
3. Add 2 mL of methanol to the test tube, and agitate until the powder has dissolved into the methanol.
4. Prepare a mixture of 100 mL of each TLC development solvent system.
5. Pour each reagents into a TLC development tank. Place enough of the developing solvent so that its depth is approximately 0.5 cm.
6. Place the glass lid over the development tanks, and let them stand until you are ready to use them.
7. Prepare the TLC plates for each of the TLC solvent systems.

8. Apply your samples and standards on the TLC plates, at a point 1 cm from the bottom of the plate. Use a capillary melting-point tube for application. Apply a very small spot of extract, let dry, and then apply a small spot again in the same place. Let dry thoroughly. Be sure the spots are separated. Care should be taken to keep the spots small. This will take patience.

9. Hold the spotted plate along the side of the developing tank containing the solvent. Make certain that the level of solvent in the tank will be below, but still close to, the applied sample on the plate when placed inside the tank. If it is at too high a level, remove some solvent with a small disposable pipette.

10. Place the TLC plates in the developing tanks of solvent. Be certain that they are properly identified. Place the glass top back on top of the tanks and let them stand until the solvent front has moved about three-quarters up the plate.

11. Remove the plates, and mark the solvent front.

12. Let them dry, and follow the development sequence outlined in this experiment.

13. Document the color(s) of each spot(s).

14. Measure the distance each band moved from the point of application to the front of the band.

15. Measure the distance the solvent front moved from the point of application of the spot.

16. Calculate the R_f value for each band by use of the relationship given earlier:

$$R_f = \frac{\text{distance of sample band front from application}}{\text{distance of solvent front from application point}}$$

17. Compare the known drug R_f values and colors with that of the unknown(s).

18. Do any of the drugs have a common origin? If so, which ones?

19. Can you determine conclusively the identity of the drugs?

20. Attach your TLC plates to the data sheet using transparent tape.

21. Answer all questions, and turn in the data sheet and questions to the laboratory instructor.

22. Clean all equipment used, and return it to its proper place. Dispose of all solvents in an appropriate waste container.

DEVELOPMENT SEQUENCE

Ensure that all solvents and ammonia have dried prior to the visualization process. You may use a hand blow dryer to expedite this process.

1. View under UV light (short and long wave).

2. Spray with Fluram (view under UV light).

3. Overspray with Iodoplatinate solution.

SELECTED SOURCES FOR ADDITIONAL INFORMATION

Bell, S., *Forensic Chemistry*, 2nd ed. Upper Saddle River, NJ: Pearson Prentice Hall, 2013 (ISBN: 978-0-321-76575-8).

Moffat, A.C., Osselton, D., Widdop, B., and Watts, J. eds., *Clarke's Analysis of Drugs and Poisons*, vol. 1, 4th ed. London, UK: Pharmaceutical Press, 2011, 471–495.

Saferstein, R., *Criminalistics: An Introduction to Forensic Science*, 10th ed. Upper Saddle River, NJ: Prentice Hall, 2011.

SWGDRUG Recommendations, Edition 6.0, www.swgdrug.com, July 7, 2011 (accessed 11 Nov. 2013).

EXPERIMENT 19   Name _____

DATA SHEET   Date _____

SEPARATION OF DRUGS USING THIN-LAYER CHROMATOGRAPHY

1. Attach the plates to the data sheet.

2. R_f values obtained with drug standards _____ R_f values obtained for the unknown (drugs) _____

    Band 1

    Band 2

    Band 3

3. Compare the R_f values and draw conclusions concerning the identity of the drug(s).

4. Do you think a different mobile phase would improve the separation of the drug(s)?

5. What types of other tests should be performed to confirm the identity of the drug(s)?

EXPERIMENT 20

Identification of Drugs and Poisons by Infrared Spectroscopy (Advanced)

In previous experiments you have identified a single drug using a specific reagent, and classes of drugs using spot tests. This experiment will show you one way to provide a positive identification of a drug and, if necessary, how to determine how much of the drug is present. The infrared (IR) spectrophotometer is used by the criminalist to determine drugs and organic poisons in powders, urine, and tablets. It measures the frequencies at which atoms and groups of atoms rotate and vibrate in a molecule and plots these on a sheet of paper. Each molecule has its own pattern, different from all other molecules. This pattern is called a **spectrum** (*spectrum* is singular; *spectra* is plural).

IR spectrophotometers are delicate instruments and quite expensive. They are called *instruments*, not *machines*. You mow the lawn with a **machine**, but you make measurements with an **instrument**. If you call it a machine you will treat it like a machine, and it will not last very long. Treat it with tender loving care and it will reward you with accurate data and less downtime.

There are many different manufacturers of IR spectrophotometers, and although they may look very different, the major components are the same, and they all operate on the same principle. Therefore, if you learn the basic techniques on one instrument, you will be able to work with almost any other instrument.

Most often in criminalistics, IR spectroscopy is used to determine what is present (qualitative analysis), not how much is there (quantitative analysis). Following the acquisition of the IR spectrum for the unknown sample, some preliminary work is done in the class determination, and then catalogs (or computer files) of reference spectra are consulted for comparison. When a match is found, a confirmatory spectrum is obtained on the same instrument for conclusive proof of identity.

The interpretation of IR spectra must be practiced before the analyst can become very certain of the conclusions. In this exercise, you are not expected to be, or to become, an expert or even a competent novice; however, you will gain an insight into the methods and problems of an IR spectroscopist. If you are interested, you may do an extension of this exercise. You will be working with liquid samples. The analysis is often performed on solid and gaseous samples as well. If you wish to try solid samples yourself, see your laboratory instructor for the procedures.

Figure 20–1 shows the IR spectra of two compounds. Notice how different they are. Each drug has its own characteristic spectrum. In fact, no two pure chemical substances have exactly the same IR spectrum. For this reason, an IR spectrum may be thought of as a *fingerprint* of a chemical compound.

Once we have a catalog of these spectra of known drugs and poisons, it is then a matter of matching the unknown with the standard in order to identify it. However, street drugs contain many compounds in addition to the drug, and preliminary extraction procedures are often necessary to obtain the drug in a form pure enough for identification.

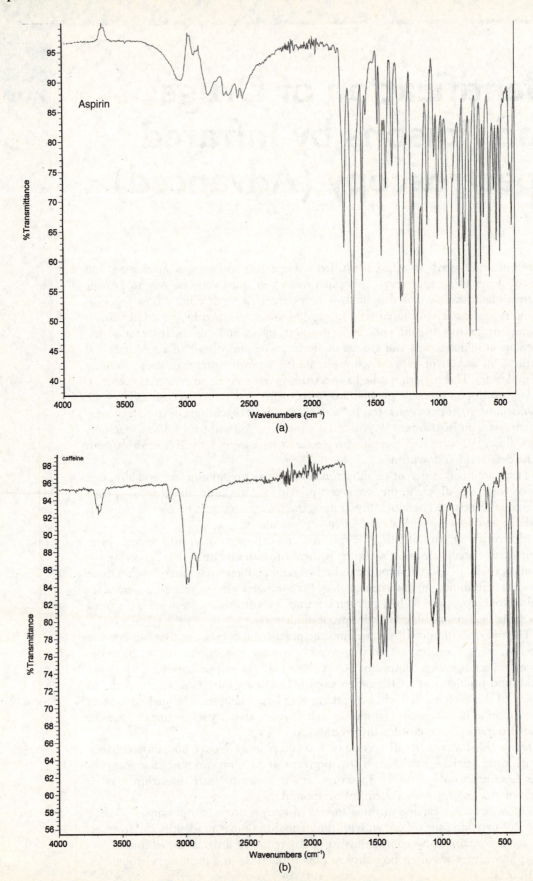

FIGURE 20-1 (a) Infrared spectrum of aspirin. (b) Infrared spectrum of caffeine.

Identification of Drugs and Poisons by Infrared Spectroscopy (Advanced)

CRIME SCENE

A law enforcement agency is alerted to the apparent sale of drugs by two persons living in a house located in a middle-class residential area. The information states that an excessively large number of persons have been visiting this house and that in one or two instances there have been sounds of violent arguments coming from within the house. The person requesting police investigation, a resident of the area, says that he is apprehensive of the violence that may result from these arguments.

After obtaining a search warrant, the law enforcement officials enter the premises and find only a bottle of liquid, which is not labeled. The occupants of the house profess ignorance of the identity of the bottle's contents.

The bottle of liquid has been transferred to the state forensic laboratory for analysis. You now have a sample of the contents of that bottle and will attempt to identify its contents by the following experiment.

EQUIPMENT

- 1 Calibration film, polystyrene
- 6 Corks, for the Erlenmeyer flasks
- 6 Flasks, Erlenmeyer, 25 mL
- 1 pr Goggles, safety
- 1 Spectrophotometer, infrared
- 1 bx Kimwipes
- 1 Liquid sample cell or demountable cell with salt plate
- 6 Medicine droppers
- 1 Wash bottle

MATERIALS

Acetone
Knowns: 5 liquid samples of known identity
Unknown: 1 liquid sample of unknown identity

METHOD

1. There are a number of manufacturers of IR spectrophotometers. Because the designs vary slightly, the operating instructions will as well. See your laboratory instructor for instructions on the proper use of the instrument available to you.

2. Obtain a demountable IR sample cell from your laboratory instructor. Assemble it and fill it with your sample as described in the steps that follow.

3. Remove the knurled nuts from the bolts that hold the plate holder together.

   NOTE: Steps 4 through 8 must be performed quickly. Read all of these steps before proceeding.

4. Obtain a salt plate from the desiccator. Be very careful not to touch the faces of the plates with your fingers, as the moisture on your skin will dissolve some of the salt from the plate and cause it to be cloudy and inaccurate. Place the salt plate on the cell plate with the bolts attached to it. Center the salt plate over the cell plate window.

5. Place the Teflon spacer on the salt plate and align the edges of the spacer and the salt plate.

6. Use a medicine dropper to transfer enough of your unknown sample to the cavity of the spacer to fill it completely. (This will require 3 or 4 drops.)

7. Place a second salt plate on top of the spacer and align the edges. Again, be careful not to touch the faces of the salt plate with your fingers.

8. Place the metal plate with the holes in it over the bolts of the lower metal plate; replace the knurled nuts and tighten them evenly and securely to hold the liquid sample in place between the salt plates.

9. Place the filled cell in the sample cell holder on the spectrophotometer and obtain the IR spectrum of your known liquid according to the operating instructions you were given earlier.

158 Experiment 20

10. After you have obtained your spectrum, disassemble the cell and rinse both faces of each salt plate and both sides of the Teflon spacer with acetone, using a polystyrene squeeze bottle and holding the parts to be cleaned over a laboratory sink. **Never clean the salt plates with water; they will be ruined.** Take our word for it and don't try it for yourself.

11. Repeat steps 3 through 10 for each of the known compounds.

12. Look carefully at each spectrum you have just obtained and notice that different groups of atoms produce specific bands in the spectra.

13. Repeat steps 3 through 10 for the unknown, and compare its spectrum with the spectra you have just obtained.

14. After you have finished the exercise, clean the salt plates and return them to the desiccator. Replace the desiccator cover. Turn the IR spectrophotometer off or leave it on standby, as directed by your laboratory instructor.

SELECTED SOURCES FOR ADDITIONAL INFORMATION

Cartier, J., Gueniat, O., and Cole, M.D., "Headspace analysis of solvents in cocaine and heroin samples," *Sci. & Just.*, 37 (3), (1997), 175.

Causin, V., Marega, C., Guzzini, G., and Margio, A., "The effect of exposure to the elements on the forensic characterisation by infrared spectroscopy of poly(ethylene terephthalate) fibers," *J. Forens. Sci.*, 50 (4), (2005), 887.

Chappell, J.S., Meyn, A.W., and Kangim, K., "The extraction and infrared identification of Gamma-hydroxybutyric acid (GHB) from aqueous solutions," *J. Forens. Sci.*, 49 (1), (2004), 52.

Flynn, K., O'Leary, R., Lennard, C., Roux, C., and Reedy, B.J., "Forensic application of infrared chemical imaging: multi-layered paint chips," *J. Forens. Sci.*, 50 (4), (2005), 832.

Lopez-Artiguiz, M., Camean, A., and Repetto, M., "Unequivocal identification of several common adulterants and solvents in street samples of cocaine by infrared spectroscopy," *J. Forens. Sci.*, 40 (4), (1995), 602.

Sakayanagi, M., Konda, Y., Watanabe, K., and Harigaya, Y., "Identification of pressure-sensitive adhesive polypropylene tape," *J. Forens. Sci.*, 48 (1), (2003), 68.

Sugawara, S., "Comparison of near infrared light photograsphy and middle infrared light photography for deciphering obliterated writings," *J. Forens. Sci.*, 49 (6), (2004), 1349.

Tahtouh, M., Kalman, J.R., Roux, C., Lennard, C., and Reedy, B.J., "The detection and enhancement of latent fingermarks using infrared chemical imaging," *J. Forens. Sci.*, 50 (1), (2005), 64.

EXPERIMENT 20   Name _____

DATA SHEET   Date _____

IDENTIFICATION OF DRUGS AND POISONS BY INFRARED SPECTROSCOPY (ADVANCED)

Fill in the data portion of your infrared spectrum chart paper. Give this spectrum, along with any others you have obtained, to your laboratory instructor.

Questions

1. What are the characteristic absorption peaks that classify your compound as to type? The following are some characteristic absorption ranges and peaks:

   Alkanes: $2,900$–$3,000$ cm^{-1}

   Aromatics: $3,000$–$3,200$ cm^{-1} (maximum near $3,030$ cm^{-1})

   Ethers: aliphatic, $1,070$–$1,150$ cm^{-1}; aromatic, $1,200$–$1,270$ cm^{-1}

   Alcohols: $3,610$–$3,640$ cm^{-1}; also $1,050$ cm^{-1}

   Ketones: $1,715$ and $1,100$ cm^{-1}

   Aldehydes: $1,725$, $2,820$, and $2,720$ cm^{-1}

   Acids: $1,760$, $1,710$, and $2,500$–$3,000$ cm^{-1}

   Esters: $1,735$ cm^{-1}; two between $1,300$ and $1,050$ cm^{-1}

2. What causes the length of the absorption peaks? How could you lengthen or shorten them?

3. Why would you have problems if you washed the salt plates with a liquid such as alcohol? What did you notice about the rate of evaporation of the acetone from the salt plates? How does this characteristic make the acetone useful as a washing liquid?

Salicylates in Blood by Visible Spectroscopy

Visible spectroscopy is the measurement of the amount of light absorbed by a solution, the amount absorbed being proportional to the concentration of the compounds in the solution. Each compound has a select few wavelengths that it will absorb in preference to other wavelengths. Therefore, by carefully selecting the wavelengths, it is often possible to measure the amount of one compound in the presence of several others.

Salicylates react with ferric salts (iron) to produce a violet color, which is proportional to the concentration of the salicylate. For the detection of salicylates, we shall use the wavelength at 540 nm to measure light absorption. Because of the simplicity of this salicylate procedure, the assumption of salicylate poisoning may be verified within minutes, especially as severe poisoning produces a very strong and easily seen violet color with the color reagent.

This experiment consists of two parts. The first involves developing the purple salicylate colors for several known solutions, preparing a calibration curve, and then determining an unknown. In the second part, you will determine salicylate in a blood serum sample.

EQUIPMENT

- 1 Brush, test tube
- 1 Bulb, pipet
- 8 Cuvettes to fit the spectrophotometer
- 1 pr Goggles, safety
- 1 bx Kimwipes
- 2 Pipets, Mohr, 1.0 mL
- 1 Rack, test tube
- 1 Spectrophotometer for operation in the visible range of the electromagnetic spectrum
- 1 Sponge
- 5 Test tubes, 10 cm and 0.1 mL

MATERIALS

Ferric nitrate, 1%   Nitric acid, 0.07 M

Dilute ferric nitrate solution: 5 parts of 1% and 4 parts of 0.07 M HNO_3

Nitric acid, 0.039 M: 5 parts of 0.07 M and 4 parts of distilled water

Salicylic acid stock solution, 100 mg/dL (100 mg/100 mL): Transfer 1.16 g of sodium salicylate to a 1-L flask, and dilute to 1 L with distilled water. Add a few drops of chloroform as a preservative, then store the solution in a refrigerator. Discard the solution after 6 months. This solution is equivalent to 100 mg/dL of salicylic acid. The use of salicylic acid as a standard is not recommended.

Salicylic acid standard solution, 5.0 mg/dL: Transfer 5 mL of the salicylic acid stock solution to 95 mL of water.

Solution of unknown salicylate concentration

PART A: BASIC SPECTROPHOTOMETRY

1. Place seven spectrophotometer cuvettes in a small test tube rack.

2. Pipet the appropriate amounts of material into 6 cuvettes as shown in Table 21–1, and shake to mix thoroughly. Calculate the salicylate concentration in mg/dL for each known salicylate sample and record the value in the space provided in the data sheet at the end of this experiment. (Hint: Cuvette 2 has a salicylate concentration of 0.25 mg/dL.)

3. The procedure described is written for use with the Spectronic 20D (Thermo Fisher Scientific) spectrophotometer. Some minor changes may be required with other types of spectrophotometers.

4. Turn on the instrument and allow the instrument to warm up for 15–20 minutes to stabilize the source and detector.

5. Adjust the wavelength to 540 nm.

6. Set the display mode to transmittance.

7. Adjust the 0% T with the "power switch/zero" control. Make sure the sample compartment is empty and the cover is closed.

8. Insert the cuvette containing the blank all of the way down into the sample compartment. Align the guide mark on the cuvette with the mark on the instrument. Make a mark on the side of the cuvette if ordinary test tubes are used.

9. Adjust the display to 100% T with the "transmittance/absorbance" control. Remove the cuvette from the compartment.

    NOTE: A flashing display indicates that the reading is out of range. Dilute the sample.

10. Insert each of the known salicylic acid standards in the sample compartment, and obtain a transmittance reading for each sample. Record each reading on the data sheet.

11. Plot percent transmittance (% T) on the vertical axis of a sheet of graph paper and the concentration (C) in mg/dL along the horizontal axis for cuvettes 1–6. Draw the best straight line through these points. This is called a calibration curve.

12. Pipet 1.0 mL of the unknown solution into a cuvette, and mix with 1.0 mL of dilute ferric nitrate. Determine its absorbance.

13. From the calibration curve and the absorbance reading you obtained for the unknown, determine the concentration of salicylate in the unknown.

TABLE 21–1	Preparation of Salicylic Acid Standards			
	5.0 mg/dL Standard	Distilled H_2O	Dilute Ferric-Nitrate	0.039 M HNO_3
Cuvette 1 Blank	0.0	1.0	0.0	1.0
Cuvette 2	0.1	0.9	1.0	0.0
Cuvette 3	0.3	0.7	1.0	0.0
Cuvette 4	0.5	0.5	1.0	0.0
Cuvette 5	0.7	0.3	1.0	0.0
Cuvette 6	1.0	0.0	1.0	0.0

PART B: SALICYLATES IN BLOOD SERUM (ADVANCED)

CRIME SCENE

A police officer observes a car moving quite erratically down the highway, and, in fact, it even crosses over the centerline, forcing another vehicle off of the road. The officer stops the car, and the driver states that she had a severe headache and had taken some aspirin. She had trouble removing the safety cap on the bottle while driving, and this had caused the erratic driving. No aspirin container is found, and the driver says that she threw it away. The driver denies that she is under the influence of alcohol or other drugs. She is taken to a hospital, where she voluntarily provides blood for an alcohol and drug test. You now have a small sample of the blood serum and are to test it for the presence and/or concentration of aspirin.

METHOD

Perform this analysis in duplicate. (You will do the serum unknown and the 5.0-mg/dL standard twice each.)

1. Label two small cuvettes each for both the unknown sample and the 5.0-mg/dL standard. The unknown sample cuvettes will be labeled "Test" and "Blank," and the standard sample cuvettes will be labeled "Test" and "Blank."
2. Prepare the cuvettes as described below. Table 21–2 lists each tube and its contents.
3. Pipet 2.0 mL of distilled water into each cuvette.
4. Into the cuvettes for the unknown sample, pipet 0.2 mL of serum.
5. Into the cuvette for the standard, pipet 0.2 mL of the 5.0-mg/dL standard.
6. Into both Blank cuvettes, pipet 2.0 mL of 0.039 N nitric acid.
7. Into the Test cuvettes, pipet 2.0 mL of dilute ferric nitrate solution.
8. Shake all cuvettes to mix the contents.
9. Let all tubes stand for 5 minutes.
10. Follow the directions given in Part A for the operation of the spectrophotometer, and obtain a reading for each cuvette. Record the absorbance reading on the data sheet.

TABLE 21–2	Contents of the Various Cuvettes
Standard (5.0 mg/dL)	**Serum Unknown**
Blank	*Blank*
2.0 mL of distilled water	2.0 mL of distilled water
0.2 mL of 5.0-mg/dL standard	0.2 mL of serum
2.0 mL of 0.039 N nitric acid	2.0 mL of 0.039 N nitric acid
Test	*Test*
2.0 mL of distilled water	2.0 mL of distilled water
0.2 mL of 5.0-mg/dL standard	0.2 mL of serum
2.0 mL of dilute ferric nitrate	2.0 mL of dilute ferric nitrate

SELECTED SOURCES FOR ADDITIONAL INFORMATION

Almog, J., Cohen, Y., Azoury, M., and Hahn, T., "Genipin-a novel fingerprint reagent with colorimetric and fluorogenic activity," *J. Forens. Sci.*, 49 (2), (2004), 255.

Berger, C.H., Dekneijer, J.A., Glas, W., and Madhuizen, H.T., "Color separation in forensic image processing," *J. Forens. Sci.*, 51 (1), (2006), 100.

DuBey, I.S., and Caplan, Y.H., "The storage of forensic drug specimens as dry stains: recovery and stability," *J. Forens. Sci.*, 41 (5), (1996), 845.

Exline, D.L., Wallace, C., Roux, C., Lennard, C., Nelson, M.P., and Treado, P.J., "Forensic application of chemical imaging: latent fingerprint detection using visible absorption and luminescence," *J. Forens. Sci.*, 48 (5), (2003), 1047.

Levinton-Shamuilov, G., Cohen, Y., Azoury, M., Chaikovsky, A., and Almog, J., "Genipin, a novel fingerprint reagent with colorimetric and fluoregenic activity,"*J. Forens. Sci.*, 50 (6), (2005), 1367.

Massonnet, G., and Stoecklein, W., "Identification of organic pigments in coatings: Application to red automotive topcoats. Part I: Thin layer chromatography with direct visible microspectrophotometric detection," *Sci. & Just.*, 39 (2), (1999), 128.

Suzuki, S., Suzuki, Y., Ohta, H., Sugita, R., and Marumo, Y., "Microspectrophotometric discrimination of single fibers dyed by indigo and its derivatives using ultraviolet-visible transmittance spectra," *Sci. & Just.*, 41 (2), (2001), 107.

Vandenberg, N., and Van Oorschot, R.H., "The use of Polilight in the detection of seminal fluid, saliva, and bloodstains and comparison with conventional chemical-based screening tests," *J. Forens. Sci.*, 51 (2), (2006), 361.

Vogt, C., Becker, A., and Vogt, J., "Investigation of ball point pen inks by capillary electrophoresis (CE) with UV/vis absorbance and laser induced fluorescence detection and particle induced x-ray emission (PIXE)," *J. Forens. Sci.*, 44 (4), (1999), 819.

Voorhees, J., Ferrance, J.P., and Landers, J.P., "Enhanced elution of sperm from cotton swabs via enzymatic digestion for rape kit analysis," *J. Forens. Sci.*, 51 (3), (2006), 574.

Wilson, J.D., Laporte, G.M., and Cantu, A.A., "Differentiation of black gel inks using optical and chemical techniques," *J. Forens. Sci.*, 49 (2), (2004), 364.

EXPERIMENT 21 Name _____

DATA SHEET Date _____

SALICYLATES IN BLOOD BY VISIBLE SPECTROSCOPY

Part A: Basic Spectrophotometry

	Concentration of salicylate (mg/dL)	Absorbance
Cuvette 1		
Cuvette 2		
Cuvette 3		
Cuvette 4		
Cuvette 5		
Cuvette 6		

Absorbance of unknown: _____

Concentration of unknown obtained from the graph: _____ mg/dL

Part B: Salicylates in Blood Serum (Advanced)

	Absorbance	Absorbance
Standard blank		
Standard 5.0 mg/dL		
Unknown Blank		
Unknown		

Calculations

a. Use the following relationship to determine the concentration of salicylate in the unknown sample:

$$\text{mg/mL} = \frac{\text{absorbance of unknown} - \text{absorbance of unknown blank}}{\text{absorbance of standard} - \text{absorbance of standard blank}} \times 50$$

b. Calculate each sample of the unknown separately, and average the results. If the individual results do not agree within 2 to 3 mg/dL, perform the analysis a third and a fourth time. Calculate and compare the results obtained before. Average the values that agree within 2 to 3 mg/dL of each other.

Questions

1. Do you suppose that there would normally be salicylate in human blood? Give reasons for your answer.

2. Why does the analyst perform the determination in duplicate?

3. Give an instance, other than the example cited, where this analysis might be applicable.

Salicylates in Blood by Fluorometry (Advanced)

Salicylate, in various forms, is the most widely used of all drugs. Determining the presence of salicylate is important in toxicology. The accessibility of aspirin (acetylsalicylic acid) and oil of wintergreen (methyl salicylate) has led to frequent reported poisonings.

CRIME SCENE

A young woman confides to a friend of hers that she is very depressed. An argument with her fiancé has resulted in the breaking of their engagement. She says that she does not want to live if the problem cannot be resolved and the quarrel resolved. Her friend offers what little consolation she can and says that she will call her later that evening. However, when she calls no one answers the telephone. She then calls the police, gives them the address, and someone is sent to investigate. On entering the distressed girl's apartment, the officers find her lying on the bed in a coma. An empty aspirin bottle is found in the bathroom. The girl is taken to a local hospital by ambulance and a sample of blood drawn from her arm. You now have that sample of blood to analyze for salicylate content.

This procedure measures salicylic acid and its conjugates (related compounds). Acetylsalicylic acid is readily, but incompletely, hydrolyzed to salicylic acid in the intestines and in the blood. The strongly alkaline conditions utilized in this experiment will largely complete the hydrolysis, yielding a substantially quantitative assay. The fate of oil of wintergreen is less certain. Such esters of salicylic acid are absorbed after hydrolysis. The procedure will detect ingestion with certainty, but the determined levels may be *low*.

Acetylsalicylic acid

Salicylic acid

168 Experiment 22

EQUIPMENT

1	Beaker, 100 mL	1 bx	Kimwipes
2	Cuvettes to fit fluorometer	1	Pipet bulb
1	Cylinder, graduated, 100 mL	1	Pipet, Mohr, 10 mL
1	Flask, Erlenmeyer, 250 mL	1	Plastic or glass funnels, 65 mm
1	Flask, volumetric, 10 mL		Stirring rods, glass
1	Flask, volumetric, 100 mL	5	Test tubes, 22 × 150 mm
1	Filter paper, 11.5 cm, Whatman grade 40 or equivalent	1	Test tube brush
		1	Test tube rack
1 pr	Goggles, safety		
1	Fluorometer (your instructor will provide information regarding settings for the excitation wave length and emission spectrum)		

MATERIALS

Sodium tungstate, 10%: Dissolve 10 g of reagent-grade sodium tungstate, $Na_2WO_4 \cdot 2H_2O$, in 100 mL of distilled water.

Sulfuric acid, 1/12 N: Add, cautiously, 2.3 mL of reagent-grade sulfuric acid to 1.0 L of distilled water.

Tungstic acid reagent: Mix 10 mL of the sodium tungstate solution and 80 mL of 1/12 N sulfuric acid. This reagent is stable for about 2 weeks. If it becomes turbid, it should be discarded.

Sodium hydroxide, 10 N: Carefully add 40 g of reagent-grade sodium hydroxide, NaOH, to 93 mL of water. Because this will become quite hot, solution should be effected by careful swirling in a borosilicate conical flask in a pan of cool water. After the solution has cooled to room temperature, it should be transferred to a polyethylene container for storage. Alternatively, 50% solutions (w/w) of reagent-grade sodium hydroxide are available. Mixing equal volumes of this and distilled water will produce, closely enough, a 10 M solution.

Salicylate stock standard, 100 mg/dL (1 mg/dL = 1 mg/100 mL of solution): Dissolve 116.0 mg of reagent-grade sodium salicylate, $NaC_7H_5O_3$, in distilled water in a 100-mL volumetric flask, and dilute to the mark with distilled water. Invert several times to ensure thorough mixing. Store in the refrigerator.

Salicylate working standard, 10 mg/dL: Pipet 1.00 mL of the stock into a 10-mL volumetric flask, and dilute to the mark with tungstic acid reagent. Prepare fresh daily.

Blood samples containing known concentrations of salicylate ion (instructor prepared)

NOTE: The older term to describe concentration, mg% (mg/100 mL of body fluid), has largely been replaced with mg/dL (also mg/100 mL). They both mean the same thing and the values are the same.

METHOD

Salicylic acid is intensely fluorescent under alkaline conditions and can be measured directly in diluted serum or plasma, following precipitation of the proteins (see Note 1 at the end of this section). This procedure is based on the method of Saltzman (1948), wherein the proteins are precipitated with tungstic acid. Following the addition of concentrated sodium hydroxide, the sample fluorescence is compared with that of a standard solution. The values are expressed as salicylic acid in accordance with routine usage. As written, the procedure uses 0.5 mL of serum.

Blank values for plasma containing no salicylate are of the order of mg/dL and are not usually taken into account in the calculation of the results. If very low levels are of interest, it is recommended that an extraction procedure be used (see Note 1).

Convenient vessels for the following operations are test tubes of about 40 mL capacity (22 × 150 mm). Each unknown will require three such tubes. In addition, one tube each will be required for a standard and a blank. All volumes called for are measured and added by pipet.

1. To 0.5 mL of serum or plasma, add 9.5 mL of tungstic acid reagent slowly and with stirring. Mix thoroughly and let stand for 10 minutes.

2. Filter the solution through a small conical funnel (50 mm) using a medium retentive paper, such as Whatman No. 40. A clear filtrate is desirable, but a slight turbidity will not interfere.

3. Tubes are now set up for unknowns (U), standard (S), and blank (B):

    U: 5 mL of filtrate from step 2.
    S: 0.5 mL of salicylate working standard plus 4.5 mL of tungstic acid reagent.
    B: 5 mL of tungstic acid reagent.

4. Add 7 mL of 10 M sodium hydroxide to each tube and mix thoroughly.

5. The solutions are poured into 12 × 75 mm cuvettes and the fluorescence read any time within 30 minutes in a fluorometer that has been blanked with the dummy cuvette.

6. Clean all glassware well. The sodium hydroxide will leave a white residue, after drying, if this is not done. (Caution: Be sure to remove all of the NaOH from your hands; it can cause severe burns. Its presence is determined by a slippery feeling when the skin is rubbed.)

7. Repeat the procedure two more times, and average the results.

NOTE 1: For the determination in tissues and other fluids, an extraction procedure is recommended.

NOTE 2: The procedure was arranged this way for convenience. The standard contains no protein, and hence requires no filtration, and preparing it directly to the volume called for in step 3 eliminates one pipetting operation. It could have been prepared from 0.25 mL of standard and 4.75 mL of tungstic acid reagent, eliminating the factor of 2 in calculation, but such volumes are difficult to read in graduated pipets.

CALCULATIONS

Because the serum is diluted 20-fold whereas the standard is diluted only 10-fold, a factor of 2 must be used in computation (see equation below). If the recommended working standard of 10 mg/dL is used, then

$$\text{mg/dL salicylate} = \frac{U - B}{S - B} \times 10 \times 2$$

SELECTED SOURCES FOR ADDITIONAL INFORMATION

Almog, J., Azoury, M., Elmaliah, Y., Berenstein, L., and Zaban, A., "Fingerprints' third dimension: The depth and shape of fingerprints penetration into paper," *J. Forens. Sci.*, 49 (5), (2004), 981.

Almog, J., Cohen, Y., Azoury, M., and Hahn, T., "Genipin: A novel fingerprint reagent with colorimetric and fluorogenic activity," *J. Forens. Sci.*, 49 (2), (2004), 255.

Gardner, S.J., and Hewlett, D.F., "Optimization and initial evaluation of 1,2-indandione as a reagent for fingerprint detection," *J. Forens. Sci.*, 48 (6), (2003), 1288.

Kurata, S., Hirano, H., and Nagai, M., "Determination of luminescent europium B-diketones used as tracers for shadowing pursuits," *J. Forens. Sci.*, 47 (4), (2002), 797.

Pretty, I.A., Smith, P.W., Edgar, M., and Higham, S.M., "The use of quantitative light-induced fluorescence (QLF) to identify composite restorations in forensic examinations," *J. Forens. Sci.*, 47 (4), (2002), 831.

Saltzman, A., "Fluorometric method for the estimation of salicylate in blood," *J. Biol. Chem.*, 174, (1948), 399.

Turner Manual of Fluorometric Procedures, Turner Instruments Corporation.

Vogt, C., Becker, A., and Vogt, J., "Investigation of ball point pen inks by capillary electrophoresis (CE) with UV/vis absorbance and laser induced fluorescence detection and particle induced x-ray emission (PIXE)," *J. Forens. Sci.*, 44 (4), (1999), 819.

EXPERIMENT 22
DATA SHEET

Name _____

Date _____

SALICYLATES IN BLOOD BY FLUOROMETRY (ADVANCED)

1. Sample   Fluorometer dial reading:

   a. Blank (B)

   b. Standard (S)

   c. Unknown (   )

   d. Unknown (   )

   e. Unknown (   )

2. Calculation

$$\text{mg/dL salicylate} = \frac{U - B}{S - B} \times 10 \times 2$$

Calculate each sample of your unknown separately. Then average the three values for your unknown if they all agree closely. If one value for the unknown is very different from the other two (>20%), do not use that value and average the other two.

Sample   mg/dL salicylate

   c. Unknown (   )

   d. Unknown (   )

   e. Unknown (   )

Average mg/dL salicylate in unknown = _____ mg/dL?

172   Experiment 22

3. Do you suppose that there would normally be salicylate in human blood?

4. What precautions do you suppose one must observe when filtering the solutions in step 2 of the analysis?

5. Give an instance, other than the example cited, where fluorometric analysis might be applicable.

EXPERIMENT 23

Quinine in Urine by Fluorometry (Advanced)

Fluorescence spectroscopy is an outgrowth of the observation that some materials will fluoresce or emit light when they are exposed to ultraviolet radiation. A characteristic property of any fluorescent compound is that it always absorbs and emits radiation at specific wavelengths. A fluorometer is an instrument designed to expose compounds to selected wavelengths of ultraviolet radiation and, at the same time, to measure the wavelengths of visible radiation they emit. Often, by utilizing a fluorometer, it is possible to detect and identify a fluorescing material that may be mixed in with other substances.

Quinine is a common adulterant of illicit heroin drug preparations. Hence, the finding of quinine in urine or blood is taken as an indication that heroin was used. If morphine is present as well, this assumption becomes very reasonable. Quinine may, however, be found in over-the-counter medications and in tonic water, and these can also cause a positive test.

CRIME SCENE

A driver is stopped by a police officer for speeding and operating his vehicle in an erratic manner. The driver fails to respond properly to the balance and coordination tests administered by the arresting officer. Upon further questioning, the driver denies being under the influence of alcohol and agrees to take a breath test in a nearby police station. Within 30 minutes the suspect is driven to the station, where the test is administered. The breath test results in a zero reading. However, the subject is observed to be sweating and drowsy. A urine specimen is requested and received from the driver for drug analysis. A short time later, a search of the driver's vehicle uncovers a syringe and other paraphernalia associated with the use of heroin. You now have the urine specimen, and as a preliminary test for the presence of heroin, you will analyze the specimen for quinine.

Quinine can be extracted out of a basic solution of urine with an organic solvent. Re-extraction of the quinine into dilute acid produces a solution whose fluorescence spectrum can be used to identify the presence of quinine.

EQUIPMENT

- 1 Bulb, for disposable pipets
- 1 Bulb, pipet
- 2 Cuvettes to fit the fluorometer
- 2 Cylinders, graduated 10 mL
- 1 Flask, volumetric, 100 mL
- 2 Flasks, volumetric, 1 L
- 5 Funnels, separatory, 125 mL
- 1 pr Goggles, safety
- 1 Paper, pH
- 1 Pipet, Mohr, 5 mL
- 3 Pipets, Pasteur
- 1 Rack, funnel
- 1 Rack, test tube
- 1 Ring stand
- Spectrofluorometer
- 1 cup Urine (from a hospital)

MATERIALS

Chloroform

Potassium hydroxide, saturated aqueous solution

Quinine sulfate stock solution: Dissolve 100 mg of quinine sulfate in 1 L of distilled water.

Quinine sulfate reference solution: Dilute 1 mL of the quinine sulfate stock solution to 100 mL with distilled water.

Sulfuric acid, 0.05 M: Dilute 2.8 mL of concentrated sulfuric acid to 1 L with distilled water.

Urine sample containing quinine (instructor prepared)

METHOD

A spectrofluorometer is set up at an excitation wavelength of 350 nm to record an emission spectrum at 445 nm. Because there are different models of fluorometers commercially available, your instructor will demonstrate the operation of the particular one being used in your laboratory. In 0.05 M sulfuric acid, quinine fluoresces at approximately 445 nm.

1. Add a drop of saturated potassium hydroxide to 5.0 mL of urine. Test the specimen for alkalinity with pH paper. Add more potassium hydroxide, if necessary, until the pH is greater than 7. In the same manner, process 5.0 mL of quinine reference solution and 5.0 mL of water for a reagent blank.

2. Place the urine specimen in a separatory funnel, and extract with 10 mL of chloroform. Shake the funnel for at least 1 minute. Allow the solvent and aqueous phases to separate completely.

3. Carefully transfer the chloroform layer to a clean separatory funnel and re-extract the solvent with 6 mL of 0.1 N (0.05 M) sulfuric acid.

4. Transfer the upper (aqueous) layer to a cuvette by means of a Pasteur pipet and place the cuvette in the fluorometer.

5. To determine if quinine is present, excite the sample at 350 nm, and read the fluorescence at 445 nm.

6. Repeat the procedure for the quinine reference solution and the water blank.

The fluorometer can also be used to measure the concentration of quinine in urine. This is done by comparing the intensity of the quinine fluorescence in the urine extract to the fluorescence of a quinine standard. These values were obtained in step 6.

CALCULATIONS

The concentration of the quinine sulfate reference solution is 0.1 mg/100 mL, or 0.1 mg/dL. Hence, the concentration of quinine in urine is found by applying the following equation:

$$\text{mg/dL quinine} = \frac{\text{fluorescence or urine extract} - \text{water blank}}{\text{fluorescence of quinine reference solution} - \text{water blank}} \times 0.1$$

SELECTED SOURCES FOR ADDITIONAL INFORMATION

Goodpaster, J.V., Howerton, S.B., and McGuffin, V.L., "Forensic analysis of commercial petroleum products using selective fluorescence quenching," *J. Forens. Sci.*, 46 (6), (2001), 1358.

Kurata, S., Hirano, H., and Nagai, M., "Development of fluorescent markers using polycyclic aromatic hydrocarbons with Vaseline," *J. Forens. Sci.*, 47 (2), (2002), 244.

Vogt, C., Becker, A., and Vogt, J., "Investigation of ball point pen inks by capillary electrophoresis (CE) with UV/vis absorbance and laser induced fluorescence detection and particle induced x-ray emission (PIXE)," *J. Forens. Sci.*, 44 (4), (1999), 819.

EXPERIMENT 23

Name _____

DATA SHEET

Date _____

QUININE IN URINE BY FLUOROMETRY (ADVANCED)

1. Sample   Fluorometer scale reading

   Blank

   Reference

   Unknown

2. Calculation for unknown sample

   mg/dL quinine sulfate in urine = _____ mg/dL

Analysis of Blood Alcohol by Gas Chromatography Using a Thermal Conductivity Detector

Gas liquid chromatography (GLC) is a means of identifying and quantitating poisons, drugs, and alcohol in blood or urine samples. It is a rapid, simple, and specific procedure, assuming the availability of standard samples for comparison and quantitation. If the instrument is warmed up and ready to operate, the determination of alcohol can be performed in 6 to 8 minutes.

A sample (liquid or gaseous) is injected onto a heated column packed with a material capable of separating the components of a mixture into their individual parts. This packing material is determined by reference to the literature or by the analyst, who tries various materials and determines the best one for use by means of the separation data obtained.

Known and unknown samples are injected into the same column under identical conditions, and by comparing the time it takes for the peaks to emerge from the column (retention time), the components in the unknown are identified. Use of known concentrations of the standard samples will allow quantitation of the unknown by a comparison of sample peak areas or heights as shown on the chromatogram.

Figure 24–1 shows a typical chromatogram. For sharp peaks, the peak height is proportional to the concentration, whereas for broader peaks we find that the peak area gives a more accurate measure of the concentration.

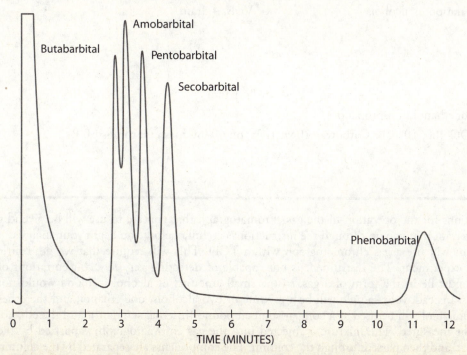

FIGURE 24–1 A typical gas chromatogram. *Courtesy Varian, Inc., Palo Alto, Calif.*

Operating instructions vary slightly, depending upon the particular instrument used; your instructor will explain how to use the gas chromatograph assigned to you.

Two procedures will be given, one that simulates the analysis of blood alcohol, employing an instrument with a thermal conductivity detector (TCD), and the other, in the following experiment, which uses an instrument with the flame ionization detector (FID). In either case, the principle remains the same. This choice will allow schools that have either or both types of instruments to do the analysis and help students understand the principles involved. A working forensic laboratory would make use of the FID because of its increased sensitivity and its lack of response to water.

CRIME SCENE

A law enforcement officer, in the routine performance of his duties, notices a car being operated in a rather erratic manner. The car, while not being driven excessively fast, swerves from one side of the street to the other, and the driver appears to be under the influence of alcohol or some other substance, which impairs the safe operation of his vehicle. The officer stops the driver, and as he approaches, detects the odor of alcohol on the driver's breath. The officer requests that the driver accompany him to a nearby facility to take a blood alcohol test. The driver maintains that he is not under the influence of alcohol, but that he will submit to the test. He is taken to a hospital, where a sample of his blood is taken by a certified medical technologist and sent to a forensic laboratory for analysis of blood alcohol content. You now have that blood sample and will perform the analysis.

EQUIPMENT

1	Beaker, 10 mL	1	Pencil, grease
1	Beaker, 50 mL	1	Pipet, Mohr, 2 mL
1	Bulb, pipet	1	Pipet, Mohr, 10 mL
7	Corks	1	Razor blade, single edge
7	Flasks, Erlenmeyer 25 mL	1	Ruler, metric
1	Gas chromatograph equipped with a thermal conductivity detector and a column suitable for the separation of alcohols	1	Strip chart recorder compatible with the gas chromatograph used
		1	Syringe, 10 microliter (µL)
		6	Vials, 4 dram
1pr	Goggles, safety		

MATERIALS

Absolute ethanol

n-Propanol

Unknown mixtures of ethanol in n-propanol

Suggested column: DC-200, 10%, or Carbowax 20M, 10%, on 60–80 mesh Chromosorb P

METHOD

The specific instructions for the operation of the gas chromatograph that you are to use will be given by your instructor. Be certain that you go through the instructions carefully before you begin your analysis.

This experiment will use a gas chromatograph with a TCD. This will require that we do a little "pretending" in this experiment. The instrument is not capable of detecting very low concentrations of compounds, which must be in the form of a gas, so the small amounts of alcohol in blood would not be useful for analysis. Instead, your sample will be a mixture of two alcohols, one ethanol, and the other n-propanol. The n-propanol will be used as a comparison compound (internal standard), and the ethanol is the substance to be measured. The mixture is injected into the gas chromatograph, vaporized by the heated injection block, and then passed through the column. The components are separated by the column packing material and pass over the detector element. The interaction of the molecules with the filaments in the detector is converted to an electrical signal, passed to a recording device, and printed out as a peak on a moving chart paper. The height of the peak will be used as a representation of the quantity of substance detected and, therefore, present in the sample.

An example of one workable gas chromatographic system for the typical Gow-Mac student gas chromatograph is as follows:

>   Flow rate: 60 mL/min; use helium or nitrogen carrier gas
>
>   Filament current: 180 mA
>
>   Column temperature: 90°C
>
>   Column packing: 10% DC-200 on Chromosorb P
>
>   Attenuation: 4
>
>   Sample size: 5 μL

1. Inject 5 μL of ethanol. Once it has produced a peak, then inject 5 μL of n-propanol separately to determine their retention times and to determine what attenuation to use.

2. Prepare mixtures of ethanol and n-propanol in the following proportions, in 25-mL Erlenmeyer flasks. Be sure to cork each mixture to prevent evaporation.

   >   0.1 mL of ethanol + 1.9 mL of n-propanol
   >
   >   0.2 mL of ethanol + 1.8 mL of n-propanol
   >
   >   0.3 mL of ethanol + 1.7 mL of n-propanol
   >
   >   0.4 mL of ethanol + 1.6 mL of n-propanol
   >
   >   0.5 mL of ethanol + 1.5 mL of n-propanol

3. Inject these mixtures consecutively into the gas chromatograph, waiting for each to come through before the next is injected. Use a volume of the mixture that will keep the recorded peaks on scale. Injections are performed by use of a 10-μL syringe. Use the same volume for all your injections. The easiest way to determine this volume is to find the volume that keeps all peaks on scale for the mixture containing the greatest percentage of ethanol. Then use this volume for all of the other injections, including your unknown mixture. Do not change any of the instrumental settings after you begin your injections of the known mixtures.

4. After you have injected all of the known mixtures, obtain an unknown. Inject the unknown according to the previously given instructions.

5. Turn off or place the instrument in a standby mode, according to the directions of your laboratory instructor.

6. Tear off your chart paper and proceed as follows.

7. Measure the height of the ethanol peak for each of the known mixtures.

8. Calculate the percentage of ethanol in each mixture and prepare a calibration curve on graph paper of percentage ethanol versus peak height. Use the vertical axis for peak height and the horizontal axis for concentration.

9. Measure the ethanol peak height for your unknown, and determine the percentage ethanol from your calibration curve.

10. Report the value obtained for percentage ethanol in your sample on the data sheet.

11. Staple your calibration curve and the chart paper with your recorded peaks to the data sheet, answer all questions, and turn this material in to your laboratory instructor.

12. Clean and return all equipment and glassware to the designated locations. The actual procedure used for blood alcohol analysis differs from the one given here and is presented in Experiment 25.

SELECTED SOURCES FOR ADDITIONAL INFORMATION

Barnes, A.T., Dolan, J.A., Kuk, R.J., and Siegel, J.A., "Comparison of gasolines using gas chromatography-mass spectrometry and target ion response," *J. Forens. Sci.*, 49 (5), (2004), 1018.

DeVos, B.J., Fronman, M., Rohwer, E., and Sutherland, D., "Detection of petrol (gasoline) in fire debris by gas chromatography/mass spectrometry/mass spectrometry (GC/MS/MS)," *J. Forens. Sci.*, 47 (4), (2002), 736.

Jones, A.W., and Holmgren, P., "Comparison of blood alcohol concentration in deaths attributed to acute alcohol poisoning and chronic alcoholism," *J. Forens. Sci.*, 48 (4), (2003), 874.

EXPERIMENT 24 Name _____

DATA SHEET Date _____

ANALYSIS OF BLOOD ALCOHOL BY GAS CHROMATOGRAPHY USING A THERMAL CONDUCTIVITY DETECTOR

1. Unknown sample number _____

2. Data for calibration curve

Mixture	% Ethanol (vol.)	Height of ethanol peak (cm)
1.		
2.		
3.		
4.		
5.		
Unknown		

3. Concentration of ethanol in unknown mixture (%)

4. Do the retention times of ethanol and n-propanol compare closely with these components in each mixture? Measure each component of each standard and the sample solution. List each retention time in the space below and compare them. Calculate the average retention time for each component and list them in question five.

5. What are the retention times of each component, expressed in centimeters?

   ethanol _____ cm   n-propanol _____ cm

6. Is the plot of % ethanol by volume versus peak height linear? What might cause any deviation from linearity, if it exists? If the five points representing the five standards are not linear, draw the best straight line through the points, passing through as many points as possible, and try to position the line in such a way as to have equal numbers of outliers above and below your line. DO NOT connect dot to dot.

7. How could you change the retention times of the components in the mixture to achieve better separation between them?

8. (Optional) Peak area versus concentration could also be used to prepare the calibration curve. Extra credit points will be awarded if you choose to use peak area to determine the percentage of ethanol in your mixture. What might cause any deviation from linearity, if it exists? If the five points representing the five standards are not linear, draw the best straight line through the points, passing through as many points as possible, and try to position the line in such a way as to have equal numbers of outliers above and below your line. DO NOT connect dot to dot. How do the values compare for both calibration curve results?

Analysis of Blood Alcohol by Gas Chromatography Using a Thermal Conductivity Detector

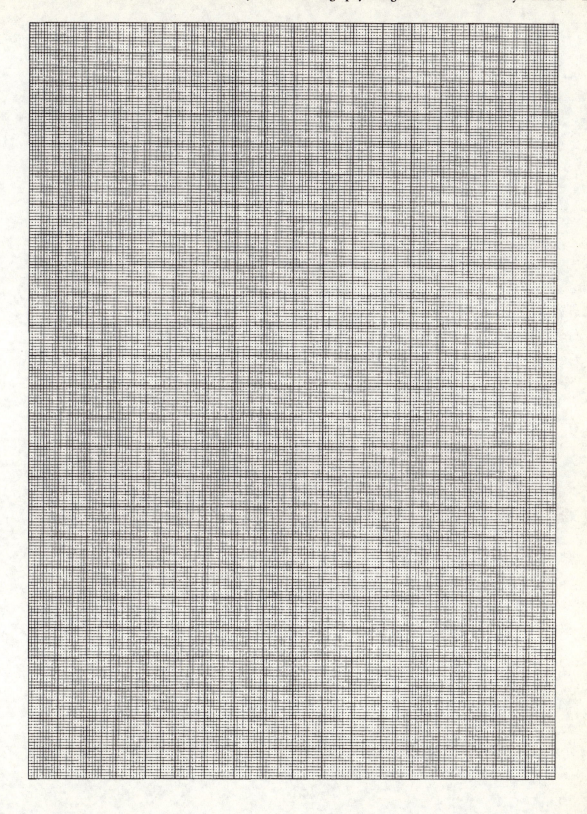

Analysis of Blood Alcohol by Gas-Liquid Chromatography Using a Flame Ionization Detector

EXPERIMENT 25

The analysis given here is a standard method for determining the alcohol content by volume percentage in a blood or urine sample. This method, with maybe a few local variations, is routinely performed in laboratories associated with local police and state highway patrol law enforcement agencies in every state. The method is rapid, accurate, and reproducible.

This analysis is useful when a vehicle operator is suspected of being under the influence of alcohol. A typical example is cited in Experiment 24, and the student is referred to it for background information.

The gas chromatograph employed in this analysis is equipped with a flame ionization detector (FID). This detector is very sensitive to small amounts of alcohol and other organic compounds, but is insensitive to water. This detector is about 100 times more sensitive than the thermal conductivity detector (TCD). This makes the detector very useful for the analysis of alcohol or drugs in blood or urine samples. The method used here will be one of headspace analysis. This means that instead of a liquid sample being injected into the gas chromatograph, a sample of the vapor above the liquid sample, produced by incubating the sample in a constant-temperature water bath at a slightly elevated temperature, is used for injection. This serves to eliminate extra peaks due to other substances in the blood or urine sample.

EQUIPMENT

- 1 Brush, test tube
- 1 Flask, volumetric, 100 mL
- 1 Holder, test tube
- 1 bx Kimwipes
- 1 Label or glass-marking pen
- 2 Pipets, Mohr, 5 mL
- 1 Rack, test tube
- 1 Ruler, metric
- 1 Gas chromatograph, equipped with a FID and column suitable for the separation of alcohols
- 1 Strip chart, recorder compatible with the gas chromatograph used
- 1 Syringe, Plastipak disposable, 3 mL
- 7 Test tubes, 10 cm, with rubber septum caps
- 1 Constant-temperature water bath, 50°C
- 7 Flasks, Erlenmeyer with rubber stoppers, 25 mL

MATERIALS

Blood samples containing varying percentages of ethanol

Ethanol, stock solutions 1%: Pipet 1.0 mL of absolute ethanol into a 100-mL volumetric flask and dilute to 100 mL with distilled water.

METHOD

The actual instructions for the operation of the gas chromatograph will vary slightly depending on the instrument used. These instructions will be provided by the person in charge of the laboratory and will not be dealt with here.

1. Prepare mixtures of the ethanol stock solution and distilled water in the proportions listed below in a 25-mL Erlenmeyer flask. Stopper the flask, shake vigorously, and transfer 4 mL to a stoppered test tube.

    1.0 mL ethanol stock solution + 9.0 mL of water
    2.0 mL ethanol stock solution + 8.0 mL of water
    3.0 mL ethanol stock solution + 7.0 mL of water
    4.0 mL ethanol stock solution + 6.0 mL of water
    5.0 mL ethanol stock solution + 5.0 mL of water

2. Place the mixtures, in the septum-stoppered test tubes, in a 50°C constant-temperature water bath for 10 minutes.

3. Obtain two blood samples.

4. Pipet 2 mL of your blood sample into a clean test tube, repeat with a second pipet, and pipet this sample into a second tube.

5. Be certain that you mark the tubes with the sample number, to avoid identification errors later.

6. Place the septum cap on each test tube, shake to mix the contents, and place both tubes in the 50°C constant-temperature water bath for 10 minutes.

7. Zero the recorder-gas chromatographic system as explained by your laboratory instructor.

8. Remove the known standard mixture containing the highest percentage of ethanol from the water bath.

9. Insert the gas-tight syringe needle through the septum cap completely, but do not allow the syringe needle to enter the liquid. We want a sample of the vapor above the liquid only.

10. Remove a 1.0-mL sample of the headspace vapor and inject it into the gas chromatograph. Set the controls of the gas chromatograph so that this sample will stay on scale and give a complete peak for each component.

11. When this is accomplished, inject ethanol and n-propanol separately to determine the identity of each component by its retention time on the gas chromatographic column.

12. Return the mixture to the water bath, as you will need to sample this mixture again later.

13. Beginning with the sample mixture containing the lowest percentage of ethanol, inject each mixture in turn, taking care to only sample headspace vapor. Wait for both peaks to be recorded before injecting the next sample. Use 1.0 mL of sample in each injection.

14. Inject the headspace vapor of each of your unknowns in the same manner as the known mixtures.

15. Leave the gas chromatograph on standby or shut it down, as your laboratory instructor has indicated.

16. Measure the height of each ethanol peak in centimeters.

17. Calculate the percentage of ethanol in each mixture.

18. Prepare a calibration curve on graph paper of percentage ethanol (by volume) on the horizontal axis and peak height on the vertical axis.

19. Determine the percentage of ethanol in each of your blood unknowns by use of your calibration curve and the measured height of the ethanol peak in each unknown.

20. Record all data values on the data sheet.

21. Answer the questions, attach the chromatogram with the recorded peaks and your calibration curve to the data sheet, and hand these in.

22. Clean all glassware and equipment. Return these items to their designated locations.

SELECTED SOURCES FOR ADDITIONAL INFORMATION

Booker, J.L., "End-position nystagmus as an indicator of ethanol intoxication," *Sci. & Just.*, 41 (2), (2001), 113.

Gullberg, R.G., and Logan, B.K., "Results of a proposed breath alcohol proficiency test program," *J. Forens. Sci.*, 51 (1), (2006), 168.

Jones, A.W., and Andersson, L., "Influence of age, gender, and blood-alcohol concentration on the disappearance rate of alcohol from blood in drinking drivers," *J. Forens. Sci.*, 41 (6), (1996), 922.

Moore, R.L., and Guillen, J., "The effect of breath freshener strips on two types of breath alcohol testing instruments," *J. Forens. Sci.*, 49 (4), (2004), 829.

Stephens, A., and Franklin, S.D.A., "Level of lung function required to use the Camic Datamaster breath alcohol testing device," *Sci. & Just.*, 41 (1), (2001), 49.

Wilson, C.I., Ignacio, S.S., and Wilson, G.A., "An unusual form of fatal ethanol intoxication," *J. Forens. Sci.*, 50 (3), (2005), 676.

EXPERIMENT 25   Name _____

DATA SHEET   Date _____

ANALYSIS OF BLOOD ALCOHOL BY GAS CHROMATOGRAPHY USING A FLAME IONIZATION DETECTOR (ADVANCED)

1. Unknown sample number _____

   Unknown sample number _____

2. Data for calibration curve

Mixture	% Ethanol (vol.)	Height of ethanol peak (cm)
1.		
2.		
3.		
4.		
5.		

   Unknown no. _____

   Unknown no. _____

3. Concentration of ethanol (vol. %)

   Unknown no. _____   conc _____

   Unknown no. _____   conc _____

4. What are the retention times of each component, expressed in centimeters?

   Ethanol _____ cm   n-Propanol _____ cm

Experiment 25

5. Is the calibration curve linear with the concentration of ethanol? How can you determine this?

6. How could you change the retention times of the components in a mixture to achieve better separation between them?

7. (Optional) Peak area versus concentration could also be used to prepare the calibration curve. Extra credit will be awarded if you choose to use your recorder peaks to determine the percentage of ethanol in your blood samples in this manner. How do the values compare for both calibration curve results?

EXPERIMENT 26

Separation of Ink Dyes Using Thin-Layer Chromatography

This experiment will demonstrate a technique that forensic scientists have developed for identifying the colored pigments in pen inks. The need for differentiating inks arises when people prepare fraudulent documents. For example, someone may alter a document long after it was originally written.

Similarly, a person intent on cheating the government may backdate a record or receipt to substantiate a false tax claim. The ability to distinguish inks will often permit the forensic scientist to determine how many inks or pens were used to prepare a document and the year(s) of manufacture for the inks used.

The actual identification of inks is made by various procedures, one of which is thin-layer chromatography (TLC). Modern-day inks actually comprise a mixture of colored dyes. These dyes can be separated by TLC.

TLC utilizes a thin film of silica gel or alumina coated onto a glass or plastic strip. As in paper chromatography, this thin film is called the **stationary phase**. A mixture of the compounds to be separated is placed in a small spot at one end of a strip, and a liquid organic solvent (**mobile phase**) is passed over the spot. As the solvent moves up the strip, it carries with it the various components in the spot. Because each compound present has a different size, shape, and distribution of electrical field, each compound will adhere to the stationary phase and dissolve in the solvent to a different extent. Thus, if two compounds are started at the same place and solvent is passed over them, one compound will move along the strip more quickly than the other. After a period of time, the flow of the mobile phase is stopped; the strip is dried and then sprayed with a reagent that will produce colored spots, if the compounds are not colored. The distance the compound moves relative to the distance the mobile phase moves is a characteristic of that compound and is known as the R_f value.

Modern inks are a mixture of different dye components. These dyes can often be separated by TLC, and the resultant separation pattern provides a useful characteristic for comparing one ink to another.

The chromatography sheets that may be used come in a variety of types. Silica-gel plastic-backed chromatogram sheets are suitable (sold by Carolina Biological Supply Company). The TLC plates may be notched as shown in Figure 26–1. This notching permits all of the solvent to move through a narrow space, with the result that the dyes will appear as thin bands of color, well separated in most instances, rather than as a gradient of unresolved, colored spots.

If the plates used in this experiment are glass or aluminum backed, they may be difficult to notch. To produce the same effect, the TLC plate coating is removed from the portion of the plate shown in Figure 26–1. This is easily accomplished by the use of a single-edged razor blade, a scalpel, or some similar sharp instrument.

Experiment 26

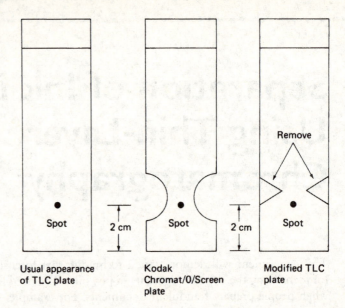

FIGURE 26-1 Notching techniques.

This type of analysis is useful for the chromatography of ballpoint pen inks and water-based inks, such as those used in fountain and felt-tip pens. The ballpoint pen inks, because of their intensity of color and their high viscosity, are best diluted with an organic solvent, such as ethyl or methyl alcohol. One can also cut or punch the ink out of a written line with a squared-off syringe needle, dissolve it in a suitable solvent, and chromatograph the extract by this method. This affords a means of comparison between written lines, which may or may not have come from a single pen.

The chromatographic developing chamber for this analysis is quite small. Capped bottles, 4 oz or smaller in size, are used. They must have a wide mouth to facilitate the introduction and removal of a TLC plate approximately 10–12 cm long and 2–3 cm wide. In most instances, this length of plate gives adequate separation in a rather short period of time. Vials fitted with corks will work very well if bottles are not available.

CRIME SCENE

A woman repeatedly receives notes of an obscene nature through the mail. This continues for a period of time, during which the woman hopes her tormentor will tire of such activity, but to no avail. The woman informs the police. She suspects a former admirer with whom she has severed all communications under quite antagonistic circumstances. The police officers call upon the man in question. He of course denies any involvement in the note-writing harassment. The officers obtain the necessary papers to search his living quarters and find some pens and some stationary samples similar to those on which the notes were written. These articles are sent to a forensic laboratory for analysis and comparison with those of the notes, both for ink and paper comparisons. The analysis you will perform in this exercise will be that of the ink comparison.

EQUIPMENT

- 1 Beaker, 100 mL
- 1 Beaker, 400 mL
-   Bottles, 16 oz, sample holders
- 1 Bulb, pipet
- 1 Burner, Bunsen
- 1 Capillary melting-point tube
- 1 Cover, metal, steam bath type
- 6 Bottles, wide mouthed, 4 oz
- 1 Bottle, wash, 250 mL
- 1 Brush, test tube
- 1 Ring, iron, 10 cm
- 4 Rods, glass, stirring
- 1 Ruler, metric
- 1 pr Scissors

1	Cylinder, graduated, 10 mL	6	Silica gel TLC plates, cut into strips to fit the bottles
1 pr	Forceps		
1	Gauze, wire	1	Spatula
1 pr	Goggles, safety	1	Stand, ring
2	Holders, test tube	1	Tape, masking
1 bx	Matches	6	Test tubes, 10 cm
2	Medicine droppers or disposable pipets	1	Tubing, burner, 1 m
1	Rack, test tube		Stoppers, small
1	Razor blade, single-edged scalpel, or other sharp-edged instrument		

MATERIALS

n-Butanol
Distilled water
Isopropanol
Methanol

Paper with notes written on it by an "admirer"
5 Pens, ballpoint, different brands, same color
Pyridine

METHOD

1. Obtain a sample of the letter upon which is written a message in ink.

2. Using scissors, cut out small portions of a few words.

3. Place the pieces of paper in a 10-cm test tube.

4. Add 1 or 2 drops of methanol to the test tube, and let it stand to extract the ink from the paper into the methanol. If the ink does not dissolve, repeat this step with pyridine in a stoppered test tube.

5. Make a heavy mark on a piece of paper with each of the test pens.

6. Cut out each mark and treat it in the same way as you did the suspect letter.

7. Prepare a mixture of 10 mL of n-butanol, 5 mL of isopropanol, and 5 mL of distilled water to use as a solvent or mobile phase in your chromatography of the ink samples. Use a 10-mL graduated cylinder, and pour the reagents into a 100-mL beaker to mix them.

8. Into each of the small bottles to be used as developing chambers, place enough of the developing solvent so that its depth is approximately 0.5 cm.

9. Cap or cork the bottles, and let them stand until you are ready to use them.

10. Prepare a strip of the TLC plate for each of the inks to be chromatographed. This is done as indicated in the discussion section at the beginning of this experiment and as shown in Figure 26–1, where the modified TLC plate is shown. Alternately, use a 5 × 10 cm TLC plate and place all of the samples on the same plate. Be sure the spots are separated.

11. Remove the inked test papers from the small test tubes.

12. Place the tubes in a steam bath, and evaporate the solvent to 1 or 2 drops. If it becomes dry, don't worry. Just add 1 drop of methanol and shake gently. You may omit this step if you added the methanol dropwise initially.

13. Apply the extracted ink in methanol solvent to the TLC plate, at a point 1 cm from the bottom of the plate, just below the constricted areas of the coating material. Use a capillary melting-point tube for application. Apply a very small spot of extract, let dry, and then apply a small spot again in the same place. Let dry thoroughly.

14. Hold the spotted plate along the side of the bottle containing the solvent. Make certain that the level of solvent in the bottle will be below, but still close to, the applied sample on the strip when placed inside the bottle. If it is at too high a level, remove some solvent with a medicine dropper.

15. Place the TLC plates in the bottles of solvent. Be certain that they are properly identified. Cap or cork the bottles, and let them stand until the solvent front has moved up about 5 cm from the sample spot.

16. Remove them, and mark the solvent front.

17. Let them dry, and compare the colored bands that have appeared.

18. Measure the distance each band moved from the point of application to the front of the band.

19. Measure the distance the solvent front moved from the point of application of the spot.

20. Calculate the R_f value for each band by use of the relationship

$$R_f = \frac{\text{distance of sample band front from application point}}{\text{distance of solvent front from application point}}$$

21. Compare the known ink chromatograms with that of the ink from the note.

22. Do any of the inks have a common origin? If so, which ones?

23. Can you determine conclusively that the inks are the same, or only that they could have come from the same manufacturer?

24. Attach your TLC plates to the data sheet using transparent tape.

25. Answer all questions, and turn in the data sheet and questions to the laboratory instructor.

26. Clean all equipment used, and return it to its proper place. Dispose of all solvents in an appropriate waste container.

SELECTED SOURCES FOR ADDITIONAL INFORMATION

Claybourn, M., and Ansell, M., "Using Raman spectroscopy to solve crime: inks, questioned documents and fraud," *Sci & Just.*, 40 (4), (2000), 261.

Gernandt, M.N., and Urlaub, J.J., "An introduction to the gel pen," *J. Forens. Sci.*, 41 (3), (1996), 503.

Gillis, T.D., Kubic, T.A., and De Forest, P.R., "An alternative method to screen for pepper spray residue," *J. Forens. Sci.*, 48 (1), (2003), 111.

Kato, N., and Ogamo, A., "A TLC visualization for dimethylamphetamine and other abused tertiary amines," *Sci. & Just.*, 41 (4), (2001), 239.

Lewis, J.A., "Thin layer chromatography of writing inks—quality control considerations," *J. Forens. Sci.*, 41 (5), (1996), 874.

Radley, R., "Determination of sequence of intersecting ESDA impressions and porous tip, fibre tip and roller ball point pen inks," *Sci. & Just.*, 35 (4), (1995), 267.

Wiggins, K.K., Holness, J., and March, B.M., "The importance of thin layer chromatography and UV microspectrophotometry in the analysis of reactive dyes released from wool and cotton fibers," *J. Forens. Sci.*, 50 (2), (2005), 364.

Wilson, J.D., Laporte, G.M., and Canta, A.A., "Differentiation of black gel inks using optical and chemical techniques," *J. Forens. Sci.*, 49 (2), (2004), 364.

EXPERIMENT 26 Name _____

DATA SHEET Date _____

SEPARATION OF INK DYES USING THIN-LAYER CHROMATOGRAPHY

1. Attach the plates to the data sheet.

2. R_f values obtained with R_f values obtained for
                         test pen _____   the unknown pen _____

   Band 1

   Band 2

   Band 3

   Band 4

   Band 5

3. Comparison of R_f values and conclusions concerning similarity or difference of inks.

4. Do you think a different mobile phase would improve the separation of the ink dyes?

Experiment 26

5. How does the analyst select the mobile phase to be used?

6. Would this method work for the separation of dyes in waterproof ink?

7. The smaller the spot applied to the TLC plate, the better the separation obtained. Why do you think this is true?

Seminal Stains by Human Prostatic Acid Phosphatase

Acid phosphatase is an enzyme secreted by the prostate gland into seminal fluid. Because its concentrations in seminal fluid are up to 400 times greater than those found in any other body fluid, forensic scientists use its presence to characterize human seminal stains. However, the fact that other body organs do produce this enzyme means that its presence is not a totally specific test for seminal stains. For example, acid phosphatase can also be present in female vaginal secretions.

Forensic scientists have long been searching for a technique that will distinguish acid phosphatase originating from the prostate gland as opposed to other sources. One approach used in the past stemmed from the belief that the chemical reactivity of human seminal acid phosphatase was specifically inhibited by L-tartaric acid. Thus, the presence of such inhibition was taken as proof of sexual relations. However, recent evidence has disproved this theory. It seems that a significant percentage of the female population also produces, in vaginal secretions, acid phosphatase that is inhibited by L-tartaric acid. What this test now shows is that a very high level of acid phosphatase is evidence of sexual relations and that inhibition is probably only of value if you can be sure there is no vaginal secretion contamination.

The term **acid phosphatase** is applied to enzymes, regardless of source, that can hydrolyze certain organic phosphates in slightly acid media. The substrate in the method we use in this experiment is alpha naphthylphosphate. This is incubated with suspected prostatic acid phosphatase at a pH of 4.9. The enzyme, if present, splits away the phosphate radical, liberating the alpha-naphthyl group, which in turn reacts with an added dye (naphthanil diazo blue B) to give a violet-colored complex.

CRIME SCENE

A young woman phones the police station to say that she has just been raped and that she knows the identity of the rapist. The police arrive on the scene within a few minutes. The police officer who listens to her explanation is experienced and knows that she should obtain proof of rape as soon as possible. She takes the woman to a hospital, and a doctor obtains swabs from around the genital area as well as swabs from the vagina. In addition, her skirt is kept as evidence. You have been given the swabs and the skirt, and your job is to tell the police officer if the woman has in fact had recent sexual relations or is merely telling a story to get the fellow in trouble.

Experiment 27

EQUIPMENT

- 6 Bottles, 4 oz
- 2 Bottles, wide mouth, 16 oz (samples)
- 1 Brush, test tube, small
- 1 Cylinder, graduated, 100 mL
- 1 Cylinder, graduated, 10 mL
- Disposable gloves
- 1 Flask, Dewar, 0.5 L
- 1 Flask, Erlenmeyer, 125 mL
- 1 pr Forceps
- 1 pr Goggles, safety
- 1 Lamp, UV
- 2 Medicine droppers
- 1 Pencil, grease
- 1 pH meter
- 1 Pipet, Mohr, 1 mL
- 1 Pipet, Mohr, 5 mL
- 1 Rack, test tube
- 1 Rod, glass, stirring, 15 cm
- 1 pr Scissors
- 1 Stopper, rubber, solid, No. 13
- 1 Stopper, rubber, solid, No. 6
- Swabs, cotton (Q-tips®)
- 6 Test tubes, 10 cm

MATERIALS

Glacial acetic acid, reagent-grade

Liquid nitrogen, 1 pt

Normal saline solution, 0.9%

Sodium acetate, reagent-grade

Sodium chloride, reagent-grade

Sodium hydroxide solution, 1 M

Seminal fluid: Usually several mL can be obtained from a hospital or clinic if they have a few weeks' notice. They get it from patients who have had vasectomies and are being checked for sperm. Store it in a refrigerator.

Alpha-naphthyl phosphate, calcium salt

Acetate buffer solution: Using a laboratory balance, add 23.0 g of NaCl, 2.0 g of $NaC_2H_3O_2$, and 0.5 mL of glacial acetic acid to about 90 mL of deionized water in a graduated 150-mL beaker. Stir with a glass stirring rod until the solids dissolve. Adjust the pH to 4.9. Add additional water to make the final volume about 100 mL, place the solution in a glass-stoppered 125-mL Erlenmeyer flask, and store it in a refrigerator.

Alpha-naphthyl phosphate solution: Weigh 0.30 g of alpha-naphthyl phosphate calcium salt on an analytical balance. Place it in a 30-mL dropping bottle and add 20 mL of acetate buffer solution. Swirl and suspend the powder, and store the solution in a refrigerator. This should be prepared fresh about every 2 months.

Dye solution: Weigh 0.30 g of naphthanil diazo blue B on an analytical balance. Add it to a 30-mL dropping bottle containing 20 mL of normal saline. This suspension should be kept in a refrigerator and prepared fresh about every 2 months.

Inhibitor solution: Weigh 3.0 g of L-tartaric acid on an analytical balance. Add to some deionized water and 35 mL of 1 M NaOH in a graduated 150-mL beaker, and stir until dissolved. Adjust the pH to 4.9 by adding 1 M NaOH if too low and L-tartaric acid if too high. Add deionized water to make 100 mL, and store in a refrigerator. Fresh solution should be made every 2 months.

METHOD

Laboratory Safety: Gloves and goggles should be worn routinely as good laboratory practice.

PART A: SUSPECTED STAINS ON CLOTHING OR BEDDING

1. Cut a 1 × 1 cm piece of the material including or containing the suspected seminal stain. Place it in a 10-cm test tube with 3 mL of deionized water. Label this T for test.

2. Cut a 1 × 1 cm piece from an unstained area and place it in a 10-cm test tube with 3 mL of deionized water. Label the tube C for control.

3. After 15 minutes, prepare four additional 10-cm test tubes as follows:

T (test)	3 drops of phosphate solution
TI (test inhibitor)	3 drops of phosphate solution
	3 drops of inhibitor solution
C (control)	3 drops of phosphate solution
CI (control inhibitor)	3 drops of phosphate solution
	3 drops of inhibitor solution

Swirl each tube to mix the contents.

4. Transfer 0.5 mL from the test solution prepared in step 1 to each of the T and TI tubes prepared in step 3. Swirl to mix.

5. Transfer 0.5 mL from the control solution prepared in step 2 to each of the C and CI tubes prepared in step 3. Swirl to mix.

6. Add 3 drops of the dye solution to each of the T, TI, C, and CI tubes. Swirl to mix.

7. If the T tube turns reddish-brown to violet in less than 30 seconds, while the TI tube remains clear to a pale yellow, the test is positive. The C and CI tubes, however, must also remain clear to pale yellow, or the result is suspect. Another control portion should be prepared and run to determine if a seminal stain was included in the "control" or if one or more of the reagents has deteriorated.

8. If T turns reddish-brown to purple in 30 seconds or less, and no purple color is imparted to TI, C, or CI, report the test as positive for acid phosphatase.

PART B: EXAMINATION OF SWABS

1. Place the swab in a 10-cm test tube containing 3 mL of deionized water, label it T for test, and proceed as in Part A. Use deionized water as the control or blank.

PART C: VAGINAL WASHINGS

1. Place 3 drops of wash in each of two 10-cm test tubes containing 0.5 mL of deionized water. Label one tube T and the other TI. Add 3 drops of phosphate solution to tube T and 3 drops of phosphate solution plus 3 drops of inhibitor to TI. Use deionized water for the control. Add 3 drops of the dye solution to each tube. Swirl to mix.

2. If the wash sample contains too much acid phosphatase, it may exceed the inhibiting capacity of the L-tartrate solution. Both T and TI would turn purple. To eliminate this possibility, repeat the test using only one drop of aspirate or some further dilution made in deionized water.

PART D: LOCATION OF SEMINAL STAINS BY THEIR PHOSPHORESCENCE (ADVANCED)

1. Obtain a 0.5-L Dewar flask and fill it with liquid nitrogen. (Caution: The temperature of liquid nitrogen is −320° F, and it freezes fingers quickly! You should wear insulated gloves.)

2. Hold a piece of the suspect stain with a forceps, carefully lower it into the solution, and hold it there until rapid bubbling ceases.

3. Turn out the lights or go into a dark room and direct the rays from a UV lamp on the stain. A seminal stain should glow. Record what you see.

4. Repeat the procedure with a blank piece of cloth.

SELECTED SOURCES FOR ADDITIONAL INFORMATION

Allard, J.E., "The collection of data from findings in cases of sexual assault and the significance of spermatozoa on vaginal, anal and oral swabs," *Sci. & Just.*, 37 (2), (1997), 99.

Allery, J., Telmun, N., Mieusset, R., Blanc, A., and Rouge, D., "Cytological detection of spermatozoa comparisons of three staining methods," *J. Forens. Sci.*, 46 (2), (2001), 288.

Berti, A., Virgill, A., D'Errico, G., Vespi, G., Lago, G., and Cavazzana, A., "Expression of seminal vesicle specific antigen in serum of lung tumor patients," *J. Forens. Sci.*, 50 (5), (2005), 1114.

Chen, J., Kobilinsky, L., Wolosiu, D., Shaler, R., and Baum, H., "A physical method for separating spermatozoa from epithelial cells in sexual assault evidence," *J. Forens. Sci.*, 43 (1), (1998), 114.

Khaldi, N., Miras, A., Botti, K., Benali, L., and Gromb, S., "Evaluation of three rapid detection methods for the forensic identification of seminal fluid in rape cases," *J. Forens. Sci.*, 49 (4), (2004), 754.

Kobus, H.J., Silenieks, E., and Schamberg, J., "Improving the effectiveness of fluorescence for the detection of semen stains on fabrics," *J. Forens. Sci.*, 47 (4), (2002), 819.

Montagna, C.P., "The recovery of seminal components and DNA from the vagina of a homicide victim 34 days after postmortem," *J. Forens. Sci.*, 41 (4), (1996), 700.

EXPERIMENT 27 Name _____

DATA SHEET Date _____

SEMINAL STAINS BY HUMAN PROSTATIC ACID PHOSPHATASE

Part A: Suspected Stains on Clothing or Bedding

    Observations

    Tube T	Tube C

    Tube TI	Tube CI

    Conclusions

Part B: Examination of Swabs

    Observations

    Tube T	Tube C

    Tube TI	Tube CI

    Conclusions

Part C: Vaginal Washings

Observations

Tube T

Tube C

Tube TI

Tube CI

Conclusions

Part D: Location of Seminal Stains by Their Phosphorescence (Advanced)

Observations

Stained material

Blank material

Question

1. How do you think you could use this test to determine the order of deposition of overlapping seminal stains and bloodstains?

Arson Detection: The Recovery of Flammable Liquids

EXPERIMENT 28

Fires generally burn from the point of origin upward and outward; therefore, if a liquid accelerant has been used to start a fire, some of it will probably have soaked downward and not have been entirely consumed. The fire investigator attempts to trace the fire to its point or points of origin and then digs down and collects samples. To prevent the evaporation and loss of volatile liquids, samples must be placed in air-tight containers. Frequently, new quart- or gallon-size paint cans are used, as are 1-quart fruit jars.

Once the samples arrive at the laboratory, the forensic chemist may use any of a number of procedures to recover and identify the accelerants from the collected debris. One popular method is the headspace technique, in which a portion of the debris is placed in a glass jar or empty paint can that has a small hole punched in the lid. This hole is covered with a silicone septum glued on with Super Glue. When the container is heated, any volatile residue present in the debris will be driven off and trapped in the container's enclosed air space. A few milliliters of the vapor is removed with a syringe and analyzed by gas chromatography. This procedure will be followed in Part A. A recent modification involves adding a charcoal trap. This technique will be explained in Part B. An older technique involves the use of an immiscible solvent distillation with toluene and water and the collection of any volatile materials in the toluene layer. Again, gas chromatography (GC) is used to analyze the recovered liquid. GC will be used to identify the recovered accelerant as to general type, such as gasoline, kerosene, etc.

CRIME SCENE

The fire department is called to put out a fire in a furniture warehouse. The fire appears to have started in one of the large wooden storage containers. A check of the storage records indicates that nothing spontaneously combustible was in the container, so the fire chief suspects foul play. He has collected some of the charred wood from where the fire appears to have started and a few partially burned rags lying nearby. You have one of these samples, and your job is to determine if gasoline, kerosene, lighter fluid, or some similar material was present.

EQUIPMENT

- 1 Beaker, 250 mL
- 1 Brush, test tube, small
- 1 Gas chromatograph, preferably equipped with flame ionization detector
- 1 pr Goggles, safety
- 1 Holder, test tube
- 1 Hot plate
- 1 Pipet, 1 mL
- 1 Pipet, Pasteur
- 1 Rack, test tube
- 1 Syringe, 10 μL
- 1 Syringe, gas tight, 5 mL, or Plastipak disposable syringe, 3 mL
- 1 Test tube, 50 mm

Fruit jar, 1 quart, or paint can, 1 gallon (preferred); or 4 test tubes, 20 × 150 mm, with rubber septum caps. If fruit jars or paint cans are available, then a drying oven is necessary, but the hot plate and test tubes indicated are not needed.

MATERIALS

Accelerants (kerosene, gasoline, lighter fluid)

Activated charcoal, 50–200 mesh

Carbon disulfide

Copper wire, 22 ga × 4 cm, flattened on one end for a distance of 5 mm

Samples of burned fabric or wood with accelerants on them

SE-30, 3%, on Chromosorb W, 60–80 mesh, TCD or 10% DC-200 on Chromosorb P

SE-30, 10%, on Chromosorb P, 60–80 mesh, FID

Sodium silicate solution

METHOD

PART A: HEADSPACE ANALYSIS

We will assume that you do not have glass jars or clean metal cans.

1. Obtain a sample from your instructor.

2. Place a portion of your sample into the bottom third of a test tube. Place a septum cap on the test tube.

3. Fill a 250-mL beaker with water and heat it to boiling on a hot plate. Place the test tube in the hot water for 3–5 minutes, holding it steady with the aid of a test tube holder.

4. Remove the tube from the water, and insert the syringe needle through the septum cap to obtain a sample of vapor.

5. Remove 1 mL of vapor, and inject it into the gas chromatograph. Obtain directions on the use of the gas chromatograph from your instructor.

6. Pipet 1 mL of each accelerant into separate test tubes. Cover each with a septum cap, and at room temperature remove 1 mL of vapor from each tube for analysis.

7. Compare the general profile of each accelerant to that obtained in step 5 to identify the accelerant present in the debris. Table 28–1 shows one set of GC conditions.

    Figure 28–1 shows the results obtained for gasoline.

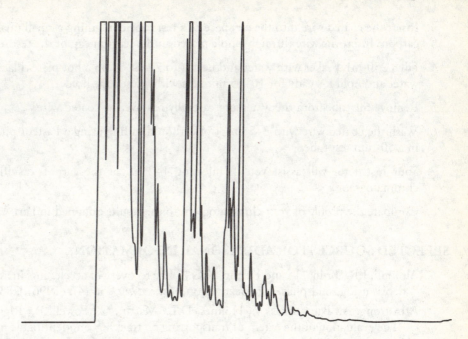

FIGURE 28-1 A gas chromatogram of one brand of regular gasoline.

PART B: VAPOR CONCENTRATION ON CHARCOAL (ADVANCED)*

Often headspace analysis is not sufficiently sensitive to detect minute traces of flammable hydrocarbons that may be present in debris collected at the scene of a suspected arson. One approach for enhancing the sensitivity of detecting small quantities of flammable residues is to improve the collection process so that a significant quantity of flammable hydrocarbons can be removed from the debris for analysis by GC. For this purpose the use of absorbent materials for trapping hydrocarbons has achieved wide use in the crime laboratory. Commonly, activated charcoal is used as an absorbent.

Activated charcoal particles readily absorb hydrocarbons, and when they are exposed to hydrocarbon vapor, they are able to trap a large quantity of material on a small number of charcoal particles. The trapped hydrocarbon molecules can then be recovered by washing them off of the charcoal with a solvent, carbon disulfide (CS_2).

METHOD

1. Obtain a piece of copper wire from your instructor and flatten one end with a hammer if it is not already flattened.

2. Dip the flattened end of the wire in sodium silicate solution and then into activated charcoal. Dry the wire in an oven at 70°C for 15 minutes.

TABLE 28-1	Conditions for Using the Gow-Mac Gas Chromatograph
Flow rate	60 mL/min, N_2
Column	10% DC-200 on Chromosorb P, 4 ft
Temperature	85°C
Filament current	180 mA
Attenuation	4
Sample size	5 μL

---

* This method is based on a procedure developed by John A. Juhala, PhD, published in *Arson Analysis Newsletter*, Vol. 6, No. 2, 1982.

3. Insert the coated wire into the air space of a test tube containing a small quantity of a volatile hydrocarbon. Insert the wire through a hole placed in the septum cap of the test tube.

4. Fill a 250-mL beaker with water and heat it to 70–80°C on a hot plate. Place the test tube in the hot water and hold it steady for 10–15 minutes with a test tube holder.

5. Remove the tube from the water and carefully remove the coated wire.

6. Wash the coated wire with 3–5 drops of carbon disulfide using a Pasteur pipet. Collect the washings in a 50-mm test tube.

7. Your instructor will assist you in injecting 1–2 μL of the carbon disulfide washings into a gas chromatograph.

8. Compare the profile of your chromatogram to the results obtained in Part A of this experiment.

SELECTED SOURCES FOR ADDITIONAL INFORMATION

Almirall, J.R., Bruna, J., and Furton, K.G., "The recovery of accelerants in aqueous samples from fire debris using solid-phase microextraction," *Sci. & Just.*, 36 (4), (1996), 283.

Armstrong, A., Babrauskas, V., Holmes, D.L., Martin, C., Powell, R., Riggs, S., and Young, L.D., "The evaluation of the extent of transporting or 'tracking' an identifiable ignitable liquid (gasoline) throughout fire scenes during the investigative process," *J. Forens. Sci.*, 49 (4), (2004), 741.

Barshick, S., "Analysis of accelerants and fire debris using aroma detection technology," *J. Forens. Sci.*, 43 (2), (1998), 284.

Berrett, R.R., and Candy, C.F., "The training of fire investigators in the UK," *Sci. & Just.*, 38 (3), (1998), 195.

Coulombe, R., "Chemical markers in weathered gasoline," *J. Forens. Sci.*, 40 (5), (1995), 867.

Dhole, V.R., Kurhekar, M.P., and Ambade, K.A., "Detection of petroleum accelerant residues on partially burnt objects in burning/arson offences," *Sci. & Just.*, 35 (3), (1995), 217.

Fernandes, M.S., Lau, C.M., and Wong, W.C., "The effect of volatile residues in burnt household items on the detection of fire accelerants," *Sci. & Just.*, 42 (1), (2002), 7.

Furton, K.G., Almirall, J.R., and Bruna, J.C., "A novel method for the analysis of gasoline from fire debris using headspace solid-phase microextraction," *J. Forens. Sci.*, 41 (1), (1996), 12.

Holleyhead, R., "Ignition of flammable gases and liquids by cigarettes: A review," *Sci. & Just.*, 36 (4), (1996), 257.

Kurz, M.E., Schultz, S., Griffith, J., Broadus, K., Sparks, J., Dabdour, G., and Brock, J., "Effect of background interference on accelerant detection by canines," *J. Forens. Sci.*, 41 (5), (1996), 868.

Lewis, R.J., Denieul, S.E., Chem, C., Langford, A.M., and Okley, M., "The analysis of fire debris for the presence of propan-2-ol using dynamic head space concentration and gas chromatography with flame ionization detection," *J. Forens. Sci.*, 44 (5), (1999), 1061.

Lloyd, J.A., and Edmiston, P.L., "Preferential extraction of hydrocarbons from fire debris samples by solid phase microextraction," *J. Forens. Sci.*, 48 (1), (2003), 130.

McGee, E., Dip, N., and Lang, T.L., "A study of the effects of a micelle encapsulation fire suppression agent on dynamic head space analysis of fire debris samples," *J. Forens. Sci.*, 47 (2), (2002), 267.

Newman, R., Dietz, W.R., and Lothridge, K., "The use of activated charcoal strips for fire debris extractions by passive diffusion. Part I: The effects of time, temperature, strip size, and sample concentration," *J. Forens. Sci.*, 41 (3), (1996), 361.

Ren, Q., and Bertsch, W., "A comprehensive sample preparation scheme for accelerants in suspect arson cases," *J. Forens. Sci.*, 44 (3), (1999), 504.

EXPERIMENT 28

Name _____

DATA SHEET

Date _____

ARSON DETECTION: THE RECOVERY OF FLAMMABLE LIQUIDS

Record all instrumental settings (parameters) on your chromatograms. Be sure also to record the column packing material. These are to be turned in to your instructor along with the identity of the accelerant used in starting the fire, if you have determined that one was present.

Identity of accelerant (if present) _____

Questions

1. A suspect is apprehended, and his lawyer questions your results. She says that what you found was a cleaning rag used on a forklift and no arson was committed. How could you go about verifying the truth or fiction of her statement?

2. Suppose you determine that the fire started on a cement pad. How might you get a sample out of the cement without destroying the pad?

3. Why might there still be accelerant present on materials found at the base of the fire even though the building was almost entirely burned down?

4. How might one determine the physical location of the origin of the fire, so that he or she might know where to look for evidence of accelerants?

EXPERIMENT 29

Metal Residues on Hands from Guns, Knives, and Other Metal Weapons

There are many crimes committed in which hand guns are not used, and with stricter gun laws in force, the possibility of weapons other than guns being used is even greater. What is needed is a simple, inexpensive test to determine whether a subject has recently handled a metallic object.

Such a test was proposed in 1970, in which the reagent 8-hydroxyquinoline is used to chelate with any trace metallic fragments left on the palm of the hand when a metal object was handled. These chelates fluoresce when exposed to UV radiation and often indicate the imprint of the object handled. There are many variables, however, such as how tightly the object was held, how old it was, whether it was oiled, how sweaty the suspect's hand was, and the kinds of metals involved. Our own success with this approach has been excellent. Other investigators have had good success also. The interpretation of the imprint requires a great deal of experience and a large file of photographs of known objects in order to draw definite conclusions. Nonetheless, you will perform the test so that you understand how it works. We believe that the potential for this test is better than the results you will obtain.

In 1976 a new reagent, ferrozine, was suggested as a better test for weapons containing iron (Goldman and Thornton, 1976). You will experiment with this reagent in Part B.

PART A: THE 8-HYDROXYQUINOLINE METHOD

Basically, this procedure involves applying a 0.1 to 0.2% solution of 8-hydroxyquinoline (oxine) in alcohol to the subject's hands, either by immersion or by spraying from an entirely metal-free system, and allowing them to air dry. The 8-hydroxyquinoline undergoes a chelating reaction with various metallic ions present on the skin's surface to form oxine complexes. When viewed under short-wavelength UV radiation, these complexes either emit various fluorescent colors or cause a quenching of the light-yellow background fluorescence imparted to areas of the skin treated by the solution. The fluorescent color observed depends upon the particular metal present, with different metals producing different colors. When viewed under UV radiation, any metallic residue left on the hands after handling a particular object will appear as various colored patterns outlining those areas of the hand that were in contact with the object. Each of the various objects, held in the usual manner for its intended use, produces a distinctive pattern that can be recognized and identified by the observer, once he or she has gained sufficient experience in observing such patterns. The color of the pattern gives information concerning the metallic composition of the object, with the position, shape, and extent of the pattern indicating the shape of the object.

CRIME SCENE

A highway patrol officer responding to an emergency call arrives at the scene of a roadside beating. The victim has apparently been struck by a heavy object, possibly a jack handle or a tire iron. The witness who called 911 states that, from a distance, he thought he saw a semi-trailer pull away, but he can't be sure. The highway patrol officer calls the local forensic lab. You have been rushed out to a truck stop just outside of town accompanied by the sheriff. All of the truck drivers deny knowing anything about the crime. They may be telling the truth, and admittedly it is a long shot, but you decide to test their hands for metal particles, which you do according to the following procedure.

EQUIPMENT

- 1 pr Goggles, safety
- 1 Hair dryer
- 1 Jar, wide mouth, gallon size
- 1 Lamp, UV, 6 watts preferred
- 1 Towel, cloth
- 1 Viewing box or darkened room
- Several metal test objects, such as a jack handle, pipe wrench, scissors, knife, etc.

MATERIALS

8-Hydroxyquinoline, 0.15% in isopropanol: Prepare 2 L in a wide-mouthed plastic bottle. It is good for 40 to 50 immersions, or until pronounced discoloration occurs. Store in a dark plastic bottle.

3-(2-Pyridyl)-5,6-diphenyl-1,2,4-triazine-p-p'-disulfonic acid, disodium salt trihydrate: Also known as PDT or ferrozine, it is capable of detecting 0.090 mg of iron.

METHOD

Prior to this experiment the lab instructor will take 4 or 5 students into another room and have one of them hold a metal object and strike a surface with it 2 or 3 times. When the group comes back, you will test all the suspects to see if you can tell which one handled the weapon.

1. Place each hand of the first suspect into the jar containing the 8-hydroxyquinoline in isopropanol for a period of 3 to 5 seconds.

2. Dry the suspect's hands with a hair dryer.

3. Take the suspect into a dark room or place his or her hands in a UV viewing box, and examine them under a UV lamp (a 6-watt UV lamp works best). Record what you see.

4. Repeat this procedure with each of the suspects, and record what you see. Can you identify which one handled the weapon?

5. Have 3 or 4 students who have not touched a metal object today (including door handles) each handle a specific "weapon" just as they might if they were to use it in a crime. They must grip the weapon very tightly for a realistic simulation. A person involved in a crime is under tension, so he or she grips the weapon tightly; and the person usually sweats, so good contact is made.

6. Test each student and see if you can (1) see any metal evidence at all, and (2) distinguish any pattern related to the weapon.

7. If you have good results and are in fact able to detect metal residuals, then have the person wet his or her hands and repeat the test. Record your results.

8. Clean up the area, and replace the lid tightly on the reagent solution container.

PART B: THE FERROZINE METHOD

METHOD

1. Spray the reagent (1 mg/mL of methanol) over the subject's hands.
2. Follow the steps listed in Part A.

SELECTED SOURCES FOR ADDITIONAL INFORMATION

Almog, J., and Glattstein, B., "Detection of firearms imprints on hands of suspects. Study of the PDT based field test," *J. Forens. Sci.*, 42 (6), (1997), 993. [Forms a magenta color with submicrograms of Fe.]

Basu, S., Boone, C.E., Denio, D.S., and Miazga, R.A., "Fundamental studies of gunshot residue deposition by glue-lift," *J. Forens. Sci.*, 42 (4), (1997), 571.

Collins, P., Coumbaros, L., Horsley, G., Lynch, B., Kirkbride, K.P., Skinner, W., and Klass G., "Glass containing gunshot residue particles: A new type of highly characteristic particle?" *J. Forens. Sci.*, 48 (3), (2003), 538.

Goldman, G.L., and Thornton, J.I., "A new trace ferrous metal detection reagent," *J. Forens. Sci.*, 21 (3), (1976), 625.

Jalanti, T., Henchoz, P., Gallusser, A., and Bonfanti, M.S., "The persistence of gunshot residue on shooter's hands," *Sci. & Just.*, 39 (1), (1999), 48.

Leifer, A., Avissar, Y., Berger, S., Wax, H., Donchin, Y., and Almog, J., "Detection of firearm imprints on the hands of suspects: Effectiveness of PDT reaction," *J. Forens. Sci.*, 46 (6), (2001), 1442.

Meng, H., and Caddy, B., "Gunshot residue analysis: A review," *J. Forens. Sci.*, 42 (4), (1997), 553.

Migeot, G., and De Kinder, J., "Gunshot residue deposits on the gas pistons of assault rifles," *J. Forens. Sci.*, 47 (4), (2002), 808.

Reardon, M.R., and MacCrehan, W.A., "Developing a quantitative extraction technique for determining the organic additives in smokeless hand gun powder," *J. Forens. Sci.*, 46 (4), (2001), 802.

Reis, E.L., Souza Sarkis, J.E., Neto, O.N., Rodrigues, C., Kakazu, M.H., and Viebig, S., "A new method for collection and identification of gunshot residues from the hands of shooters," *J. Forens. Sci.*, 48 (6), (2003), 1269.

Schyma, C., and Placidi, P., "The accelerated polyvinyl alcohol-alcohol method for GSR collection-PVAL 2.0," *J. Forens. Sci.*, 45 (6), (2000), 1303.

Stahling, S., "Modified sheet printing method (MSPM) for the detection of lead in determination of shooting distance," *J. Forens. Sci.*, 44 (1), (1999), 179.

Stahling, S., and Karlsson, T., "A method for collection of gunshot residues from skin and other surfaces," *J. Forens. Sci.*, 45 (6), (2000), 1299.

Wallace, J.S., "Discharge residue from mercury fulminate-primed ammunition," *Sci. & Just.*, 38 (1), (1998), 7.

Zeichner, A., and Eldar, B., "A novel method for extraction and analysis of gunpowder residues on double side adhesive coated stubs," *J. Forens. Sci.*, 49 (6), (2004), 1194.

Zeichner, A., Eldar, B., Glattstein, B., Koffman, A., Tamiri, T., and Muller, D., "Vacuum collection of gunpowder residues from clothing worn by shooting suspects and their analysis by GC/TEA, IMS, and GC/MS," *J. Forens. Sci.*, 48 (5), (2003), 961.

EXPERIMENT 29

DATA SHEET

Name _____

Date _____

METAL RESIDUES ON HANDS FROM GUNS, KNIVES, AND OTHER METAL WEAPONS

Part A: The 8-Hydroxyquinoline Method

Record your observations below, with both a brief description of colors and a sketch of any patterns related to the weapon.

Suspect 1

Suspect 2

Suspect 3

Suspect 4

Suspect 5

Part B: The Ferrozine Method

Record your observations below, with both a brief description of colors and a sketch of any patterns related to the weapon.

Suspect 1

Suspect 2

Suspect 3

Suspect 4

Suspect 5

Can you tell who handled the weapon? If so, on what do you base your conclusions?

Sketch any weapon patterns that you detect and indicate the colors involved.

EXPERIMENT 30

The Emission Spectrum of Elements

Criminalists are often asked to identify materials by the chemical elements of which they are composed, for example, in the identification of poisons or the analysis of coins, weapons, or tools. Additionally, most manmade and natural materials contain small quantities of elements known as trace elements. Often, by comparing the trace elements contained within physical evidence it is possible to successfully link evidence to a particular source or location. The analytical techniques used for the identification of elements can be quite lengthy and often involve the application of sophisticated and expensive equipment. This experiment does not utilize such instrumentation; instead, the objective here is for you to learn about the underlying principles of one important technique, **emission spectroscopy**.

You will see that elements emit radiation when they are heated to high temperatures, as in a flare. All elements are composed of atoms. Each atom has electrons in orbit around a central nucleus, a situation analogous to the planets in orbit around the sun. When heat is applied to an element, many of its atoms will become **excited**; that is, their electrons will jump into higher-energy orbitals. These electrons will stay in these higher-energy orbitals for only a very short time. When the excited electrons fall back to a lower level, energy is emitted in the form of radiation. This radiation, called **light**, if our eyes are sensitive to it, when analyzed will show a characteristic spectrum consisting of discrete lines of differing wavelengths. The simplest instrument used to separate light into its component wavelengths is known as a **spectroscope**. What makes this technique so valuable to the criminalist is the fact that no two elements emit the same combination of wavelengths; in essence, the emission spectrum of an element is a fingerprint. In this exercise we will study the colors and wavelengths of visible radiation (light) that different elements emit when they are heated. You will also learn to use a simple spectroscope.

EQUIPMENT

1 Beaker, 25 mL
1 Burner, Bunsen
1 pr Goggles, safety
1 Spectroscope
   Wire, Nichrome
1 Tube, helium discharge
1 Tube, hydrogen discharge

MATERIALS

Barium chloride
Calcium chloride
Hydrochloric acid
Potassium chloride
Sodium chloride
Strontium chloride

PART A: OBTAINING FLAME EMISSIONS

METHOD

1. Place a small quantity of sodium chloride on a loop of Nichrome wire, and hold it in the flame of a Bunsen burner. Record the color you see on your data sheet.

2. Clean the wire by heating it in the flame until the color imparted to the flame by sodium disappears. If this color does not disappear after the wire becomes red hot, allow it to cool for 10 seconds and immerse it in a beaker of concentrated hydrochloric acid, then return the wire to the flame. Repeat until the wire no longer imparts a color to the flame.

3. Next, repeat steps 1 and 2 with each of the following substances: potassium chloride, calcium chloride, strontium chloride, and barium chloride. Record the colors you see on the data sheet.

PART B: THE SPECTROSCOPE

In Part A you found that some elements are easy to distinguish by the colors they emit in a hot flame, but many elements are not so easily identified. We need a way to separate the mixed colors that elements emit so that we can notice slight differences in the color emissions of elements. This can be accomplished by spreading out the various colors of emitted light in a way similar to the formation of a rainbow. This spread of colors is called a spectrum. As noted earlier, the instrument used for separating the colors of light is called a spectroscope; it contains a prism or grating to separate light into its component wavelengths.

Radiation from the excited atoms enters the spectroscope through a narrow slit and passes through the prism or grating, where it is separated into various colors; the radiation then passes through a tube and into the viewer's eye. Your instructor will show you the parts of your spectroscope and how to operate it.

Your spectroscope may contain a scale for measuring the wavelengths of the separated light. The numbers on the scale are arbitrary and do not correspond to any particular wavelength. Therefore, it is necessary to calibrate the spectroscope against a known standard, in this case, helium. The purpose of the calibration is to relate the numbers of your scale to the wavelength values of helium.

METHOD

1. Place a helium discharge tube directly in front of the spectroscope's slit. Make sure that the slit is very nearly closed; if not, the helium lines will not be well separated.

2. Focus the spectroscope and adjust the width of the slit so that you can see the first red line on the left side of the spectrum. Record on your data sheet the scale reading for this line.

3. Moving from left to right along the spectrum, record the scale readings for each of the 5 or 6 additional colored lines in the helium spectrum. You will notice that the known wavelengths of each helium line are recorded in a table on the data sheet.

4. Draw a graph with wavelengths in nanometers as the abscissa and with the scale reading as the ordinate for the lines of the helium spectrum. The smooth curve so obtained is the calibration curve of the instrument. This curve is obtained by plotting the scale readings of each of the known lines of an element against the corresponding wavelength. From this curve, the wavelength of the lines observed in other spectra may be calculated.

5. Substitute a hydrogen discharge tube for the helium source, and record the scale readings for the observed lines. Record these readings along with the line colors on your data sheet. From your calibration curve, identify the wavelength for each scale reading.

6. Look at the radiation from an ordinary tungsten bulb through your spectroscope. What difference do you observe between this source of radiation and that of helium and hydrogen?

PART C: THE EMISSION SPECTRA OF ELEMENTS

In this portion of the experiment you will examine the emission spectra of various elements.

1. Place a lighted Bunsen burner in front of the slit of the spectroscope, but far enough away so that the flame will not damage the instrument.

2. Clean the Nichrome wire as described in Part A.

3. Individually introduce each of the following materials into the flame: sodium chloride, potassium chloride, calcium chloride, strontium chloride, and barium chloride. It may be necessary to add the powder to the flame several times to observe all the spectral lines.

4. Record the number of lines and colors that you observe for each material. If your spectroscope has a scale reading, you may want to record the reading for each line observed. Your instructor may ask you to determine the emission wavelengths for some of these elements.

5. Your instructor may issue you an unknown containing one or more elements for you to identify.

SELECTED SOURCES FOR ADDITIONAL INFORMATION

Almirall, J.R., Cole, M.D., Gettinnby, G., and Furton, K.G., "Discrimination of glass sources using elemental composition and refractive index: Development of predictive models," *Sci. & Just.*, 38 (3), (1998), 93.

Curran, J.M., Triggs, C.M., Almarall, J.R., Buckleton, J.S., and Walsh, K.A.J., "The interpretation of elemental composition measurements from forensic glass evidence: I," *Sci. & Just.* 37 (4), (1997), 241, 245.

Kasamatsu, M., Suzuki, Y., Sugita, R., and Suzuki, S., "Forensic determination of match heads by elemental analysis with inductively coupled plasma-atomic emission spectrometry," *J. Forens. Sci.*, 50 (4), (2005), 883.

Kinoshita, H., Ameno, K., Sumi, Y., Kumihashi, M., Ijiri, J., Ameno, S., Kubota, A., and Hishida, S., "Evidence of hexavalent chromium ingestion," *J. Forens. Sci.*, 48 (3), (2003), 633.

Koons, R.D., and Buscaglia, J., "Forensic significance of bullet lead compositions," *J. Forens. Sci.*, 50 (2), (2005), 352.

Koons, R.D., and Grant, D., "Compositional variation in bullet lead manufacture," *J. Forens. Sci.*, 47 (5), (2002), 950.

Poolman, D.G., and Pistorius, P.C., "The possibility of using elemental analysis to identify debris from the cutting of mild steel," *J. Forens. Sci.*, 41 (6), (1996), 998.

EXPERIMENT 30

DATA SHEET

Name _____

Date _____

THE EMISSION SPECTRUM OF ELEMENTS

Part A: Obtaining Flame Emissions

Compound   Color observed

    Sodium chloride

    Potassium chloride

    Calcium chloride

    Strontium chloride

    Barium chloride

Part B: The Spectroscope

Helium spectrum:

Color	Wavelength (nm)	Scale reading
Red	668	
Yellow	588	
Green	502	
Green	492	
Blue-green	471	
Blue-violet	447	
Violet	403	

Hydrogen spectrum:

Color	Scale reading	Calculated wavelength (nm)

Part C: The Emission Spectra of Elements

List the elements examined, along with the color of each of their spectral lines. You may also be asked to record the scale readings of each line and to find its wavelength from the calibration curve prepared in Part B.

Element	Color of line	Scale reading	Calculated wavelength (nm)

1. Unknown Number _____

    Element(s) present in the unknown:

2. Does the chlorine have any effect on the spectra of the compounds analyzed?

EXPERIMENT 31

Determination of Blood-Spatter Angles of Impact

The solution of violent crimes can often be aided by the determination of certain aspects of the commission of the crime. Two of these aspects are the relationship of the victim and the perpetrator with respect to each other and the location of the victim at the time of occurrence. Was he or she standing, sitting, or reclining? Some of these questions perhaps may be answered by the application of the procedure that you are about to follow. Maybe the pattern and shape of blood spots can be of help. It has been found that when a drop of blood strikes a surface it tends to spread out, longer in the direction of impact. If you measure the width of the spot and compare it to the length, making a ratio, you can determine the angle at which the drop of blood was traveling at the moment of impact. Ratios are used to eliminate the effect of different sizes of drops. It has been suggested that the average height of a drop of blood falling from either a wounded person or a person carrying a wounded person would be about 42 inches. Large differences in height can make a difference because the blood tends to cool and start to coagulate shortly after exposure to air, thus altering the pattern.

According to *Webster's New College Dictionary*, there is not much difference between the definitions of the words *spatter* and *splatter*. In fact, at the entry for splatter, one is referred to the definition of *spatter*, which is defined as "to scatter by splashing; to sprinkle around" and also as "to spurt forth in drops." The latter definition best suits our purpose here. You will make some careful measurements of blood spatters on a surface at various angles. These measurements, when properly applied, can be used to determine the angle at which the spatter struck the surface. This angle can then be used to determine a very close approximation of the location in three-dimensional space where the blood spatters originated. This would be valuable information for the crime-scene analyst.

CRIME SCENE

A person has been found in the living room of his home. The person has been determined to be dead, apparently of wounds sustained from a severe beating. There is evidence of blood on the floor, walls, and ceiling of the room. It is the task of the crime-scene investigator, in this case you, to determine a variety of factors: information pertaining to the position of the victim when the beating occurred, the location in the room of the victim when the beating was initiated, and subsequent movements of the victim during the beating. These questions may be all or partially answered by the measurements that you will learn to make in this experiment. The scene just described will be used in both parts of this experiment. In the first part, it will be used only as a basis for the necessity of making the determinations with which you will be involved.

222 Experiment 31

EQUIPMENT

- 1 Medicine dropper
- 1 Meter stick or yard stick
- 1 Protective paper, to place under tag board
- 1 Protractor
- 1 Ruler
- 1 pr Scissors, or a razor blade
- 1 Table of trigonometric sine values
- 4–6 Tag board (poster board) rectangles, approximately 6 × 8 inches

MATERIALS

The following recipes have been proposed for simulated blood[1]:

1. Mix 4 oz. evaporated milk, 2 to 3 tablespoons tomato paste and red food coloring. Add water as needed to achieve the approximate consistency of blood. Store in refrigerator for up to two days.

2. Mix dry milk powder, water, and red food coloring to desired thickness. Store in refrigerator.

3. Mix white corn syrup and red food coloring. Add water to desired thickness. Store at room temperature.

METHOD

Your course instructor may have provided surfaces upon which you will find dried blood spatters. If so, proceed to Part B of this experiment. If not, you will make your own spatters and you will begin with Part A. The first item needed to accomplish this production of your own is either bovine blood or simulated blood. Human blood is not used due to the risk of exposure to certain health hazards contained in the blood. Among these hazards are hepatitis and the immune-destroying factor HIV. The experiment can be conducted through the use of simulated blood, such as honey diluted with water to make a viscosity similar to that of real blood and colored with red food coloring. Another preparation is to use red food coloring, water, and dry milk powder to produce a liquid with a viscosity similar to that of blood. The viscosity is important in trying to reproduce the spatter patterns of human blood. If you are to produce your own blood spatters using simulated or bovine blood, you will need to use a protractor to measure angles. When you have prepared the liquid that you are going to use in the experiment, you are ready for the next steps. You will need to perform the following steps with a partner or in small groups of students.

PART A: OBTAINING BLOOD SPATTERS

If your course instructor has provided you with previously prepared blood spatters, begin the experiment at Part B.

1. Obtain six pieces of precut tag board, approximately 6 × 8 inches.

2. Your partner, or one person in your group, will place the tag board on the protective paper at an angle of 0 degrees with the floor—in other words, lying flat on the floor. Be sure to place some protective paper under the tag board to avoid getting stains on the floor.

3. Draw some of the liquid being used into your medicine dropper. Be careful not to expel any of the liquid before you are ready to do so. It may stain cloth, so be aware of this possibility.

4. Place one end of the meter stick vertically on the floor next to the tag board. Place your hand holding the medicine dropper at some distance on the meter stick that is near the full length of the stick. Remember what this distance is for later reference. Incline the meter stick slightly so that the opening of the medicine dropper will be over the center portion of the tag board.

5. Very carefully squeeze the bulb of the medicine dropper to expel a single drop of the fluid. It will strike the tag board and produce a "blood" spatter.

---

[1] T. Kubic and N. Petraco, *Forensic Science Laboratory Manual and Workbook, Revised Ed.* (Boca Raton, FL: CRC Press, 2005).

6. Very carefully move the tag board aside and replace it with another piece. One person will hold this piece of tag board at an angle of 30 degrees to the floor, with the 6-inch edge on the floor, as determined through the use of the protractor.

7. Repeat the expulsion of a drop of the liquid onto the surface of this piece of tag board. If you desire, you may expel more than one drop of liquid on each tag board, but you must move your hand slightly, so that each drop will strike the tag board in a different place, not on top of each other. Separate the drops completely. The height at which the medicine dropper is held should remain as constant as possible.

8. Repeat steps 6 and 7 with other pieces of tag board, changing the angle of the tag board to 45°, 60°, and 75°.

9. Allow all of the spatters to dry thoroughly before proceeding.

PART B: MEASURING ANGLES OF IMPACT

10. All of your measurements must be made as accurately as possible, given the tools that you are working with. You will notice that, with the exception of the spatter made when the tag board was lying flat on the floor, all of the spatters have an elliptical shape. The ellipse becomes more pronounced as the angle of the target with the floor becomes greater, as illustrated in Figures 31–2 through 31–5. You must create all 5 spatters (Part A) to complete the ellipse before making your measurements.

Measure the length of each spatter as illustrated in Figures 31–2 through 31–5, omitting from this measurement the "tail" of the spatter, if one is present. Record the measurements on the data sheet at the end of this experiment.

11. Carefully measure the width of each spatter at its widest point, as shown in Figures 31–2 through 31–5, and record it on the data sheet.

12. You only need to measure one spatter on each piece of tag board, but if you are interested you can measure others as well.

Now it is time for an explanation of trigonometric functions. These functions give the relationships between the sides and angles of a right triangle—that is, a triangle with one 90° angle contained in it.

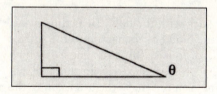

FIGURE 31–1 Right triangle with θ being the angle of impact, measured from the horizontal (floor) side.

FIGURE 31–2

FIGURE 31–3

FIGURE 31–4

FIGURE 31–5

TABLE 31-1 Impact Angle Determinations

One of the methods of determining the impact angle of a blood drop is based on the following trigonometric relationship:

$$\frac{\text{Width of stain}}{\text{Length of stain}} = \text{Sine of the impact angle}$$

Thus, by locating the width-to-length ratio of the bloodstain in the following sine table, the angle of impact of the drop causing the stain can be obtained directly.

Degs.	Sine	Degs.	Sine	Degs.	Sine	Degs.	Sine	Degs.	Sine
0	0.00	19	0.33	37	0.60	55	0.82	73	0.956
1	0.02	20	0.34	38	0.62	56	0.83	74	0.961
2	0.03	21	0.36	39	0.63	57	0.84	75	0.966
3	0.05	22	0.37	40	0.64	58	0.85	76	0.970
4	0.07	23	0.39	41	0.66	59	0.86	77	0.974
5	0.09	24	0.41	42	0.67	60	0.87	78	0.978
6	0.10	25	0.42	43	0.68	61	0.87	79	0.982
7	0.12	26	0.44	44	0.69	62	0.88	80	0.985
8	0.14	27	0.45	45	0.71	63	0.89	81	0.988
9	0.16	28	0.47	46	0.72	64	0.90	82	0.990
10	0.17	29	0.48	47	0.73	65	0.91	83	0.993
11	0.19	30	0.50	48	0.74	66	0.914	84	0.995
12	0.21	31	0.52	49	0.75	67	0.921	85	0.996
13	0.23	32	0.53	50	0.77	68	0.927	86	0.997
14	0.24	33	0.54	51	0.78	69	0.934	87	0.998
15	0.26	34	0.56	52	0.79	70	0.940	88	0.9994
16	0.28	35	0.57	53	0.80	71	0.946	89	0.9998
17	0.29	36	0.59	54	0.81	72	0.951	90	1.00
18	0.31								

In our case, this is the angle made by the junction of the meter stick with the floor. In a crime scene, this would be the vertical distance from the point of origin of the blood of the victim to the surface upon which that victim is standing, sitting, or lying. The angle of impact (θ) is the angle at which the blood spatter strikes the surface upon which it comes to rest (see Figure 31–1). In this case it is the angle between the floor and the edge of the piece of tag board. You can make the extension to the situation of the crime scene. The sine of the angle of impact is the function that we are interested in. This is illustrated in Table 31–1. To determine the angle of impact from its sine, you may use your calculator or Table 31–1. Your course instructor has probably given you an explanation of this procedure. This may serve as a reminder. Now we will go back to work.

13. Determine the sine of the angle of impact for each of the cards that you are working with. The use of your calculator will make the next step a little more accurate, but the table of sine values will also give good results. However, the results will only be as good as your measurement of the spatters.

14. Look in the table for the value that is the closest to your calculated result. If you are using your calculator for this step, you must use the second function button and then the "arc sin" button. This will provide you with the angle that has that value as its sin(e).
15. Record the value of each angle in the table on the data sheet. Compare it with the value that the angle was supposed to have, either from the use of the protractor or from the data provided by your instructor for each of the cards you are using.

SELECTED SOURCES FOR ADDITIONAL INFORMATION

Burnett, B.R., Orantes, J.M., and Pierson, M.L., "An unusual bloodstain case," *J. Forens. Sci.*, 42 (3), (1997), 519.

Raymond, M.A., Smith, E.R., and Liesegang, J., "Oscillating blood droplets: implications for crime scene reconstruction," *Sci. & Just.*, 36 (3), (1996), 161.

EXPERIMENT 31

DATA SHEET

Name _____

Date _____

DETERMINATION OF BLOOD-SPATTER ANGLES OF IMPACT

"Target" in the table below refers to the piece of tag board used in this experiment.

Angle of Target in Degrees	Width of Spatter in mm	Length of Spatter in mm	Width/Length Ratio	Impact Angle from the Sine Table
0				
30				
45				
60				
75				

Questions

1. How closely do the known values of the angles of impact compare with those that you determined from the use of the sine function?

2. What is the most likely cause of any difference between the two values that you compared in question 1?

3. Do you think that the height of the medicine dropper above the target tag board has anything to do with the ratio calculated from the width/length ratio of the spatter? Why or why not?

Electrophoretic Analysis of Blood for Human Origin (Advanced)

EXPERIMENT 32

Experiments 32, 34, and 35 involve a technique called electrophoresis. Experiments 34 and 35 involve gel electrophoresis. Experiment 32 is concerned with the determination of whether or not a stain is human blood as opposed to animal blood or something that just looks like blood. Experiment 33 extends this further to introduce you to the technique of obtaining DNA, and Experiments 34 and 35 introduce you to several uses of DNA typing.

In the mid-1930s Arne Tiselius found that if ions of similar charge were placed in solution between two oppositely charged electrodes as shown in Figure 32–1, the smaller ions of the same charge move (migrate) toward the electrode of opposite charge faster than the larger ions. He also found that if ions of different charge were placed in the solution, the more highly charged ions migrate faster than the lower-charged ions.

When these factors are combined, a separation is possible. Modern techniques pass the compounds through a gel on a piece of plastic or paper because it is easier to stain and measure them later.

When a stain is analyzed in the laboratory and found to be a bloodstain, the forensic analyst will have to determine whether the stain is of human origin. For this purpose the standard test used is the **precipitin test**. Precipitin tests are based on the fact that when animals (usually rabbits) are injected with human blood, antibodies are formed that react with the invading blood to neutralize its presence. The animal's serum can be recovered and marketed commercially as human antiserum. This experiment sets forth a practical, rapid, inexpensive, and sensitive electrophoretic method for confirming the fact that a bloodstain is of human origin.

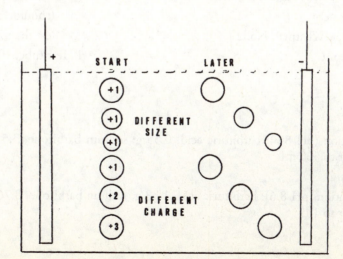

FIGURE 32–1 Diagram of electrophoretic migration.

 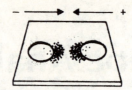 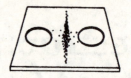

Antigen and antibody are added to their respective wells

Antigen and antibody are being moved toward each other

Antigen and antibody have formed a visible precipitin line in the gel between the wells

FIGURE 32-2 The sequence of events on the microscope slide.

The technique that we shall use in this experiment is known as **counter immunoelectrophoresis** or **crossover electrophoresis**. It takes advantage of the fact that human blood is antigenic; that is, its presence in the body of animals such as rabbits will cause the production of antibodies. In crossover electrophoresis an agar mixture is poured onto a microscope slide and allowed to harden. Then a set of holes is punched into the gel where the antigen solution (bloodstain) and the commercial human antiserum are placed. Under the influence of an electrical field, the antigens and antibodies move toward each other across the gel. If the blood is of human origin, a line of precipitation will form midway between the two holes (see Figure 32–2).

CRIME SCENE

A suspect was arrested based on a man's charge of assault and robbery. In the preliminary hearing, the defense lawyer challenged the results of the blood typing test, asserting that the blood was not of human origin. The prosecution has requested that the laboratory do a crossover electrophoresis test in order to determine human origin. You have a portion of the suspect stain to do the following experiment.

EQUIPMENT

- 1 Beaker, 25 mL
- 1 Bulb to fit the Pasteur pipets
- 1 Burner, Bunsen
- 1 Constant voltage power supply, only up to 100 volts is required
- 1 pr Goggles, safety
- 1 Paper, filter, Whatman No. 2
- 1 Pipet, 1.0 mL
- 1 Pipet, Pasteur
- Slides, microscope, 5 × 8 cm
- 1 Syringe, 10 μL
- 1 Tank, electrophoresis, to hold microscope slides in shoulders (shoulders should be placed less than 7 cm apart)
- 1 Test tube, 10 × 75 mm

MATERIALS

Agarose

Gel buffer solution (pH 8.6): barbituric acid, 0.55 g; sodium barbitone, 3.5 g; calcium lactate, 0.51 g; distilled water to 500 mL

Human antiserum

Tank buffer solution (pH 8.6): barbituric acid, 1.38 g; sodium barbitone, 8.76 g; calcium lactate, 0.38 g; distilled water to 1 L

METHOD

1. Cut a 1 × 1 cm piece of the material containing a suspected human bloodstain. Place this in a test tube with 1 mL of gel buffer. Label this tube T, for test. Allow the material to soak for 5 to 10 minutes. The ideal extract will appear as a pale straw color.

2. Cut a 1 × 1 cm piece from an unstained area and place it in a test tube with 1 mL of gel buffer. Label the tube C, for control.

3. Cut a 1 × 1 cm piece of material containing a known human bloodstain. Treat as in step 1. Label the test tube K, for known.

4. Weigh 0.1 g of agarose and add it to 5 mL of distilled water; add an equal volume of gel buffer and heat the mixture in a boiling water bath until the agarose dissolves.

5. Pour the agarose mixture onto a leveled 5 × 8 cm microscope slide. Allow the agarose to set for at least 15 minutes, scraping off any excess gel from the edges.

6. Once the gel hardens, punch three pairs of holes, or wells, in the gel with a Pasteur pipet (with suction). Position the holes about midway up the slide. The holes should be about 1.5 mm in diameter and separated from each other by about 1.5–2.0 mm. Note: Well-punching kits are commercially available.

7. Hold the coated plate lengthwise, and with a Pasteur pipet, place the test solution, known, and control extracts in the right-hand set of wells. Place the human antiserum into the left-hand set of wells. The wells should be filled to their tops, but not overflowing.

8. Place 50 mL of the tank buffer in each side of the electrophoresis tank. Saturate 22 × 4 cm strips of filter paper and place them on each side of the tank.

9. Invert the plate into the filter papers so that the antiserum wells are closest to the anode (+ electrode) and the stain extracts nearest to the cathode (− electrode).

10. Electrophoresis is carried out at 100 to 150 volts for 10 to 20 minutes.

11. A fine line of white precipitate between holes of a pair represents a positive reaction.

SELECTED SOURCES FOR ADDITIONAL INFORMATION

Buel, E., LaFountain, M., Schwartz, M., and Walkinshaw, M., "Evaluation of capillary electrophoresis performance through resolution measurements," *J. Forens. Sci.*, 46 (2), (2001), 341.

Klapec, D.J., and Ng, D., "The use of capillary electrophoresis in the detection of monomethylamine and benzoate ions in the forensic examination of explosive residues," *J. Forens. Sci.*, 46 (5), (2001), 1168.

Moretti, T.R., Baumstark, A.L., Defenbaugh, D.A., Keys, K.M., Brown, A.L., and Budowle, B., "Validation of STR typing by capillary electrophoresis," *J. Forens. Sci.*, 46 (3), (2001), 661.

Quarino, L., Samples, M., San Pietro, D., Shaler, R., Orta, A., and Jack, D., "Haptoglobin typing of bloodstains using horizontal discontinuous polyacrylamide gel electrophoresis," *Sci. & Just.*, 35 (3), (1995), 213.

EXPERIMENT 32

DATA SHEET

Name _____

Date _____

ELECTROPHORETIC ANALYSIS OF BLOOD FOR HUMAN ORIGIN (ADVANCED)

1. Attach your slide to this sheet.

2. What is agar, and what is its purpose in this experiment?

3. A person suspected of just robbing a meat market was apprehended and found to have several bills in his pockets. His explanation was that he was shooting craps in the alley and picked up the money and ran when the "cops" came. The police detective asked the lab people whether they could tell if the bills had been in a meat market. They said they could if given a little time. How could they do this using electrophoretic analysis?

EXPERIMENT 33

Nuclear DNA Extraction*

DNA evidence is used whenever possible in criminal investigations. The next several experiments involve DNA in various situations. It is therefore desirous to learn how DNA can be obtained, but in a situation that is safer than using human blood. The procedures described in this experiment can be used to isolate chromosomal DNA from a variety of sources, such as *Escherichia coli* (*E. coli*) as well as peas, onions, and other vegetable sources.

All organisms are composed of cells. Some organisms, such as bacteria and yeast, are single-celled organisms. Others, such as humans, are made of trillions of specialized cells. Cells are composed of proteins, lipids, carbohydrates, and nucleic acids. DNA (deoxyribonucleic acid) is the hereditary material found in all cells. It is the genetic material that directs the development and function of all organisms (Figure 33-1).

One of DNA's most important functions is to direct the synthesis of proteins. Genes are long segments of DNA (Figure 33-1) that encode proteins. Genes contained on one strand of DNA make up a chromosome. Humans have 23 pairs of chromosomes, one maternal set and one paternal set. If the DNA from one human cell was stretched end to end, it would be 7 feet long. Before DNA can be amplified via polymerase chain reaction or analyzed through genetic fingerprinting, the DNA must be extracted from the cell. We will review several procedures that can accomplish this goal.

In the following procedures we are going to complete three basic steps:

1. Lyse (break open) the cells
2. Separate DNA from other cellular components
3. Stain DNA for visualization

The procedures vary slightly due to the differing cellular composition between cell types. In the first procedure, you will isolate the chromosome of a rod-shaped prokaryotic bacterium called *E. coli*. Prokaryotic cells, such as bacteria, do not enclose their chromosomal DNA in a nuclear membrane. In the second procedure, you will be working with eukaryotic plant cells. Eukaryotic cells (Figure 33–2) have a nuclear membrane around the chromosomes. Plants and animals are eukaryotic organisms. Plant cells, in particular, have walls that require further enzymatic digestion for cell lysis to occur.

In the first step we will lyse the cells using a detergent. *Lysing* the cells refers to breaking the outer plasma membrane of the cell, thus releasing the internal components of the cell. This can be accomplished with most dishwashing liquid as well as some laundry detergents. The cell (plasma) membrane is composed of lipids. Detergents have

---

*Courtesy of Laura Roselli, Biotechnology Dept., Burlington County College, Mt. Laurel, NJ 08054.

236 Experiment 33

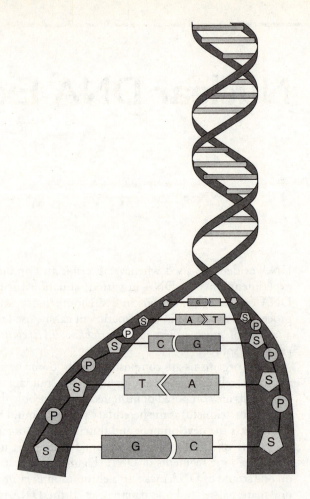

FIGURE 33-1 The double helix DNA module.
Reprinted with permission from M. F. Mallette, C. O. Clagett, A. T. Phillips, and R. L. McCarl, Introductory Biochemistry *(Baltimore: Williams and Wilkens Co., 1971).*

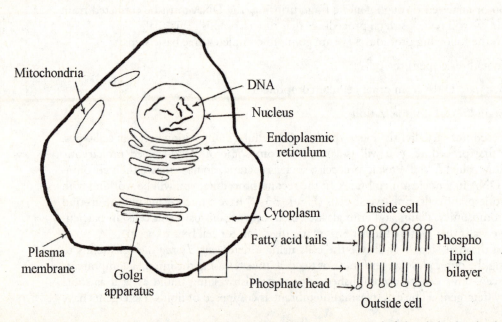

FIGURE 33-2 Eukaryotic cell, detailing the plasma membrane. The membrane is composed of phospholipid molecules.

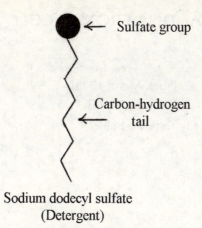

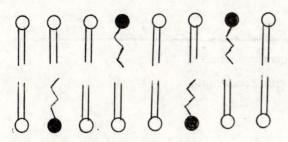

FIGURE 33-3 Diagram illustrating how a detergent disrupts the cell membrane.

a similar structure to these membrane lipids. The molecules of detergent integrate into the cell membrane and cause it to dissociate. This is shown in diagram form in Figure 33-3.

In the second step we separate the DNA from other cellular components using alcohol extraction. When the ethanol is added, two phases form in the tube, the aqueous and alcohol phases. The DNA will separate from the other two phases and precipitate at the interphase (thin layer between the aqueous and alcohol layers).

For those eukaryotic sources of DNA, an additional step of protein digestion is included. This is necessary because eukaryotic DNA is wrapped around protein molecules called *histones*. Meat tenderizers contain enzymes that will remove these proteins. The enzymes also aid in digestion of the **cell wall**.

Last, the DNA can be removed from the interphase by gently moving a rod through the two phases repeatedly. The white precipitate that begins to spool is chromosomal DNA. DNA can be visualized at higher magnification under a microscope, with the use of methylene blue, a stain that dyes DNA.

CRIME SCENE

It has been found, although in limited experiments, that plant DNA is as unique as animal DNA. This was first shown by demonstrating that trees have unique DNA. A young woman was found murdered under a group of trees. The police located a suspect who denied even being in the area. The police noticed some seed pods in the back of his pick-up truck that looked just like those on the trees where the body was found. Would the DNA of these seeds match the tree over the body and be different from those of the adjacent trees? In order to give you some practice in obtaining plant DNA before you test the evidence, you are going to experiment with the basic techniques involved.

PART A: ISOLATION OF CHROMOSOMAL DNA FROM *E. COLI*

EQUIPMENT

- 5–6 Wooden stir rods (can use the wooden end of cotton swabs)
- 1 Water bath set at 65°C
- 1 Medicine dropper
- 1 Pipet, Mohr, 10 mL
- 1 Test tube, 10 mL
- 1 Test tube holder

MATERIALS

7 mL *E. coli* (actively growing culture, 24 hrs)
4 mL Ethanol (or isopropyl alcohol)
3 mL Detergent or shampoo

METHOD

1. Make 5 milliliters of a 50 percent dilution of detergent in water.
2. Add 5 milliliters of 50 percent detergent directly to the *E. coli* culture.
3. Heat the tube for 15 minutes at 65°C.
4. Cool the bacteria to room temperature.
5. Tilt the test tube slightly and add 4 milliliters of cold ethanol dropwise down the side of the bacterial tube. Do not mix the two layers.
6. Move a stirring rod back and forth through the two phases. Do not move the rod entirely to the bottom of your broth tube. Moving the rod slightly into the aqueous phase and then slightly back into the alcohol phase will suffice.
7. Twirl the wooden rod. DNA should begin to spool around it.

PART B: ISOLATION OF DNA FROM VEGETABLE SOURCES

EQUIPMENT

- 4–5 Wooden stir rods
- 1 Water bath
- 1 Blender
- Cheese cloth, approximately 6 × 6 inches
- 1 Beaker, 250 mL
- 1 Graduated cylinder, 50 or 100 mL
- 1 Pipet, Mohr, 10 mL
- 4–5 Test tubes, 10 mL
- 1 Test tube rack

MATERIALS

DNA source (e.g., peas, onions)
Table salt
Water
Ethanol
Detergent or dish liquid
Meat tenderizer

METHOD

1. Combine 1/2 cup (or 118 milliliters) of your vegetable with 1 cup (236 milliliters) of water.
2. Blend on high or homogenize until liquid.
3. Strain through cheesecloth and catch the filtrate in a 250-milliliters beaker.
4. Place 4 milliliters aliquots of the liquid into each of four to five test tubes.
5. Add 3 milliliters of 50 percent detergent to a test tube containing strained vegetable liquid.
6. Add a pinch of meat tenderizer (contains an enzyme).
7. Tilt the test tube slightly and add 3 milliliters of cold ethanol dropwise down the side of the tube. Do not mix the two layers.
8. Move a stirring rod back and forth through the two phases. Do not move the rod entirely to the bottom of your sample tube. Moving the rod slightly into the aqueous phase and then slightly back into the alcohol phase will suffice.
9. Twirl the wooden rod. DNA should begin to spool.

PART C: STAINING OF DNA FOR VISUALIZATION (CAN BE USED SUBSEQUENT TO PART A OR PART B)

EQUIPMENT

2–3 Cover slips
2–3 Microscope slides
1 Compound microscope
1 Medicine dropper
2–3 Toothpicks

CHEMICALS

Methylene blue indicator solution

METHOD

1. Remove the isolated DNA from the wooden rod with a toothpick and place it on a glass slide.
2. Place two drops of methylene blue directly on the DNA.
3. Place a cover slip over the stained DNA.
4. View under a compound microscope. Look under two levels of magnification: 40× and 100×.

ALTERNATE EXPERIMENTS

1. Use laundry detergent vs. dishwashing detergent to compare the differences in the amounts of DNA isolated from the same vegetable source.
2. Try isolating DNA from different vegetable sources. How do the yields of DNA compare in peas vs. onions, carrots?
3. Using baker's yeast and athletic shoe cleaner, yeast genomic DNA can be isolated. (See Kelly et al., 1987, in the Selected Sources section.)

SELECTED SOURCES FOR ADDITIONAL INFORMATION

Kelly, K.F., Rankin, J.J., and Wink, R.C., "Method and application of DNA fingerprinting: a guide for the non-scientist," *Criminal Law Revi.*, (1987), 105.

Kimber, C., "Interpretation of mitochondrial DNA sequencing," *Sci. & Just.*, 40 (3), (2000), 217.

Montpetit, S.A., Fitch, I.T., and O'Donnell, P.T., "A simple automated instrument for DNA extraction in forensic casework," *J. Forens. Sci.*, 50 (3), (2005), 555.

EXPERIMENT 33 Name _____

DATA SHEET Date _____

NUCLEAR DNA EXTRACTION

1. Describe the appearance of the DNA that you have isolated on the wooden rod, and illustrate it below.

2. Describe the appearance of the DNA as viewed under the microscope, and illustrate it below.

3. After the addition of ethanol, two phases develop in your tube. Which phase is on top? Why does this phase sit on the top rather than the bottom?

Experiment 33

4. Why is the addition of detergent necessary to isolate DNA?

5. How would your results differ in Part B if you omitted the meat tenderizer?

EXPERIMENT 34

DNA Fingerprinting: EDVO-Kit # 109*

EXPERIMENT COMPONENTS

ELECTROPHORESIS SAMPLES

- Ready-to-Load™ DNA samples

    A: DNA from crime scene cut with Enzyme 1
    B: DNA from crime scene cut with Enzyme 2
    C: DNA from Suspect 1 cut with Enzyme 1
    D: DNA from Suspect 1 cut with Enzyme 2
    E: DNA from Suspect 2 cut with Enzyme 1
    F: DNA from Suspect 2 cut with Enzyme 2

REAGENTS AND SUPPLIES

- Practice gel loading solution
- UltraSpec-Agarose™ powder
- Concentrated electrophoresis buffer
- InstaStain® Methylene Blue
- Methylene Blue Plus™
- Pipet, 1 mL
- Graduated cylinder (packaging for samples), 100 mL
- Microtipped transfer pipets

THIS EXPERIMENT DOES NOT CONTAIN HUMAN DNA.

REQUIREMENTS

- Horizontal gel electrophoresis apparatus
- DC power supply
- Automatic micropipets with tips
- Balance
- Microwave or hot plate/burner
- Pipet pump

---

* © EDVOTEK, Inc. All rights reserved. www.edvotek.com

- Flasks or beakers, 250 mL
- Hot gloves
- Safety goggles and disposable laboratory gloves
- Small plastic trays or large weigh boats (for gel destaining)
- DNA visualization system (white light)
- Distilled or deionized water

INTRODUCTION TO DNA FINGERPRINTING

DNA typing (also called DNA profile analysis or DNA fingerprinting) is the process whereby the genomic DNA of an organism is analyzed by examining several specific, variable DNA sequences located throughout the genome. In humans, DNA fingerprinting is now used routinely for identification purposes.

Human DNA fingerprinting was pioneered by Dr. Alex Jeffreys at the University of Leicester in 1984. His analytical method led to the apprehension of a murderer in the first DNA fingerprinting conviction in September 1987 in the UK. Two months later, the first U.S. conviction based on DNA fingerprinting occurred in Orlando, Florida. Since then, the use of DNA fingerprinting has led to thousands of criminal convictions, as well as dozens of exonerations.

In contrast to earlier methodologies, such as blood typing, that can only exclude a suspect, DNA fingerprinting can provide positive identification with great accuracy. In addition to criminal identification cases, DNA fingerprinting is now used routinely in paternity determinations and for the identification of genetic disease "markers." It is also used for the identification of human remains, such as in war casualties, and was used extensively to identify victims of the September 11, 2001, terrorist attacks on the World Trade Center and the Pentagon.

Human cells contain two types of DNA. The first type is cellular chromosomal DNA, which is packaged in 23 sets of chromosomes in the nucleus of the cell. This DNA, obtained from both parents, reflects the combined parental genetic inheritance of an individual. DNA fingerprinting utilizing cellular DNA involves analysis of the sequence of two alleles for a particular gene.

The second type of DNA is different from cellular DNA and is present only in the mitochondria, which are the energy-producing organelles of the cell. Mitochondrial DNA is inherited maternally by both males and females and is extremely useful in the analysis of specific cases where fraternal linkages are important to determine. For example, a brother, sister, half-brother, or half-sister who share the same mother would inherit the same mitochondrial DNA. Identification is determined by sequencing a certain region within mitochondrial DNA, which is a single circular chromosome composed of 16,569 base pairs and 37 genes identified.

The DNA fingerprinting methods developed by Dr. Jeffreys utilize cellular chromosomal DNA, which is submitted to restriction enzyme digestion, followed by Southern Blot analysis. When human DNA is digested by a restriction enzyme, large numbers of DNA fragments are generated. When separated by agarose gel electrophoresis, the numerous DNA fragments appear as a "smear" on the gel. Labeled probes are used to detect **restriction fragment length polymorphic (RFLP)** regions within DNA, which will be described later in greater detail. The RFLP method is statistically very accurate but requires relatively large amounts of DNA and takes several weeks to perform.

In recent years, the method utilizing **polymerase chain reaction (PCR)** has subsequently superceded the RFLP method because of two important advantages. The first is the sensitivity of the PCR method, which allows for DNA fingerprinting identification using much smaller amounts of DNA. This is because the PCR method is able to amplify DNA to facilitate analysis. A second advantage is the speed of PCR analysis, which allows critical questions to be answered more quickly compared to Southern Blot analysis.

In the biotechnology teaching classroom, many important concepts, theories, and practice methods of molecular biology can be conveyed in the context of the various DNA fingerprinting methods. In this experiment, emphasis is placed on concepts related to the RFLP method. The experiment activities focus on the identification of DNA by analyzing restriction fragmentation patterns separated by agarose gel electrophoresis.

USE OF RESTRICTION ENZYMES IN DNA FINGPERPRINTING

DNA fingerprinting involves the electrophoretic analysis of DNA fragment sizes generated by restriction enzymes. Restriction enzymes are endonucleases that catalyze the cleavage of phosphodiester bonds within both strands of DNA. The points of cleavage occur in or near very specific palindromic sequences of bases called recognition sites, which are generally 4 to 8 base pairs in length.

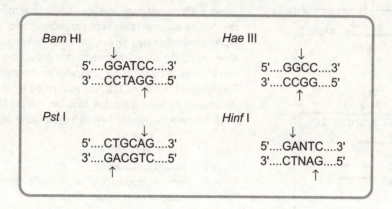

The two most commonly used restriction enzymes for DNA profile analysis are *Hae* III and *Hinf* I, which are 4-base and 5-base cutting enzymes. The examples in the figure above show recognition sites for various restriction enzymes.

The size of the DNA fragments generated depends on the distance between the recognition sites. In general, the longer the DNA molecule, the greater the probability that a given recognition site will occur. Human DNA is very large and contains approximately 3 billion base pairs. A restriction enzyme having a 6-base pair recognition site, such as *Eco* RI, would be expected to cut human DNA into approximately 750,000 different fragments.

DNA is highly polymorphic, that is, no two individuals have exactly the same pattern of restriction enzyme recognition sites in their DNA. A large number of alleles exist in the population. Alleles, which are alternate forms of a gene, result in alternative expressions of genetic traits that can be dominant or recessive.

Chromosomes occur in matching pairs, one of maternal and the other of paternal origin. The two copies of a gene (alleles) at a given chromosomal locus represent a composite of the parental genes constituting an individual's unique genotype. It follows that alleles have differences in their base sequences, which consequently creates differences in the distribution and frequencies of restriction enzyme recognition sites. Other differences in base sequences between individuals can occur because of mutations and deletions. Such changes can also create or eliminate a recognition site.

Polymorphic DNA refers to chromosomal regions that vary widely from individual to individual. By examining several of these regions within the genomic DNA obtained from an individual, one may obtain a "DNA fingerprint" for that individual. The most commonly used polymorphisms are those that vary in length; these are known as **fragment length polymorphisms (FLPs)**. There are two main reasons for the occurrence of FLPs. Restriction fragment length polymorphisms (RFLPs) are the result of variations in length of a given segment of genomic DNA between two restriction endonuclease recognition sites among individuals of the same species. RFLPs are the result of an altered restriction enzyme cut site that may be the result of a mutation of a restriction enzyme recognition site.

A second major type of FLP occurs mainly in "intergenic" or noncoding regions of DNA and is known as **variable number of tandem repeats (VNTRs)**. In this case, segments of DNA that contain sequences from 2 to 40 bases in length repeat in a tandem manner many times. The number of segments or "core units" that repeats varies among individuals of the same species. The restriction enzyme cut sites are not altered. VNTR loci are very polymorphic. There are potentially hundreds of alleles at a single locus and

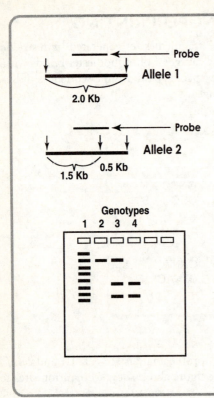

RFLP as Determined in Southern Blot analysis

An allele is recognized by a probe that spans over the internal restriction enzyme site which is present in certain alleles. In Allele 1, the internal restriction enzyme site is missing. In Allele 2, the internal restriction enzyme is present resulting in two fragments. Upon separation by agarose gel electrophoresis of the digested Allele 2, two fragments are generated. Probes will bind to the 2.0 Kb allele as well as the two smaller fragments (1.5 Kb and 0.5 Kb) generated by the restriction enzyme digestion because the probe spans over the two fragments as well as the intact allele.

Lane 1 DNA Marker
Lane 2 Homozygous allele
Lane 3 Heterozygous alleles where one can be cut with the restriction enzyme
Lane 4 Homozygous alleles where both are cut with the restriction enzyme

therefore they are very useful in DNA fingerprinting. Ten to fifteen percent of mammalian DNA consists of sets of repeated, short sequences of bases that are tandemly arranged in arrays. The length of these arrays (the amount of repeated sets) varies between individuals at different chromosomal loci.

TGTTTA|TGTTTA|TGTTTA| . . . . variable number

When these arrays are flanked by recognition sites, the length of the repeat will determine the size of the restriction enzyme fragment generated. There are several types of these short, repetitive sequences, and they have been cloned and purified.

THE DNA FINGERPRINTING PROCESS

Agarose gel electrophoresis is a procedure used to analyze DNA fragments generated by restriction enzymes. The agarose gel consists of microscopic pores that act as a molecular sieve. Samples of DNA are loaded into wells made in the gel during casting. Because DNA has a negative charge at neutral pH, it migrates through the gel toward the positive electrode during electrophoresis. DNA fragments are separated by the gel according to their size. The smaller the fragment, the faster it migrates. After electrophoresis, the DNA can be visualized by staining the gel with dyes. Restriction enzyme cleavage of relatively small DNA molecules, such as plasmids and viral DNAs, usually results in discrete banding patterns of the DNA fragments after electrophoresis. However, cleavage of large and complex DNA, such as human chromosomal DNA, generates so many differently sized fragments that the resolving capacity of the gel is exceeded. Consequently, the cleaved DNA is visualized as a smear after staining and has no obvious banding patterns.

RFLP analysis of genomic DNA is facilitated by Southern Blot analysis. After electrophoresis, the DNA fragments in the gel are denatured by soaking in an alkali solution. This causes double-stranded DNA fragments to be converted into single-stranded form (no longer base-paired in a double helix). A replica of the electrophoretic pattern of DNA fragments in the gel is made by transferring (blotting) them to a sheet of nylon membrane. This is done by placing the membrane on the gel after electrophoresis and transferring the fragments to the membrane by capillary action or suction by vacuum. The DNA, which is not visible, becomes permanently adsorbed to the membrane, which can be manipulated much more easily than gels.

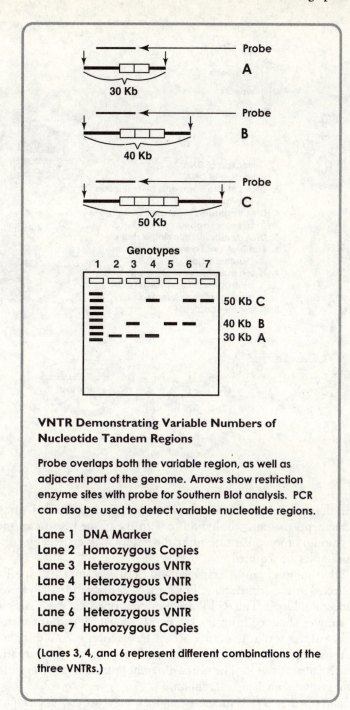

VNTR Demonstrating Variable Numbers of Nucleotide Tandem Regions

Probe overlaps both the variable region, as well as adjacent part of the genome. Arrows show restriction enzyme sites with probe for Southern Blot analysis. PCR can also be used to detect variable nucleotide regions.

Lane 1   DNA Marker
Lane 2   Homozygous Copies
Lane 3   Heterozygous VNTR
Lane 4   Heterozygous VNTR
Lane 5   Homozygous Copies
Lane 6   Heterozygous VNTR
Lane 7   Homozygous Copies

(Lanes 3, 4, and 6 represent different combinations of the three VNTRs.)

Analysis of the blotted DNA is done by hybridization with a labeled DNA probe. In forensic RFLP analysis, the probe is a DNA fragment that contains base sequences that are complementary to the variable arrays of tandemly repeated sequences found in the human chromosomes. Probes can be labeled with isotopic or nonisotopic reporter molecules, such as fluorescent dyes, that are used for detection. A solution containing the single-stranded probe is incubated with the membrane containing the blotted, single-stranded (denatured) DNA fragments. Under the proper conditions, the probe will only base-pair (hybridize) to those fragments containing the complementary repeated sequences. The membrane is then washed to remove excess probe. If the probe is isotopically labeled to the membrane, it is then placed on an x-ray film for several hours. This process is known as autoradiography. Only DNA fragments that have hybridized to the probe will reveal their positions on the film because the localized areas of radioactivity cause exposure. The hybridized fragments appear as discrete bands (fingerprint) on the film and are in the same relative

248 Experiment 34

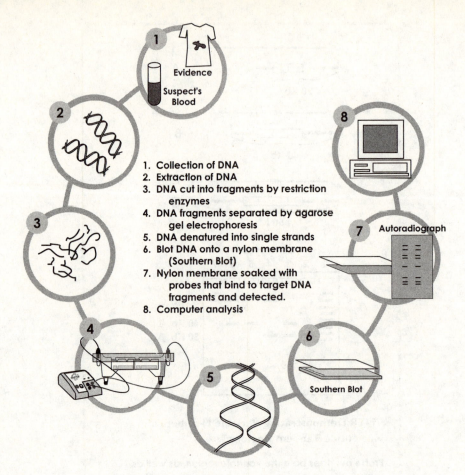

1. Collection of DNA
2. Extraction of DNA
3. DNA cut into fragments by restriction enzymes
4. DNA fragments separated by agarose gel electrophoresis
5. DNA denatured into single strands
6. Blot DNA onto a nylon membrane (Southern Blot)
7. Nylon membrane soaked with probes that bind to target DNA fragments and detected.
8. Computer analysis

positions as they were in the agarose gel after electrophoresis. Only specific DNA fragments, of the hundreds of thousands of fragments present, will hybridize with the probe because of the selective nature of the hybridization (base pairing) process. Because autoradiography is an extremely sensitive technique, only small amounts of DNA samples are required.

In forensic cases, DNA samples can be extracted and purified from small specimens of skin, blood, semen, or hair roots collected at the crime scene. DNA that is suitable for analysis can even be obtained from dried stains of semen and blood. The RFLP analyses performed on these samples is then compared to those performed on samples obtained from the suspect. If the RFLP patterns match, it is then beyond reasonable doubt that the suspect was at the crime scene. In practice, several different probes containing different types of repetitious sequences are used in the hybridizations in order to satisfy certain statistical criteria for absolute, positive identification. The use of different restriction enzymes allows for accuracies in positive identifications of greater than 1 in 100 million.

The polymerase chain reaction (PCR) method amplifies target sequences of DNA, which are referred to as AMRFLPs. PCR has made it possible for very small amounts of DNA found at crime scenes to be amplified for DNA fingerprinting analysis. Using specific probes to prime DNA polymerase, many copies of the targeted areas of DNA can be synthesized in vitro and subsequently analyzed.

In this experiment, DNA samples have been cut by restriction enzymes and the fragmentation patterns serve as the individual fingerprint. The DNA fragmentation patterns are simple enough to analyze directly in the stained agarose gel, which eliminates the need for a Southern Blot. In this hypothetical case, DNA obtained from two suspects is cleaved with two restriction enzymes in separate reactions. The objective is to analyze and match the DNA fragmentation patterns after agarose gel electrophoresis and determine if Suspect 1 or Suspect 2 was at the crime scene.

EXPERIMENT OVERVIEW

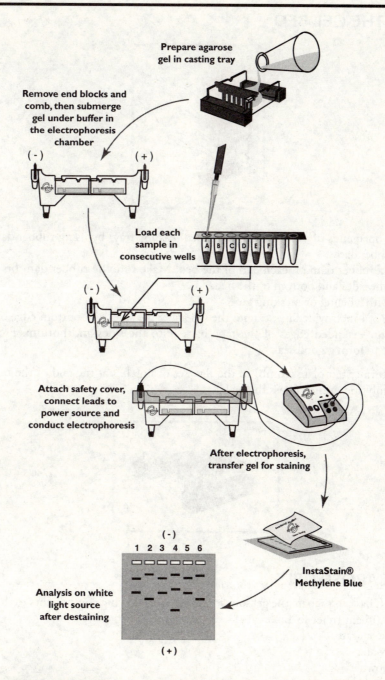

EXPERIMENT OBJECTIVE

The objective of this experiment is to develop a basic understanding of DNA fingerprinting. You will analyze variations in restriction enzyme cleavage patterns obtained from different DNA molecules and identify the possible perpetrator of a crime using the logic of DNA fingerprinting.

GEL REQUIREMENTS

- Recommended gel tray size: 7 × 7 cm or 7 × 15 cm
- Number of sample wells required: 6
- Placement of well-former template: first set of notches
- Agarose gel concentration required: 0.8%

AGAROSE GEL PREPARATION

PREPARING THE GEL BED

1. Close off the open ends of a clean and dry gel bed (casting tray) by using rubber dams or tape.
   A. Using rubber dams:
      - Place a rubber dam on each end of the bed. Make sure the rubber dam fits firmly in contact with the sides and bottom of the bed.
   B. Taping with labeling or masking tape:
      - Using 3/4-inch-wide tape, extend the tape over the sides and bottom edge of the bed.
      - Fold the extended edges of the tape back onto the sides and bottom. Press contact points firmly to form a good seal.
2. Place a well-former template (comb) in the first set of notches at the end of the bed. Make sure the comb sits firmly and evenly across the bed.

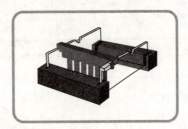

CASTING AGAROSE GELS

3. Use a 250-mL flask to prepare the gel solution. Add the following components to the flask as specified for your experiment (refer to Table 34–1).
   - Buffer concentrate
   - Distilled water
   - Agarose powder

TABLE 34–1	Individual 0.8% UltraSpec-Agarose™ Gel DNA Staining with InstaStain® MetBlue			
Size of EDVOTEK Casting Tray (cm)	Amt of Agarose (g)	Concentrated Buffer (50×) (mL)	Distilled Water (mL)	Total Volume (mL)
7 × 7	0.24	0.6	29.4	30
7 × 15	0.48	1.2	58.8	60

4. Swirl the mixture to disperse the clumps of agarose powder.

5. With a marking pen, indicate the level of the solution volume on the outside of the flask.

6. Heat the mixture to dissolve the agarose powder. The final solution should appear clear (like water) without any undissolved particles.

   A. Microwave method
   - Cover the flask with plastic wrap to minimize evaporation.
   - Heat the mixture on high for 1 minute.
   - Swirl the mixture and heat on high in bursts of 25 seconds until all the agarose is completely dissolved.

   B. Hot plate method
   - Cover the flask with aluminum foil to prevent excess evaporation.
   - Heat the mixture to boiling over a burner with occasional swirling. Boil until all the agarose is completely dissolved.

   Check the solution carefully. If you see "crystal" particles, the agarose is not completely dissolved.

   At high altitudes, it is recommended to use a microwave oven to reach boiling temperatures.

7. Cool the agarose solution to 55°C with careful swirling to promote even dissipation of heat. If detectable evaporation has occurred, add distilled water to bring the solution up to the original volume as marked on the flask in step 5.

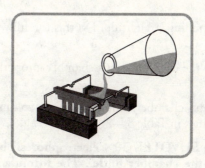

After the gel is cooled to 55°C:
If you are using rubber dams, go to step 9.
If you are using tape, continue with step 8.

8. Seal the interface of the gel bed and tape to prevent the agarose solution from leaking.
   - Use a transfer pipet to deposit a small amount of cooled agarose to both inside ends of the bed.
   - Wait approximately 1 minute for the agarose to solidify.

9. Pour the cooled agarose solution into the bed. Make sure the bed is on a level surface.

10. Allow the gel to completely solidify. It will become firm and cool to the touch after approximately 20 minutes.

PREPARING THE GEL FOR ELECTROPHORESIS

11. After the gel is completely solidified, carefully and slowly remove the rubber dams or tape from the gel bed.

    Be especially careful not to damage or tear the gel wells when removing the rubber dams. A thin plastic knife, spatula, or pipet tip can be inserted between the gel and the dams to break possible surface tension.

12. Remove the comb by slowly pulling straight up. Do this carefully and evenly to prevent tearing the sample wells.

13. Place the gel (on its bed) into the electrophoresis chamber, properly oriented, centered, and level on the platform.

14. Fill the electrophoresis apparatus chamber with the required volume of diluted buffer for the specific unit you are using (see guidelines in Table 34–2).

    For DNA analysis, the same EDVOTEK 50× electrophoresis buffer is used for preparing both the agarose gel buffer and the chamber buffer. The formula for diluting EDVOTEK (50×) concentrated buffer is 1 volume of buffer concentrate to every 49 volumes of distilled or deionized water.

TABLE 34–2	Dilution of Electrophoresis (Chamber) Buffer			
EDVOTEK Model #	Concentrated Buffer (50×) (mL)	+	Distilled Water (mL) =	Total Volume (mL)
M6+	6		294	300
M12	8		392	400
M36 (blue)	10		490	500
M36 (clear)	20		980	1000

The electrophoresis (chamber) buffer recommended is Trisacetate-EDTA (20 mM Tris, 6 mM sodium acetate, 1 mM disodium ethylenediamine tetraacetic acid) pH 7.8. Prepare the buffer as required for your electrophoresis apparatus.

15. Make sure the gel is completely covered with buffer.

16. Proceed to loading the samples and conducting electrophoresis.

SAMPLE DELIVERY (GEL LOADING)

PRACTICE GEL LOADING

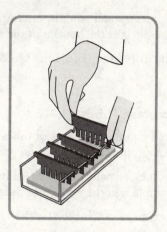

Accurate sample delivery technique ensures the best possible gel results. Pipetting mistakes can cause the sample to become diluted with buffer, or cause damage to the wells with the pipet tip while loading the gel.

If you are unfamiliar with loading samples in agarose gels, it is recommended that you practice sample delivery techniques before conducting the actual experiment. EDVOTEK electrophoresis experiments contain a tube of practice gel loading solution for this purpose. Casting of a separate practice gel is highly recommended. One suggested activity is outlined as follows:

1. Cast a gel with the maximum number of wells possible.

2. After the gel solidifies, place it under buffer in an electrophoresis apparatus chamber. Alternatively, your instructor may have cut the gel into sections between the rows of wells. Place a gel section with wells into a small, shallow tray and submerge it under buffer or water.

   Note: The agarose gel is sometimes called a "submarine gel" because it is submerged under buffer for sample loading and electrophoretic separation.

3. Practice delivering the practice gel loading solution to the sample wells. Take care not to damage or puncture the wells with the pipet tip.
   - For electrophoresis of DNA to be stained with InstaStain® Methylene Blue, load the sample well with 35–38 µL of sample.
   - If using transfer pipets for sample delivery, load each sample well until it is full.

4. If you need more practice, remove the practice gel loading solution by squirting buffer into the wells with a transfer pipet.

5. Replace the practice gel with a fresh gel for the actual experiment.

   Note: If practice gel loading is performed in the electrophoresis chamber, the practice gel loading solution will become diluted in the buffer in the apparatus. A small amount of practice gel loading solution (filling up to 12 wells) will not interfere with the experiment, so it is not necessary to prepare fresh buffer.

CONDUCTING AGAROSE GEL ELECTROPHORESIS

ELECTROPHORESIS SAMPLES

Samples in EDVOTEK Series 100 and Sci-On® Series electrophoresis experiments are packaged in one of two different formats:

- Pre-aliquoted QuickStrip™ connected tubes (new format)
     or
- Individual 1.5-mL or 0.5-mL microtest tubes

Pre-aliquoted QuickStrip™ Connected Tubes

- Each set of QuickStrip™ connected tubes contains pre-aliquoted ready-to-load samples for one gel. A protective overlay covers the strip of QuickStrip™ sample tubes.
- Check the sample volume. Sometimes a small amount of sample will cling to the walls of the tubes. Make sure the entire volume of sample is at the bottom of the tubes before starting to load the gel.
- Tap the overlay cover on top of the strip, or tap the entire QuickStrip™ on the table, to make samples fall to the bottom of the tubes

Individual 1.5-mL or 0.5-mL Microtest Tubes

- Your instructor may have aliquoted samples into a set of tubes for each lab group. Alternatively, you may be required to withdraw the appropriate amount of sample from the experiment stock tubes.
- Check the sample volume. Sometimes a small amount of sample will cling to the walls of the tubes. Make sure the entire volume of sample is at the bottom of the tubes before starting to load the gel.
- Briefly centrifuge the sample tubes, or tap each tube on the tabletop, to get all of the sample to the bottom of the tubes.

QUICKSTRIP™ SAMPLES

Successful Pipetting with Micropipets

1. Do not disturb the samples in the QuickStrip™. Gently tap the QuickStrip™ tubes on the lab bench to ensure that the samples are at the bottom of the tubes.
2. Stabilize the QuickStrip™ by firmly anchoring it on the lab bench.
3. Gently pierce the printed protective overlay with the pipet tip attached to a micropipet. Depress the micropipet plunger to the first stop before the tip is placed in contact with the sample.
4. With the pipet plunger depressed to the first stop, insert the tip into the sample.
5. Raise the plunger of the micropipet to withdraw the sample.
6. Load the sample into the appropriate well of the gel. Discard the tip.
7. Repeat steps 3–6 for each sample.

Delivering QuickStrip™ Samples with Transfer Pipets

If using disposable transfer pipets for sample delivery, pierce the protective overlay with a paper clip before inserting the transfer pipet to withdraw the sample.

If a sample becomes displaced while inserting the pipet tip in the tube, gently tap the QuickStrip™ on the lab bench to concentrate the sample to the bottom of the tube. With the pipet plunger depressed to the first stop, re-insert the tip into the sample and raise the micropipet plunger to withdraw the sample.

Loading the Samples

For either the QuickStrip™ or individual microtest tube format, samples should be loaded into the wells of the gel in consecutive order.

Load the DNA samples in tubes A–F into the wells into consecutive order. The amount of sample that should be loaded is 35–38 µL.

A: DNA from crime scene cut with Enzyme 1
B: DNA from crime scene cut with Enzyme 2
C: DNA from Suspect 1 cut with Enzyme 1

D: DNA from Suspect 1 cut with Enzyme 2
E: DNA from Suspect 2 cut with Enzyme 1
F: DNA from Suspect 2 cut with Enzyme 2

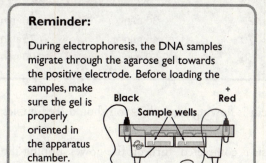

Running the Gel

1. After the DNA samples are loaded, carefully snap the cover down onto the electrode terminals.

   Make sure that the negative and positive color-coded indicators on the cover and apparatus chamber are properly oriented.

2. Insert the plug of the black wire into the black input of the power source (negative input). Insert the plug of the red wire into the red input of the power source (positive input).

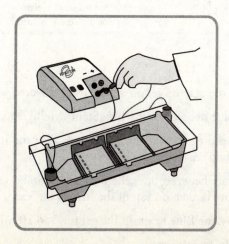

3. Set the power source at the required voltage and conduct electrophoresis for the length of time determined by your instructor. General guidelines are presented in Table 34–3.

TABLE 34–3	Time and Voltage Electrophoresis of DNA	
	Recommended Time	
Volts	**Minimum**	**Maximum**
125	30 min	40 min
70	40 min	75 min
50	60 min	100 min

4. Check to see that current is flowing properly—you should see bubbles forming on the two platinum electrodes.

5. After the electrophoresis is completed, turn off the power, unplug the power source, disconnect the leads, and remove the cover.

6. Remove the gel from the bed for staining with InstaStain® Methylene Blue.

STAINING AND VISUALIZATION OF DNA: INSTASTAIN® METHYLENE BLUE

Place gel on a flat surface covered with plastic wrap

Place the InstaStain® card on the gel.

Press firmly.

Place a small weight for approx. 5 minutes.

STAINING OF DNA

1. After electrophoresis, place the agarose gel on a flat surface covered with plastic wrap.

2. Wearing gloves, place the blue dye side of the InstaStain® Methylene Blue card on the gel.

3. Firmly run your fingers several times over the entire surface of the InstaStain® card to establish good contact between the InstaStain® card and the gel.

4. To ensure continuous contact between the gel and the InstaStain® card, place a gel casting tray and weight, such as a small empty beaker, on top of the InstaStain® card.

5. Allow the InstaStain® Methylene Blue to sit on the gel for 5 to 10 minutes.

6. After staining, remove the InstaStain® card.

IF THE COLOR OF THE GEL APPEARS VERY LIGHT, WET THE GEL SURFACE WITH BUFFER OR DISTILLED WATER AND PLACE THE INSTASTAIN® CARD BACK ON THE GEL FOR AN ADDITIONAL 5 MINUTES.

DESTAINING AND VISUALIZATION OF DNA

7. Transfer the gel to a large weigh boat or small plastic container.

Transfer to a small tray for destaining.

8. Destain with distilled water.
   - Add approximately 100 mL of distilled water to cover the gel.
   - Repeat destaining by changing the distilled water as needed.

Destain with 37°C distilled water

The larger DNA bands will initially be visible as dark blue bands against a lighter blue background. When the gel is completely destained, the larger DNA bands will become sharper and the smaller bands will be visible. With additional destaining, the entire background will become uniformly light blue.

Destaining Notes

- Warmed distilled water at 37°C will accelerate destaining. Destaining will take longer with room-temperature water.
- DO NOT EXCEED 37°C! Warmer temperatures will soften the gel and may cause it to break.
- The volume of distilled water for destaining depends upon the size of the tray. Use the smallest tray available that will accommodate the gel. The gel should be completely submerged during destaining.
- Do not exceed 3 changes of water for destaining. Excessive destaining will cause the bands to be very light.

9. Carefully remove the gel from the destain solution and examine the gel on a Visible Light Gel Visualization System. To optimize visibility, use the amber filter provided with the EDVOTEK equipment.

10. If the gel is too light and the bands are difficult to see, repeat the staining and destaining procedures.

Easy One-Step Staining and Destaining Overnight with InstaStain® Metblue

Agarose gels can be stained overnight with InstaStain™ Methylene Blue cards in one easy step. This one-step method is an excellent alternative if time does not permit staining during a regular class session. Instructions for staining a 7 × 7 cm gel after electrophoresis follow.

1. Remove the 7 × 7 cm agarose gel from its bed and totally submerse the gel in a small, clean tray containing 75 mL of distilled or deionized water, or used electrophoresis buffer. The agarose gel should be completely covered with liquid.

   Examples of small trays include large weigh boats or small plastic food containers. Do not stain gel(s) in the electrophoresis apparatus.

2. Gently float a 7 × 7 cm card of InstaStain® MetBlue with the stain side (blue) facing the liquid.

3. Let the gel soak undisturbed in the liquid overnight. The gel will be stained, destained, and ready for photography the next day.

Storage and Disposal of Instastain® Methylene Blue Cards and Gels

- Stained gels may be stored in the refrigerator for several weeks. Place the gel in a sealable plastic bag with destaining liquid.

  DO NOT FREEZE AGAROSE GELS!

- Used InstaStain® cards and destained gels can be discarded in the container for solid waste disposal.
- Destaining solutions can be disposed of down the drain.

STAINING AND VISUALIZATION OF DNA: METHYLENE BLUE PLUS™ LIQUID STAINING

LIQUID STAINING AND DESTAINING OF DNA

1. Remove each agarose gel from its bed and totally submerse up to 6 gels in a tray containing 600 mL of diluted Methylene Blue Plus™ stain. Do not stain gel(s) in the electrophoresis apparatus.

   Each group should mark its gel, such as by removing a small slice, or making a small hole in a designated corner, to facilitate identification after staining and destaining.

2. Stain gel(s) for a minimum of 30 minutes, with occasional agitation

3. Destain in 600 mL of distilled water that has been warmed to 37°C.
   - Completely submerse the gel(s) in 600 mL of 37°C distilled water for 15 minutes with occasional agitation, then discard the destaining solution.
   - Change the distilled water for a second destain for another 15 minutes with occasional agitation.

   Bands will become visible after the second destain. You may also leave the gel(s) in destain overnight.

4. Carefully remove the gel from the destain solution and examine on a Visible Light Gel Visualization System. To optimize visibility, use the amber filter provided with the EDVOTEK equipment.

5. If the gel is too light and bands are difficult to see, repeat the staining and destaining procedures.

Storage and Disposal of Methylene Blue Plus™ Stain and Gel

- Gels stained with Methylene Blue Plus™ may be stored in the refrigerator for several weeks. Place the gel in a sealable plastic bag with destaining liquid.

  DO NOT FREEZE AGAROSE GELS.

- Stained gels that are not kept can be discarded in the container for solid waste disposal.
- Methylene Blue Plus™ stain and destaining solutions can be disposed of down the drain.

EXPERIMENT RESULTS AND STUDY QUESTIONS

LABORATORY NOTEBOOK RECORDINGS

Address and record the following in your laboratory notebook or on a separate worksheet.

Before Starting the Experiment

- Write a hypothesis that reflects the experiment.
- Predict experimental outcomes.

During the Experiment
- Record (draw) your observations, or photograph the results.

Following the Experiment
- Formulate an explanation from the results.
- Determine what could be changed in the experiment if the experiment were repeated.
- Write a hypothesis that would reflect this change.

Study Questions
Answer the following study questions in your laboratory notebook or on a separate worksheet.

1. Define FLPs and explain their significance.
2. What is the most likely cause of restriction fragment length polymorphisms (RFLPs)?
3. What are variable number of tandem repeats (VNTRs)?
4. Who are the only individuals possessing the same DNA fingerprints?
5. List the steps involved in DNA fingerprinting, from extraction of DNA through the matching of a suspect to a crime-scene sample.
6. What type of human cells can be utilized for this technique?

SELECTED SOURCES FOR ADDITIONAL INFORMATION

Esslinger, K.J., Siegel, J.A., Spillane H., and Stallworth, S., "Using STR analysis to detect human DNA from exploded pipe bomb devices," *J. Forens. Sci.*, 49 (3), (2004), 481.

Melton, T., Dimick, G., Higgins, B., Lindstrom, L., and Nelson, K., "Forensic mitochondrial DNA analysis of 691 casework hairs," *J. Forens. Sci.*, 50 (1), (2005), 73.

Montpetit, S.A., Fitch, I.T., and O'Donnell, P.T., "A simple automated instrument for DNA extraction in forensic casework," *J. Forens. Sci.*, 50 (3), (2005), 555.

Nakazono, T., Kashimura, S., Hayashiba, Y., Hara, K., and Miyoshi, A., "Successful DNA typing of urine stains using a DNA purification kit following dialfiltration," *J. Forens. Sci.*, 50 (4), (2005), 860.

Rankin, D.R., Narveson, S.D., Birkby, W.H., and Lai, J., "Restriction fragment length polymorphism (RFLP) analysis on DNA from human compact bone," *J. Forens. Sci.*, 41 (1), (1996), 40.

Smith, S., and Morin, P.A., "Optimal storage conditions for highly dilute DNA samples: A role for Trehalose as a preserving agent," *J. Forens. Sci.*, 50 (5), (2005), 1101.

Thompson, W.C., Taroni, F., and Aitken, C.G.G., "How the probability of a false positive affects the value of DNA evidence," *J. Forens. Sci.*, 48 (1), (2003), 47.

EXPERIMENT 35

PCR Amplification of DNA for Fingerprinting: EDVO-Kit # 130*

EXPERIMENT COMPONENTS

ELECTROPHORESIS SAMPLES

- Ready-to-Load™ DNA samples

  A: DNA Standard marker
  B: Crime-scene PCR reaction
  C: Suspect 1 PCR reaction
  D: Suspect 2 PCR reaction
  E: Suspect 3 PCR reaction

REAGENTS AND SUPPLIES

- Practice gel loading solution
- UltraSpec-Agarose™ powder
- Concentrated electrophoresis buffer
- InstaStain® Methylene Blue
- Methylene Blue Plus™
- Pipet, 1 mL
- Graduated cylinder (packaging for samples), 100 mL
- Microtipped transfer pipets

THIS EXPERIMENT DOES NOT CONTAIN HUMAN DNA.

REQUIREMENTS

- Horizontal gel electrophoresis apparatus
- DC power supply
- Automatic micropipets with tips
- Balance
- Microwave, or hot plate/burner

---

* © EDVOTEK, Inc. All rights reserved. www.edvotek.com.

- Pipet pump
- Flasks or beakers, 250 mL
- Hot gloves
- Safety goggles and disposable laboratory gloves
- Small plastic trays or large weigh boats (for gel destaining)
- DNA visualization system (white light)
- Distilled or deionized water

DNA FINGERPRINTING

Deoxyribonucleic acid (DNA), present in the nucleus of every living cell, is the genetic material that acts as a blueprint for all of the proteins synthesized by cells. In mammals, a large fraction of the total DNA does not encode for proteins. Polymorphic DNA refers to chromosomal regions that vary widely from individual to individual. By examining several of these regions within the genomic DNA obtained from an individual, one may determine a "DNA fingerprint" for that individual. DNA polymorphisms are now widely used for determining paternity/maternity, kinship, identification of human remains, and the genetic basis of various diseases. The most widely used and far-reaching application, however, has been in the field of criminal forensics. DNA from both crime victims and offenders can now be definitively matched to crime scenes, often affecting the outcome of criminal and civil trials.

The beginning of DNA fingerprinting occurred in the United Kingdom in 1984, following the pioneering work of Dr. Alex Jeffreys at the University of Leicester. Analysis by Jeffreys led to the apprehension of a murderer in the first DNA fingerprinting case in September 1987. The first U.S. conviction occurred on November 6, 1987, in Orlando, Florida. Since then, DNA analysis has been used in thousands of convictions. Additionally, to date, 250 convicted prison inmates have been exonerated by DNA testing, including 17 who served time on death row.

In 1990, the Federal Bureau of Investigation (FBI) established the Combined DNA Index System (CODIS), a system that allows comparison of crime-scene DNA to DNA profiles in a convicted offender and a forensic (crime-scene) index. A match of crime-scene DNA to a profile in the convicted offender index indicates a suspect for the crime, whereas a match of crime-scene DNA to the forensic index indicates a serial offender. CODIS has now been used to solve dozens of cases where authorities had no suspect for the crime under investigation.

The first step in forensic DNA fingerprinting is the collection of blood or tissue samples from the crime scene or victim (Figure 35–1). A blood sample, often present as a stain, is treated with detergent to rupture the cell membranes and obtain DNA for further analysis. The early method, called **restriction fragment length polymorphism (RFLP)** analysis, involves digesting the DNA with restriction enzymes, separation on an agarose gel, transferring the DNA to a membrane, and hybridizing the DNA on the membrane with probes to polymorphic regions. This method requires relatively large amounts of DNA and takes several weeks to complete.

More recently, the **polymerase chain reaction (PCR)** has been used in forensics to analyze DNA (Figure 35–2). This technique requires about 500 times more DNA than RFLP analysis and is less time consuming. PCR amplification (Figure 35–2) uses an enzyme known as Taq polymerase. This enzyme, originally purified from a bacterium that inhabits hot springs, is stable at very high (near boiling) temperatures. Also included in the PCR reaction mixture are two synthetic oligonucleotides known as "primers" and the extracted DNA. The region of DNA to be amplified is known as the "target."

In the first step of the PCR reaction, the template complementary DNA strands are separated (denatured) from each other at 94°C, while the Taq polymerase remains stable. In the second step, known as annealing, the sample is cooled to an intermediate temperature, usually 40–65°C, to allow hybridization of the two primers, one to each of the two strands of the template DNA. In the third step, known as

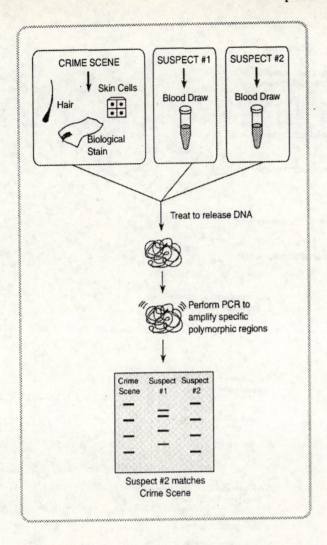

FIGURE 35–1 Comparison of crime-scene DNA to DNA from suspects.

extension, the temperature is raised to 72°C and the Taq polymerase adds nucleotides to the primers to complete the synthesis of the new complementary strands. These three steps—denaturation, annealing, and extension—constitute one PCR "cycle." This process is typically repeated for 20–40 cycles, amplifying the target sequence within DNA exponentially (Figure 35–2). PCR is performed in a thermal cycler, an instrument that is programmed to rapidly heat, cool, and maintain samples at designated temperatures for varying amounts of time.

In forensics, PCR is used to amplify and examine highly variable (polymorphic) DNA regions. These are regions that vary in length from individual to individual and fall into two categories: (1) **variable number of tandem repeats (VNTRs)**, and (2) **short tandem repeats (STRs)**. A VNTR is a region that is variably composed of a 15–70 base-pair sequence, typically repeated 5–100 times. An STR is similar to a VNTR except that the repeated unit is only 2–4 nucleotides in length. By examining several different VNTRs or STRs from the same individual, investigators obtain a unique DNA profile for that individual that is unlike the profile of any other person (except for in the case of identical twins).

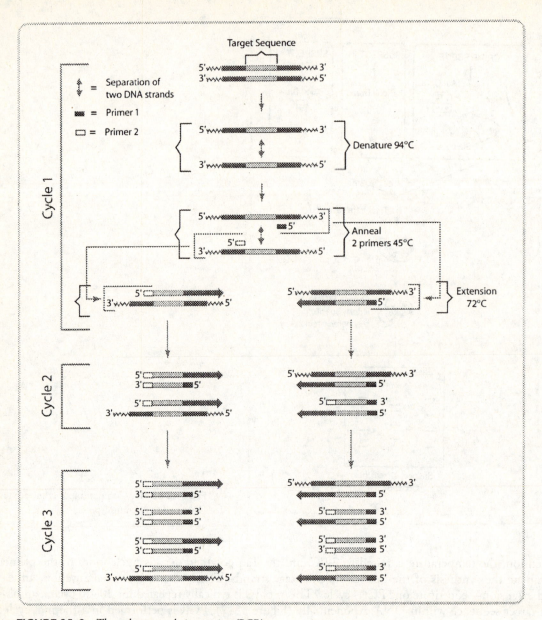

FIGURE 35-2 The polymerase chain reaction (PCR).

EXPERIMENT OVERVIEW

EXPERIMENT BRIEF DESCRIPTION

This experiment demonstrates a PCR that has been performed on hair obtained from a murder scene. You will separate this DNA sample by agarose gel electrophoresis and compare the preamplified DNA from two possible suspects to determine if either suspect was present at the crime scene.

EXPERIMENT OBJECTIVE

The objective of this experiment is to develop a basic understanding of DNA fingerprinting. You will analyze PCR reactions obtained from different suspects and compare them to a crime-scene sample.

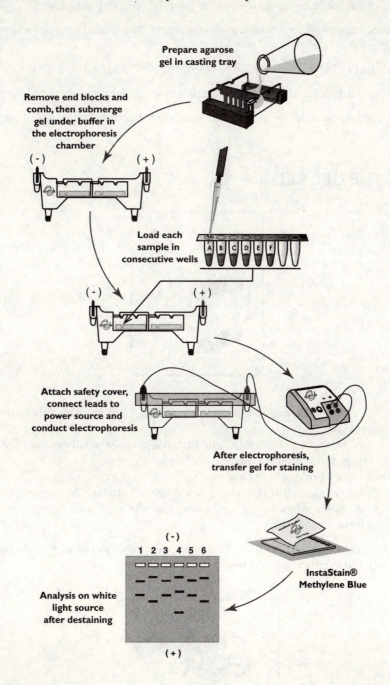

GEL REQUIREMENTS

- Recommended gel tray size: 7 × 7 cm or 7 × 15 cm
- Number of sample wells required: 5
- Placement of well-former template: first set of notches
- Agarose gel concentration required: 0.8%

AGAROSE GEL PREPARATION

LABORATORY SAFETY

1. Gloves and goggles should be worn routinely as good laboratory practice.
2. Exercise extreme caution when working with equipment that is used in conjunction with the heating and/or melting of reagents.
3. DO NOT MOUTH PIPET REAGENTS—USE PIPET PUMPS.
4. Exercise caution when using any electrical equipment in the laboratory.
5. Always wash hands thoroughly with soap and water after handling reagents or biological materials in the laboratory.

PREPARING THE GEL BED

1. Close off the open ends of a clean and dry gel bed (casting tray) by using rubber dams or tape.
   A. Using rubber dams:
      - Place a rubber dam on each end of the bed. Make sure the rubber dam fits firmly in contact with the sides and bottom of the bed.
   B. Taping with labeling or masking tape:
      - Using 3/4-inch-wide tape, extend the tape over the sides and bottom edge of the bed.
      - Fold the extended edges of the tape back onto the sides and bottom. Press contact points firmly to form a good seal.
2. Place a well-former template (comb) in the first set of notches at the end of the bed. Make sure the comb sits firmly and evenly across the bed.

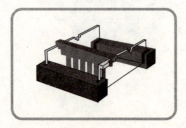

CASTING AGAROSE GELS

3. Use a 250-ml flask to prepare the gel solution. Add the following components to the flask as specified for your experiment (refer to Table 35–1).
   - Buffer concentrate
   - Distilled water
   - Agarose powder

TABLE 35-1	Individual 0.8% UltraSpec-Agarose™ Gel DNA Staining with InstaStain® MetBlue			
Size of EDVOTEK Casting Tray (cm)	Amt of Agarose (g)	Concentrated Buffer (50×) (mL)	Distilled Water (mL)	Total Volume (mL)
7 × 7	0.24	0.6	29.4	30
7 × 15	0.48	1.2	58.8	60

4. Swirl the mixture to disperse the clumps of agarose powder.

5. With a marking pen, indicate the level of the solution volume on the outside of the flask.

6. Heat the mixture to dissolve the agarose powder. The final solution should appear clear (like water) without any undissolved particles.
   A. Microwave method:
      • Cover the flask with plastic wrap to minimize evaporation.
      • Heat the mixture on high for 1 minute.
      • Swirl the mixture and heat on high in bursts of 25 seconds until all the agarose is completely dissolved.
   B. Hot plate method:
      • Cover the flask with aluminum foil to prevent excess evaporation.
      • Heat the mixture to boiling over a burner with occasional swirling. Boil until all the agarose is completely dissolved.

Check the solution carefully. If you see "crystal" particles, the agarose is not completely dissolved.

At high altitudes, it is recommended to use a microwave oven to reach boiling temperatures.

7. Cool the agarose solution to 55°C with careful swirling to promote even dissipation of heat. If detectable evaporation has occurred, add distilled water to bring the solution up to the original volume as marked on the flask in step 5.

After the gel is cooled to 55°C:
If you are using rubber dams, go to step 9.
If you are using tape, continue with step 8.

8. Seal the interface of the gel bed and tape to prevent the agarose solution from leaking.
   • Use a transfer pipet to deposit a small amount of cooled agarose to both inside ends of the bed.
   • Wait approximately 1 minute for the agarose to solidify.

9. Pour the cooled agarose solution into the bed. Make sure the bed is on a level surface.

10. Allow the gel to completely solidify. It will become firm and cool to the touch after approximately 20 minutes.

PREPARING THE GEL FOR ELECTROPHORESIS

11. After the gel is completely solidified, carefully and slowly remove the rubber dams or tape from the gel bed.

    Be especially careful not to damage or tear the gel wells when removing the rubber dams. A thin plastic knife, spatula, or pipet tip can be inserted between the gel and the dams to break possible surface tension.

12. Remove the comb by slowly pulling straight up. Do this carefully and evenly to prevent tearing the sample wells.

13. Place the gel (on its bed) into the electrophoresis chamber, properly oriented, centered, and level on the platform.

14. Fill the electrophoresis apparatus chamber with the required volume of diluted buffer for the specific unit you are using (see guidelines in Table 35–2).

    For DNA analysis, the same EDVOTEK 50× electrophoresis buffer is used for preparing both the agarose gel buffer and the chamber buffer. The formula for diluting EDVOTEK (50×) concentrated buffer is 1 volume of buffer concentrate to every 49 volumes of distilled or deionized water.

TABLE 35–2	Dilution of Electrophoresis (Chamber) Buffer				
EDVOTEK Model #	Concentrated Buffer (50×) (mL)	+	Distilled Water (mL)	=	Total Volume (mL)
M6+	6		294		300
M12	8		392		400
M36 (blue)	10		490		500
M36 (clear)	20		980		1000

The electrophoresis (chamber) buffer recommended is Trisacetate-EDTA (20 mM Tris, 6 mM sodium acetate, 1 mM disodium ethylenediamine tetraacetic acid) pH 7.8. Prepare the buffer as required for your electrophoresis apparatus.

15. Make sure the gel is completely covered with buffer.

16. Proceed to loading the samples and conducting electrophoresis.

SAMPLE DELIVERY (GEL LOADING)
PRACTICE GEL LOADING

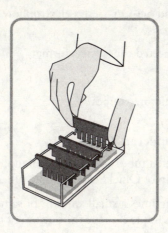

Accurate sample delivery technique ensures the best possible gel results. Pipeting mistakes can cause the sample to become diluted with buffer, or cause damage to the wells with the pipet tip while loading the gel.

If you are unfamiliar with loading samples in agarose gels, it is recommended that you practice sample delivery techniques before conducting the actual experiment. EDVOTEK electrophoresis experiments contain a tube of practice gel loading solution for this purpose. Casting of a separate practice gel is highly recommended. One suggested activity is as follows:

1. Cast a gel with the maximum number of wells possible.

2. After the gel solidifies, place it under buffer in an electrophoresis apparatus chamber.

   Alternatively, your instructor may have cut the gel into sections between the rows of wells. Place a gel section with wells into a small, shallow tray and submerge it under buffer or water.

   Note: The agarose gel is sometimes called a "submarine gel" because it is submerged under buffer for sample loading and electrophoretic separation.

3. Practice delivering the practice gel loading solution to the sample wells. Take care not to damage or puncture the wells with the pipet tip.
   - For electrophoresis of DNA to be stained with InstaStain® Methylene Blue, load the sample well with 35–38 µL of sample.
   - If using transfer pipets for sample delivery, load each sample well until it is full.

4. If you need more practice, remove the practice gel loading solution by squirting buffer into the wells with a transfer pipet.

5. Replace the practice gel with a fresh gel for the actual experiment.

Note: If practice gel loading is performed in the electrophoresis chamber, the practice gel loading solution will become diluted in the buffer in the apparatus. A small amount of practice gel loading solution (filling up to 12 wells) will not interfere with the experiment, so it is not necessary to prepare fresh buffer.

CONDUCTING AGAROSE GEL ELECTROPHORESIS

ELECTROPHORESIS SAMPLES

Samples in EDVOTEK Series 100 and Sci-On® Series electrophoresis experiments are packaged in one of two different formats:

- Pre-aliquoted QuickStrip™ connected tubes (new format)

or

- Individual 1.5-mL or 0.5-mL microtest tubes

Pre-aliquoted QuickStrip™ Connected Tubes

- Each set of QuickStrip™ connected tubes contains pre-aliquoted ready-to-load samples for one gel. A protective overlay covers the strip of QuickStrip™ sample tubes.

- Check the sample volume. Sometimes a small amount of sample will cling to the walls of the tubes. Make sure the entire volume of sample is at the the bottom of the tubes before starting to load the gel.

- Tap the overlay cover on top of the strip, or tap the entire QuickStrip™ on the table, to make the samples fall to the bottom of the tubes.

Individual 1.5-mL or 0.5-mL Microtest Tubes

- Your instructor may have aliquoted samples into a set of tubes for each lab group. Alternatively, you may be required to withdraw the appropriate amount of sample from the experiment stock tubes.

- Check the sample volume. Sometimes a small amount of sample will cling to the walls of the tubes. Make sure the entire volume of sample is at the the bottom of the tubes before starting to load the gel.

- Briefly centrifuge the sample tubes, or tap each tube on the tabletop, to get all of the sample to the bottom of the tubes.

QUICKSTRIP™ SAMPLES

Successful Pipetting with Micropipets

1. Do not disturb the samples in the QuickStrip™. Gently tap the QuickStrip™ tubes on the lab bench to ensure that the samples are at the bottom of the tubes.

2. Stabilize the QuickStrip™ by firmly anchoring it on the lab bench.

3. Gently pierce the printed protective overlay with the pipet tip attached to a micropipet. Depress the micropipet plunger to the first stop before the tip is placed in contact with the sample.

4. With the pipet plunger depressed to the first stop, insert the tip into the sample.

5. Raise the plunger of the micropipet to withdraw the sample.

6. Load the sample into the appropriate well of the gel. Discard the tip.

7. Repeat steps 3–6 for each sample.

Delivering QuickStrip™ Samples with Transfer Pipets

If using disposable transfer pipets for sample delivery, pierce the protective overlay with a paper clip before inserting the transfer pipet to withdraw the sample.

   *If a sample becomes displaced while inserting the pipet tip in the tube, gently tap the QuickStrip™ on the lab bench to concentrate the sample to the bottom of the tube. With the pipet plunger depressed to the first stop, re-insert the tip into the sample and raise the micropipet plunger to withdraw the sample.

Loading the Samples

For either QuickStrip™ or individual microtest tube format, samples should be loaded into the wells of the gel in consecutive order.

Load the DNA samples in tubes A–E into the wells in consecutive order. The amount of sample that should be loaded is 35–38 μL.

- A: DNA Standard marker
- B: Crime-scene PCR reaction
- C: Suspect 1 PCR reaction
- D: Suspect 2 PCR reaction
- E: Suspect 3 PCR reaction

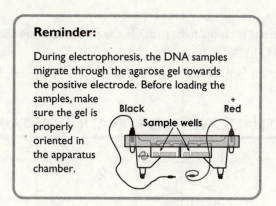

Reminder:

During electrophoresis, the DNA samples migrate through the agarose gel towards the positive electrode. Before loading the samples, make sure the gel is properly oriented in the apparatus chamber.

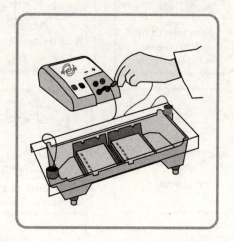

Running the Gel

1. After the DNA samples are loaded, carefully snap the cover down onto the electrode terminals.

   Make sure that the negative and positive color-coded indicators on the cover and apparatus chamber are properly oriented.

2. Insert the plug of the black wire into the black input of the power source (negative input). Insert the plug of the red wire into the red input of the power source (positive input).

3. Set the power source at the required voltage and conduct electrophoresis for the length of time determined by your instructor. General guidelines are presented in Table 35–3.

Experiment 35

TABLE 35-3	Time and Voltage Electrophoresis of DNA	
	Recommended Time	
Volts	Minimum	Maximum
125	30 min	40 min
70	40 min	75 min
50	60 min	100 min

4. Check to see that current is flowing properly—you should see bubbles forming on the two platinum electrodes.

5. After the electrophoresis is completed, turn off the power, unplug the power source, disconnect the leads, and remove the cover.

6. Remove the gel from the bed for staining with InstaStain® Methylene Blue.

STAINING AND VISUALIZATION OF DNA: INSTASTAIN® METHYLENE BLUE

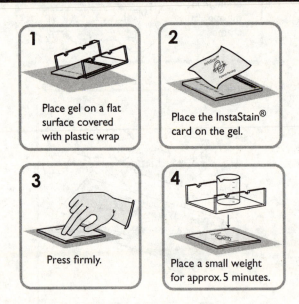

STAINING OF DNA

1. After electrophoresis, place the agarose gel on a flat surface covered with plastic wrap.

2. Wearing gloves, place the blue dye side of the InstaStain® Methylene Blue card on the gel.

3. Firmly run your fingers several times over the entire surface of the InstaStain® card to establish good contact between the InstaStain® card and the gel.

4. To ensure continuous contact between the gel and the InstaStain® card, place a gel casting tray and weight, such as a small empty beaker, on top of the InstaStain® card.

5. Allow the InstaStain® Methylene Blue to sit on the gel for 5 to 10 minutes.

6. After staining, remove the InstaStain® card.

   IF THE COLOR OF THE GEL APPEARS VERY LIGHT, WET THE GEL SURFACE WITH BUFFER OR DISTILLED WATER AND PLACE THE INSTASTAIN® CARD BACK ON THE GEL FOR AN ADDITIONAL 5 MINUTES.

DESTAINING AND VISUALIZATION OF DNA

7. Transfer the gel to a large weigh boat or small plastic container.

Transfer to a small tray for destaining.

8. Destain with distilled water.
   - Add approximately 100 milliliters of distilled water to cover the gel.
   - Repeat destaining by changing the distilled water as needed.

Destain with 37°C distilled water

The larger DNA bands will initially be visible as dark blue bands against a lighter blue background. When the gel is completely destained, the larger DNA bands will become sharper and the smaller bands will be visible. With additional destaining, the entire background will become uniformly light blue.

Destaining Notes

- Warmed distilled water at 37°C will accelerate destaining. Destaining will take longer with room-temperature water.
- DO NOT EXCEED 37°C! Warmer temperatures will soften the gel and may cause it to break.
- The volume of distilled water for destaining depends upon the size of the tray. Use the smallest tray available that will accommodate the gel. The gel should be completely submerged during destaining.
- Do not exceed 3 changes of water for destaining. Excessive destaining will cause the bands to be very light.

9. Carefully remove the gel from the destain solution and examine the gel on a Visible Light Gel Visualization System. To optimize visibility, use the amber filter provided with the EDVOTEK equipment.

10. If the gel is too light and the bands are difficult to see, repeat the staining and destaining procedures.

Easy One-Step Staining and Destaining Overnight with Instastain® Metblue

Agarose gels can be stained overnight with InstaStain™ Methylene Blue cards in one easy step. This one-step method is an excellent alternative if time does not permit staining during a regular class session. Instructions for staining a 7 × 7 cm gel after electrophoresis are as follows:

1. Remove the 7 × 7 cm agarose gel from its bed and totally submerse the gel in a small, clean tray containing 75 ml of distilled or deionized water, or used electrophoresis buffer. The agarose gel should be completely covered with liquid.

   Do not stain gel(s) in the electrophoresis apparatus.

Examples of small trays include large weigh boats, or small plastic food containers.

2. Gently float a 7 × 7 cm card of InstaStain® MetBlue with the stain side (blue) facing the liquid.

3. Let the gel soak undisturbed in the liquid overnight. The gel will be stained, destained, and ready for photography the next day.

Storage and Disposal of Instastain® Methylene Blue Cards and Gels

- Stained gels may be stored in the refrigerator for several weeks. Place the gel in a sealable plastic bag with destaining liquid.

  DO NOT FREEZE AGAROSE GELS!

- Used InstaStain® cards and destained gels can be discarded in the container for solid waste disposal.

- Destaining solutions can be disposed of down the drain.

STAINING AND VISUALIZATION OF DNA: METHYLENE BLUE PLUS™ LIQUID STAINING

LIQUID STAINING AND DESTAINING OF DNA

1. Remove each agarose gel from its bed and totally submerse up to 6 gels in a tray containing 600 ml of diluted Methylene Blue Plus™ stain. Do not stain gel(s) in the electrophoresis apparatus.

   Each group should mark its gel, such as by removing a small slice, or making a small hole in a designated corner, to facilitate identification after staining and destaining.

2. Stain gel(s) for a minimum of 30 minutes, with occasional agitation.

3. Destain in 600 ml of distilled water that has been warmed to 37°C.
   - Completely submerse the gel(s) in 600 ml of 37°C distilled water for 15 minutes with occasional agitation. Then discard the destaining solution
   - Change the distilled water for a second destain for another 15 minutes with occasional agitation. Bands will become visible after the second destain. You may also leave the gel(s) in destain overnight.

4. Carefully remove the gel from the destain solution and examine on a Visible Light Gel Visualization System. To optimize visibility, use the amber filter provided with the EDVOTEK equipment.

5. If the gel is too light and the bands are difficult to see, repeat the staining and destaining procedures.

Storage and Disposal of Methylene Blue Plus™ Stain and Gel

- Gels stained with Methylene Blue Plus™ may be stored in the refrigerator for several weeks. Place the gel in a sealable plastic bag with destaining liquid.

  DO NOT FREEZE AGAROSE GELS.

- Stained gels that are not kept can be discarded in the container for solid waste disposal.

- Methylene Blue Plus™ stain and destaining solutions can be disposed of down the drain.

EXPERIMENT RESULTS AND STUDY QUESTIONS
LABORATORY NOTEBOOK RECORDINGS

Address and record the following in your laboratory notebook or on a separate worksheet.

Before Starting the Experiment
- Write a hypothesis that reflects the experiment.

- Predict experimental outcomes.

During the Experiment
- Record (draw) your observations, or photograph the results.

Following the Experiment
- Formulate an explanation from the results.

- Determine what could be changed in the experiment if the experiment were repeated.

- Write a hypothesis that would reflect this change.

STUDY QUESTIONS
Answer the following study questions in your laboratory notebook or on a separate worksheet.

1. What is polymorphic DNA? How is it used for identification purposes?

2. What is CODIS? How is it used to solve crimes?

3. What is an STR? A VNTR? Which (STR or VNTR) is predominantly now used in law enforcement? Why?

EXPERIMENT 36

The Comparison Microscope

The comparison microscope is one of the most valuable instruments of the forensic scientist. It first came to public attention during the Sacco-Vanzetti trial of the 1920s, when the markings on a bullet obtained from the victim matched the markings made by a gun owned by the suspects.

A photo of one type of professional comparison microscope is shown in Figure 36–1. Basically, this microscope permits the forensic examiner to simultaneously view and compare two specimens side by side. The unique feature of this microscope is an optical bridge consisting of a number of mirrors and lenses. This bridge joins two separate objective lenses into a single eyepiece lens.

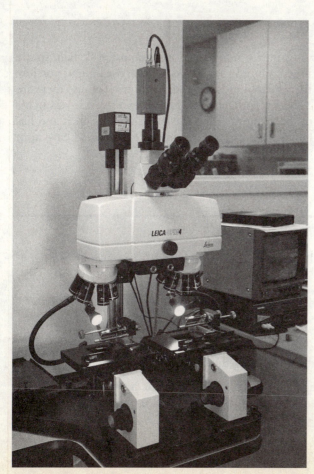

FIGURE 36–1 A comparison microscope. *Courtesy of Leica Microsystems,* © *2013, all rights reserved.*

278 Experiment 36

When looking through the eyepiece lens of a comparison microscope, a specimen mounted under the left objective is seen in the left half of the field, and the specimen mounted under the right objective is seen in the right half of the field.

To illustrate some of the microscope's capabilities, you will compare toolmarks, bullets, and shell cases in this experiment.

EQUIPMENT

- 1 Aluminum sheet
- 1 Balance, ±0.001 g
- Bullets and bullet casings
- Camera attachments
- 1 Comparison bridge, including 10× eyepieces and eyepiece holder
- 1 Hand magnifying glass
- 1 Micrometer
- 2 Microscopes
- 3 Screwdrivers

PART A: COMPARISON OF TOOLMARK SCRATCHES

The scrapings of a tool against a softer surface at a crime scene will frequently leave scratch marks that are unique to that tool and no other. These scratch markings arise from imperfections present on the tool's edge. Once a suspect tool is seized, the forensic examiner will attempt to duplicate the suspect scratch markings by scraping the tool against a soft metal—of the same type if possible—at various angles and pressures. The test and suspect markings are compared under the comparison microscope. A sufficient number of similarities between the two will ultimately lead to the conclusion that the suspect tool did indeed produce the markings found at the crime scene.

CRIME SCENE

A sporting goods store has been broken into. Entry was gained through an aluminum panel skylight in the back of the store. The detective at the scene examined the frame and suspected the tool used might possibly be a screwdriver or something similar. It is apparent that the tool must have slipped once because there are scratch marks on the window frame. The next day a suspect is apprehended. He has two screwdrivers in his tool chest. The detective has obtained that portion of the frame that has the scratch marks on it and has given it to you, as well as the two screwdrivers. Your job is to see if the marks on the frame could have been made by either of the screwdrivers.

METHOD

1. Obtain a small piece of aluminum, and place it on a flat surface.
2. Take one of the screwdrivers, and with a pencil, mark one side of the blade as side 1 and the other as side 2.
3. Hold the screwdriver at about a 30- to 45-degree angle and make about a 2-cm-long scrape on the aluminum sheet.
4. Turn the blade over, and make a second scrape about 1 cm away from the first scrape. Label these.
5. Repeat steps 2 through 4 with the other screwdriver, labeling the blade sides 3 and 4.
6. Examine the scratches on the frame with a magnifying glass to see if there is any obvious pattern of scratch marks. Then do the same with the first scratches to see if there appears to be a side that might match or if there are sides that can readily be discounted.
7. Place the frame metal under the lens of the left microscope. Pull the halving-line control to the right. Turn on the left light and focus the lowest-power optics. Turn the frame so that the scratches are horizontal with your viewing direction.

8. Place the most likely test scratch portion under the right microscope. Push the halving-line control knob to the left. Turn on the right light and focus with the lowest-power lens.
9. Move the halving line to the middle of the field of view.
10. Sharpen the focus if necessary with the halving-line focus knob.
11. Slowly and carefully move one set of scratch marks to see if it is possible to line up an adjacent series of scratch marks. If you believe you have a match, record what you see.
12. Repeat steps 7 through 11 with each blade side. Record any match on the data sheet.
13. Turn off the lights, and clean up the area.

PART B: COMPARISON OF SHELL CASES AND SLUGS

There is no way that this experiment will make you an expert on ballistics; that takes many years of experience. What we hope to do is show you the general areas that are examined.

1. Obtain three casings from the instructor, two of which are from the same weapon and the third of the same caliber, but from a different weapon.
2. Weigh each casing to the nearest milligram.
3. Using a micrometer, measure the length of the casings and their diameter.
4. Examine the head of each casing with a magnifying glass, and sketch the markings you see.
5. Look at the rim of the head, noticing any extractor or ejector marks. The extractor pulls the casing out of the breech, and the ejector throws the casings out of the weapon if the weapon is a rifle or an automatic pistol.
6. Mount each casing on a ball of clay so that the head end is up and flat. Focus on the head with low power.
7. Repeat step 6 with a second casing. Orient this casing so that it is turned in the same manner as the other casing.
8. Move the halving line to the center. Turn the casings so that it appears that only one head is in view.
9. When a gun is fired, the head of the shell is forced back against the breech block, and imprints of the breech block are pressed onto the back of the casing. Slowly turn the two casings to see if any marks on the heads match up.
10. Try different combinations of casings to see if you find any scratch and firing-pin identification matchups.
11. Remove the casings from the microscope stage.
12. Obtain three slugs from the instructor, two of which are from the same weapon and one that is from a different weapon.
13. Repeat step 2.
14. Repeat step 3.
15. Repeat step 4, if the slugs are not too distorted, and record any manufacturer's mark.
16. Examine the sides of the slugs with a magnifying glass, and record the gross general characteristics, such as the number of lands and grooves.
17. If your comparison microscope does not have slug rotators, the slugs must be turned by hand. Place the slugs on a small block of wood with a half-circle groove cut into its surface, just slightly larger than the object. Between the wood block and the slug, place a long, narrow piece of tissue paper. When this paper is gently pulled, the slug will rotate, and can be used to rotate the slug without any danger of putting additional scratches on it.

18. Place a slug on each stage of the microscope, and center the halving line. Focus each with the lowest power.

19. Slowly rotate one of the slugs to see if a match can be made. Look carefully at the fine structure because these are the critical markings. Record any matchups you see.

20. Return all casings and slugs to your instructor and clean up the microscope.

PART C: PHOTOMICROGRAPHS

Figure 36-1 shows a camera attachment mounted on a comparison microscope and a coupling attachment that links two regular microscopes together to make a comparison microscope. If you have a photographic attachment on your microscope, take a photograph of what you believe is a matchup. Obtain the exposure times and camera settings from your instructor. Attach any clear photos to your data sheet.

SELECTED SOURCES FOR ADDITIONAL INFORMATION

Bonfanti, M.S., and DeKinder, J., "The influence of manufacturing processes on the identification of bullets and cartridge cases," *Sci. & Just.*, 39 (1), (1999), 3.

Warlow, T. A., "Ballistics examination of British citizens from Waco siege," *Sci. & Just.*, 38 (4), (1998), 255.

EXPERIMENT 36   Name _____

DATA SHEET   Date _____

THE COMPARISON MICROSCOPE

Part A: Comparison of Toolmark Scratches

1. Sketch what you believe to be a match. If no match was found with any of the blades, so indicate.

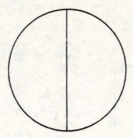

2. Conclusions:

3. Suppose that the screwdriver had not slipped. Do you believe that you could make a comparison from the impression material?

Part B: Comparison of Shell Cases and Slugs

Weight of Shell	Length of Shell	Diameter of Shell
Case 1	Case 1	Case 1
Case 2	Case 2	Case 2
Case 3	Case 3	Case 3

282   Experiment 36

Shell case base markings

Case 1

Case 2

Case 3

Shell case comparison matchup

Weight of shell	Length of shell	Diameter of shell
Shell 1	Shell 1	Shell 1
Shell 2	Shell 2	Shell 2
Shell 3	Shell 3	Shell 3

Base markings

Side markings on the slugs

Slug 1   Slug 2   Slug 3

Comparison view of fine structure

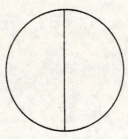

Conclusions

Burglaries and Murders: The Final Exam

Previously, you have concentrated on only one type of evidence. Now you will be allowed to examine a crime scene and you will decide what evidence to collect and how to measure it. We will provide you with a brief introduction and then present some different crimes. Your instructor may choose one of these or think up something else.

The names of all persons and the crime situations themselves, presented below, are fictitious and any similarity to persons living or dead is purely coincidental.

PART A: A BUNGLED BURGLARY

We are confronted with a crime in which there is evidence of a physical nature that will strongly link one of two suspects with the crime scene, and show that the other suspect could not have been present at the scene.

The type of crime perpetrated is a burglary—the breaking and entering of a suburban home. A window is broken, and one can see the fragments of glass strewn about. The soil below the window is damp, and it is likely that the person committing the crime transported some of this soil away from the scene on his shoes or clothing. During the course of breaking the window glass, or in reaching inside to unlock the window sash, the burglar was cut quite badly. There are bloodstains on some of the glass fragments and also on a piece of cloth that was picked up inside the house, apparently in an attempt to stem the flow of blood from the wound.

A powdered material is found scattered about the floor, apparently left by the burglar. Perhaps he had a box of some sort of pills with him, and in removing the handkerchief to stop the flow of blood from his cut, he dropped the box of pills on the floor. Some of the pills apparently broke on impact, and he did not completely remove this powder.

A locked drawer has been pried open with some sort of tool that had been covered with a protective coat of paint. Small flakes of paint are found adhering to the drawer and on the carpet immediately below this drawer. These flakes have been dissolved in an appropriate solvent and are now ready for the analysis. In the cars of both suspects, tools suitable for the purpose of prying open a drawer have been found. Both are painted, and both have chips or flakes of paint missing. Samples from both tool paints have been removed.

It is thought that this burglary may have been for the purposes of financing the purchase of drugs of abuse. Some powdered material was found on the carpet of the cars of both suspects. This has been dissolved in a suitable solvent for gas chromatographic analysis. The solvent used is methanol, and the suspected drug is phenobarbital. Standard solutions of various drugs in methanol are available for comparison by this means.

A number of analyses can be performed in an effort to link one of the two possible suspects with the scene of the crime. Both suspects are employed in work that could involve contact with glass fragments, and both claim to have cut themselves on their hands while working.

It is the task of the laboratory personnel to perform the analysis of the physical evidence collected. The matching of the glass fragments can be quite easily done by measurement of their density or refractive index. Although the results cannot be conclusive, they may contribute toward a final decision.

Matching of the soil samples also serves only to supply raw data upon which to base a conclusion; in itself, such evidence is not conclusive.

There may be stains at the scene that were not associated with the crime at all, such as spilled coffee, shoe polish, and the like. It may be well to test any apparent bloodstains first to make certain they are blood before any attempt is made to establish the blood group of the stain. Blood typing may help to eliminate one of the suspects, if the blood type does not belong to the same group as the bloodstains found at the scene. It will not prove a suspect guilty, as many persons have the same general blood type.

The paint samples may also help link the suspect to the scene, as will the analysis of the spilled powders. If the spilled powder proves to be aspirin, or some other common medicinal tablet, perhaps the suspect is a habitual user of aspirin. If this is the case, then a blood sample will perhaps yield this information. The powdered material found in the cars of the suspects may be analyzed by infrared spectrophotometry and by gas chromatography to establish its identity.

Hair samples found at the scene of the crime may be used to aid in the case presented against a suspect, but, as noted earlier, this is not conclusive in itself.

The goal is to establish with as much certainty as possible that one of the suspects was involved in the perpetration of this crime and that the other could not have been present at the crime scene.

You do not have to work on these analyses during your regularly scheduled laboratory period. You have two weeks to get everything done. You must write up your analyses in a clear, readable fashion, with a summary of your findings presented at the end. All data obtained in the laboratory must be included. Each analysis will involve three samples: suspect A, suspect B, and the physical evidence found at the scene of the crime.

PART B: CAMPSITE CRIME

The circumstances surrounding the crime to which you will be assigned as analysts are described below.

County law enforcement officers were summoned to a campground owned and operated by the state. They were notified of an apparent homicide by the park ranger. The slain woman had been discovered by persons camping at a nearby site. The time of discovery was approximately 9:15 a.m. Plans had been made the evening before to go on a morning nature hike. When the victim and her friends did not meet at the designated time, the members of the other party went to the campsite to awaken them. It was presumed that they had overslept. There was no answer to their wake-up calls, so one of the women in the party entered the victim's tent. There she found the deceased, fully clothed as if all ready for the outing, lying on the floor of the tent. She was obviously dead, lying in a stained area of what appeared at first glance to be blood. What appeared to be stab wounds were seen on the neck and chest area of the body. The hikers immediately notified the park ranger of what they had found.

Crime-scene investigators were called to the campground. They sealed off the scene to preserve any physical evidence that might yield clues as to the cause of death and the identity of any person or persons who might have been involved in the perpetration of the crime.

An extensive, careful search of the interior of the tent was conducted after the body of the victim was photographed and removed to the County Medical Examiner's morgue for a postmortem examination.

Campers occupying neighboring sites were questioned by the investigating officers. The following information was compiled. There had been three women occupying the tent the evening previous to the slaying. It was not definitely known if all of the women were actually camping together, or whether some of them were only there for a campfire visit and meant to return home that same night. The nature hike invitation had been extended to whoever might be interested in accompanying the other groups of campers.

The tent search showed the contents to be the following: one sleeping bag, two unopened packages of Marlboro Lights filter-tip cigarettes, and another pack of the same brand with only three cigarettes remaining. Within a small overnight case inside the tent were the following items: a stainless steel fork and spoon, a hairbrush, a cotton handkerchief, one fountain pen, one ballpoint pen, a tube of lipstick, a small bottle of aspirin that contained three tablets, and coins whose sum totaled $0.82. In addition, the tent inventory included a small can of green paint, a ½-inch-wide nylon-bristle paint brush, used but not cleaned, and a small amount of a white powdered substance, found beneath the edge of the sleeping bag. The crime-scene investigators properly packaged and labeled all of the above list items for transport to the State Crime Laboratory for analysis. The tent and the sleeping bag were also included for a more careful search at the lab.

The campsite area in front of the tent contained the following: ashes of a smoldering campfire; three pieces of unburned firewood; one small hand axe; a folding wire grill; a green painted folding campstool; a length of one-quarter-inch diameter rope, 7 feet 2 inches long; a waterproof match container with 9 matches inside; and a 24-quart Thermos brand portable cooler, in which were various foodstuffs. A 750-mL bottle of bourbon containing approximately one quarter of the original contents was also found along with 2 unused paper cups.

The area immediately behind the tent contained two empty 2-liter disposable plastic carbonated beverage containers.

The campsite was also found to contain—in locations surrounding the tent site—11 burned, filter-tip cigarette stubs. Four of the cigarettes were Marlboro Lights brand; the others were Eve brand filter-tip cigarettes. All of these stubs were collected, packaged, labeled as to their location, and included in the items sent to the laboratory.

The rest of the materials contained in the immediate vicinity of the tent area were of natural origin and not of evidential value in the opinion of the scene investigators.

A grid search of the wooded area surrounding the site led to the discovery of a stainless steel table knife of a design matching that of the fork and spoon found in the dead woman's tent. The blade of the knife was seen to be stained with what appeared to be blood of human or animal origin, not definable at the site. It was packaged for analysis of blood type, blood species, fingerprints, and comparison of manufacture with the utensils found in the tent. The dead woman's car was also impounded, sealed, and transported to the laboratory to be searched for physical evidence that might aid in the investigation.

The following day, the coroner's office reported to the Sheriff's Department that the woman died of multiple stab wounds to the neck and chest area, producing massive hemorrhage and a blood clot in the brain. Her clothes were transferred to the crime laboratory, along with some strands of hair caught under her fingernails. Her shirt was stained with blood and what at first glance appeared to be lipstick. Samples of her own hair, different in color from that found under her fingernails, were also taken to the lab.

The crime laboratory analysts, in working with the physical evidence from the crime scene and the body of the victim, have compiled the following information. The blood of the deceased was Type B, the bloodstains found on the edge of the victim's sleeping bag were found to be of Type O in some cases and of Type B in others. The bloodstains on the tent floor were of Type B. A more thorough search of the tent interior produced a small wad of paper, which, when unfolded, contained an inked name of the campground where the murder occurred. Analysis of the extracted ink has shown that it was not written with either of the pens found in the tent contents. Comparison of hairs from the head of the slain woman and of those found under her fingernails did not produce a match. Although this comparison is never conclusive, there were distinct differences between the two, primarily in color. Analysis of the shirt of the dead woman, with regard to the stain identified as lipstick and the contents of the tube of lipstick found in her tent, showed them to be dissimilar.

A search of the victim's car produced a small purse in the glove compartment. The driver's license showed the identity of the victim to be Ms. Inez Montego. Letters also found in the glove compartment were responses from two women, Ms. Prunella Pruitt and Ms. Hortense Hochstedtler, accepting invitations to a weekend of camping with the murdered woman for the same campground and the same weekend during which the crime was committed. The former invited guest will be called suspect A and the latter suspect B during the remainder of this narrative and for purposes of your cataloging of evidence results.

Return addresses on the envelopes found in the slain woman's car enabled the sheriff's deputies to locate the two women, presumed to be suspects in the case. Both women were brought to the sheriff's office for questioning. These are the stories that they gave as statements.

Suspect A, Ms. Prunella Pruitt, stated that she had not been at the campsite of the victim the previous evening. She was shocked to learn of the death of her friend, Ms. Montego. Ms. Pruitt said that she had known the deceased for approximately 4 years, had been good friends with Ms. Montego, and had gone camping with her many times. She stated that she had intended to meet her friend at the campground, but that she had remembered a previous commitment and had not been able to go camping. She said that she had been alone the previous evening, preparing some papers that were due at her office the following morning. The investigating officer requested that she give a blood sample to be analyzed as to type and content of foreign substances. She was fingerprinted and photographed. Various items in her possession were impounded for comparative analysis at the crime laboratory. Lipsticks, writing pens, some samples of her hair, and some white medication tablets found in her purse were also collected. A search warrant was issued and a search of her home produced a pair of jeans, stained with what appeared to be blood. The suspect, when asked about the jeans, said that she had cut her hand on her garage door the day before and had gotten some blood on her clothing. The search unit also noticed paint stains on the suspect's jeans. She said that she was an amateur furniture refinisher and had been working on a project the day before, prior to remembering the office work that she had to complete. Investigators did find a partially refinished small table in the kitchen of the suspect's home. It was newly painted, with what had been subsequently analyzed to be lead-free green paint. Ms. Pruitt was released, but informed that she was to remain available for further questioning, if needed in the future.

Sheriff's Department officials also located the other woman whose name appeared on the letters found in the car of the murdered woman. Ms. Hochstedtler stated, in response to questioning, that she had indeed been invited on the campout. She had accepted the invitation and then had changed her plans at the last minute. She had informed Ms. Montego that she would not be able to stay the night. She had indeed gone to the campground that evening, but had left just after another woman, whom she described as Ms. Pruitt, had also gone home. She apparently was the last person to see the slain woman alive. The investigating officers collected the same samples and items from Ms. Hochstedtler as they did from Ms. Pruitt. A legal search of suspect B's home produced a pair of slacks containing apparent bloodstains and paint stains. The suspect could offer no explanation for their presence, saying she had not noticed the stains and had no idea as to where she might have gotten them.

The descriptions of the two women who were with the slain woman, as given by the persons at the campground, were sufficiently vague, due to poor lighting conditions, as to be applicable to any number of persons.

You are the crime lab analyst. It is your task to analyze the physical evidence that has been collected, or that you will collect from the simulated crime scene, in some instances. Maintain an unbiased viewpoint throughout your laboratory work. Do not consciously try to make the results come out in favor of either of the suspects. Impersonal, honest, analytical work is essential if the data are to be useful in exonerating or implicating the innocent or the guilty. You are not the attorney or the judge. Your assistance to the Sheriff's Department will include a percent certainty of the connection between the crime and each of the two suspects, based upon your laboratory results.

PART C: A PARKING RAMP RUMBLE

Police authorities were called to a public parking ramp where the body of a young woman had been found beside a parked car. She had apparently met her death by stab wounds to the neck and chest areas of her body. Signs of a struggle were evident, her clothing was torn, and the contents of her purse strewn about. The driver's door of the car was open and there were bloodstains on the seat of the car on the driver's side. The victim was found in a position suggesting that she may have fallen from the car when attempting to reach for her keys. The keys were found to be just under the body of the vehicle, on the parking ramp floor.

Investigators found the following physical evidence associated with the scene of the crime: The window glass in the left front door of the vehicle had been broken. There were pieces of glass found on the floor of the parking ramp and left in the window itself. Perhaps the woman's assailant may have carried some of this glass away from the scene, lodged in clothing or soles of shoes. There were found to be some small chips of paint on the floor near the door of the vehicle. The paint apparently was chipped from the vehicle door, as there was a dented area with paint missing, freshly removed, and no rust or dirt was found on this location. The remainder of the vehicle was quite dirty and did not appear to have been washed recently.

A careful search of the vehicle and the parking ramp produced a knife, believed to be the murder weapon. It was found to have stains on the blade that might be blood. The knife was transported to the crime lab for fingerprint examination.

Among the articles from the victim's purse was a small scrap of paper upon which was written a telephone number. This was sent to the lab for ink analysis.

The body of the deceased was taken to the medical examiner's office for autopsy. During the course of his postmortem examination of the victim, the coroner found hair and small bits of skin under the victim's fingernails. The victim's blood was determined to be Type A.

The medical examiner found stains on the shirt of the deceased that he determined to be smears of lipstick. Perhaps they came from her attacker during the struggle that took place before her death.

An examination of the victim's purse contents produced a small vial of a powdered material. Analysis shows this to be a drug cut with a substance of rather unusual composition.

Analysis of the victim's blood shows no presence of alcohol or any drug.

An address book in the purse contents contained a number of names, but only two of these were women. Due to the presence of the lipstick stains on the victim's shirt, these two women were questioned by police investigators.

The following information was obtained and evidence collected. Ms. Franc Dorant, hereafter called suspect A, denied being at the parking ramp at any time. She stated that she was acquainted with the murdered girl, but had not seen her for some time. At the time of her interrogation, Ms. Dorant seemed slightly disoriented. She said that she had not been feeling well, due to having attended a party the evening before and having drank too heavily. She was suffering from a headache and had slept only a short time before the police arrived at her apartment. She was taken to police headquarters for fingerprinting, the collection of a blood specimen for typing, and alcohol and drug analyses. Police collected an article of clothing from her apartment containing bloodstains. The woman stated that she had gone fishing with a friend a few days before and in cleaning the catch had gotten blood on her clothes. Two tubes of lipstick were also taken to the lab, of a color appearing to be similar to the stains on the victim's shirt. A white, powdered material found in a bathroom cabinet was also sent to the lab. The vial container was similar to that found in the dead woman's possession. Some pens with ink similar in color to that on the paper in the victim's purse were found.

The other woman, Ms. Abigail Adamson, denoted suspect B, was not home when authorities called on her, but returned to her apartment later in the day. She said she had stayed at the home of a friend the evening before and was not in the vicinity of the parking ramp the previous night. Her friend, upon questioning, said that Ms. Adamson had come to see her late on the night in question and, after having been there for a time, seemed quite upset. She asked if she might stay at her friend's home that night, as she did not feel like being alone. Her friend agreed. Police found an article of bloodstained clothing in Ms. Adamson's apartment. She said she had been working on an art project and had cut herself on the hand. The blood had stained her clothing and she had not had time to wash it. Other articles collected include lipstick, ink pens, and a powdered substance, claimed to be an antacid by Ms. Adamson. Blood samples for analysis and fingerprints were taken from this suspect.

A thorough search of the suspect's shoes showed both had small bits of glass and paint in the soles and heels of one pair. This could be picked up at many locations and simply in the course of walking on the sidewalk. Analysis may show some similarities to that found at the crime scene.

Hair from each suspect had been collected and compared to that found under the victim's fingernails.

The crime lab has extracted the ink from the note and from the suspect pens. The note and ballpoint pens are also available for analysis.

The note, if written by someone other than the victim, may contain fingerprints that could be very useful evidence, if recoverable.

You have the evidence from this crime scene and from the suspects available to you. It is your task to attempt to implicate or exonerate either or both of the suspects, based upon this evidence. The evidence, by itself, may not convict, but could provide the basis for further investigation. Do the best you can. Careful work is a must.

PART D: A HOUSEHOLD HOMICIDE

Law enforcement authorities were summoned to the scene of a crime. The victim, a young woman, was found lying on a floor in her home. Signs of a struggle were evident. Some articles of furniture were overturned. A lamp with a decorative glass base was found broken on a table. A candy dish, its contents scattered, was found broken on the floor, apparently having fallen from a small stand during the assault. The police investigators proceeded to search the premises for physical evidence that might be useful in identifying the victim's assailants. This is what was found and what you have to work with.

The victim apparently met her death through stab wounds to her chest and neck. A knife that shows evidence of stains, thought to be blood, was found under a couch. A postmortem examination has confirmed the cause of death as massive internal hemorrhaging, compounded with wounds to the lungs that would have resulted in their collapse. Due to the placement of the wounds and the appearance of the room in which the victim was found, police investigators feel that she died at the hands of an assailant, and suicide is ruled out of the question.

Interrogation of persons having known or lived near the deceased has established her identity as Ms. Ann Holbook. She was 23 years of age, Caucasian, lived alone, and was employed by a pharmacy. She was known to have a large circle of friends and was the host of a number of social gatherings, some of which became quite bothersome to her neighbors. Raucousness, loud music, and sounds of physical combat had resulted in complaints that had caused law enforcement authorities to be called to the home on a few occasions. None of the victim's neighbors had known her very well, but were able to describe two other women who had been seen to visit her quite frequently. These two women were questioned that same morning and released pending further investigation. Both of these persons' homes were also searched by the police, following the acquisition of warrants obtained from the proper agency.

The remainder of this report is concerned with the physical evidence found in the victim's home and those of the two women, the only two suspects in the case thus far. Some suggestions as to possible analyses that the forensic laboratory might perform on this evidence will also be included. You are employed by the laboratory as an analyst and it will be your findings that may lead to conviction or exoneration of the persons being investigated.

The knife, which evidently was the weapon in the crime—now suspected of being homicide—is to be examined. The stains must be identified as being blood, if possible, and if positive results are obtained, the blood type determined. The victim's blood type was O. Ms. Alice Vick, one of the suspects, and the other woman being investigated, Ms. Marthe Malcomb, have submitted to blood samples being taken for typing. This will be done by the crime lab. Both of the suspects' living quarters have yielded articles of apparel exhibiting stains thought to be blood. Both women involved have logical explanations for the stains on their clothing. If the stains are indeed blood but are both of the suspect's own type, they mean nothing. If one is of the victim's blood type and one is a different type, then they could be significant. Many persons, however, possess blood of Type O. By itself, the blood type of the stains is not conclusive.

Fragments of glass were found lodged in the cuffs of slacks belonging to both suspects. Perhaps they match shards from either the candy dish or lamp. Find out, if you can.

The County Medical Examiner has fixed the time of the victim's death as somewhere between midnight and 4:00 a.m. The suspects, when questioned in their homes the following day, both appeared to be recovering from the effects of either liquor or drugs. They were not totally coherent and explained this by saying that they had been alone the evening before, had passed the time watching television, had consumed a few drinks, had awakened with headaches, and had taken aspirin to relieve the pain associated with headaches. Perhaps the incoherence may be attributed to drowsiness caused by a high concentration of blood salicylate. Perhaps the headache was due to stress caused by the perpetration of the crime. They submitted to blood samples being taken for both alcohol and drug analysis by the crime lab. The blood samples have been prepared for both of these procedures and are available to you.

A small amount of white powdered material was found on the carpet of the room in which the deceased was found. This material, if identified as a drug of abuse, may establish the victim as a supplier, something that her employment would make possible. Perhaps one of the suspects is a user, and in the course of an argument over drugs and in an alcohol-fueled rage, caused the demise of Ms. Holbrook.

The knife, suspected of being the murder weapon, must be dusted for fingerprints. One must be careful not to touch the handle because this is an area of primary interest. Both suspects' inked prints are available for comparison with any latent prints that might be found. Remember, because both suspects have been known visitors of the victim, they may have plausible explanations for the prints on the knife, if found. However, the position of the prints with respect to the knife point may be useful in reconstructing the crime. Make note of this when "lifting" any prints that you find on the weapon.

A scrap of paper was found on the floor of the room in which the victim was found. A phone number was written in ink on the paper. Perhaps ink analysis will show similarities between the written number and pens taken from the purses of each of the suspects. The ink samples have been prepared for analysis and are available for chromatographic separation of the dyes.

The paper, in addition to being utilized for ink analysis, may also contain latent prints of the person who murdered Ms. Holbook. The paper is available, and one may use a variety of methods for print development.

The victim's shirt was found to have some stained areas that appear to be lipstick smears. Perhaps they came from lipstick belonging to the victim herself, but, equally probable, they may have come from the lips of the assailant during the assault. The police have collected tubes of lipstick from each of the suspects as evidence, as well as some from the victim's purse and makeup table. A possible match would be quite useful in preparing a case against one of the suspects.

The county coroner, in conducting the examination of the victim's body, found several strands of hair lodged under the fingernails. These have been determined to have not come from the head of the deceased. Hair samples have been collected from both suspects for comparison with those from the victim's fingernails.

A small painted table was found overturned in the room where the victim was murdered. Some small chips of paint were also found caught in the fibers of the suspects' clothing. Paint fragments can be picked up on one's clothing in a variety of ways, but if the lead content of the paint from the scene table and that of the paint chips from either of the suspects' clothing are the same, this will help in the prosecution building a case against one or the other of the suspects.

A small amount of soil was found on the carpet of the room in which the deceased was found. Soil was collected from shoes belonging to each of the suspects and is available for comparison. This is not very conclusive evidence in itself, but added to other findings, it may be of considerable importance.

This constitutes the report of the crime and the evidence that has been found associated with it. You will be awarded additional points, beyond those given for the analyses results, by writing a reconstruction of the crime from your analyses, should you find that either or both of the suspects are implicated. This reconstruction is not required.

PART E: A LOVE TRIANGLE?

The body of a young woman was found in her apartment. The circumstances that led to this event were as follows. A young woman (Ms. Marquette) had confided to her friend that she was worried about a circumstance that had recently occurred. She was dating a man (Mr. Strand) who was in the process of obtaining a divorce. The man's estranged wife did not want this divorce and was trying to reconcile with her former husband. The man intended to marry Ms. Marquette when the divorce was finalized. Ms. Marquette told her friend that the man's former wife had called her a number of times and pleaded with her to break off her relationship with Strand. Strand's wife felt that this would aid in the reconciliation. Ms. Marquette refused to do this. Mrs. Strand had made vague threats to Marquette over the phone, but had not attempted to harm her, as yet. Mrs. Strand had mentioned that she could get help in persuading Marquette, if necessary.

Ms. Marquette's friend was concerned and invited her to lunch one day. The agreement was made and the meeting place decided. At the appointed time, Ms. Marquette failed to appear. Her friend called her apartment, but no one answered the phone. Marquette's friend went to her apartment later in the day, but could not get an answer to her knock. She called the police. The police gained entrance to the apartment and found the body of the woman on the floor of the living room. Death had apparently occurred sometime the previous evening. Crime-scene investigators were called in and evidence was gathered to be forwarded to the crime lab for analysis.

The victim apparently was involved in a struggle before her death. Furniture was out of place and a lamp was broken on the floor. Fragments of the lamp were collected as evidence. The victim met her death through multiple stab wounds to the neck and chest area. A bloodstained knife was found wrapped in a towel in a waste basket in the kitchen. This was sent to the crime lab for fingerprinting.

The postmortem examination of the victim by the medical examiner yielded the following: Hair was found under the fingernails of the deceased. This could have come from the head of her assailant during the struggle. The victim's blouse was found to have stains on it, which were determined to be lipstick. The blood type of the victim was Type A. Some of the stains were identified as paint. The victim was known to be an amateur furniture refinisher, and a partially completed project was seen in the kitchen. A paint brush was found containing dried paint of the same color as those on the victim's clothing.

A careful search of the deceased woman's apartment resulted in the investigators discovering a note, upon which was written a phone number. The ink from this number was extracted by crime lab analysts. Investigators identified the phone number as belonging to a Ms. Mockridge. Questioning of this person resulted in her giving this statement: She did indeed know Mrs. Strand and was aware of her impending divorce. She stated, however, that although she had heard of Ms. Marquette, she was not personally acquainted with her. On the evening when Ms. Marquette was killed, Ms. Mockridge had been attending a community education course in art. She had returned from this class with a headache, had taken some aspirin, and retired for the night. She had not seen Mrs. Strand for some time, she insisted. Ms. Mockridge could not give the name of any persons who had seen her since she left the class building and so could not substantiate her whereabouts.

Police investigators also visited Mrs. Strand, who stated that she had not seen the victim in person and had not spoken with her for some time. She did admit, however, to a phone conversation with the deceased during which she had asked her not to see her husband anymore. On the evening that Ms. Marquette was killed, she had not left her apartment. She said she had not been feeling well and had decided to stay home and take care of some correspondence.

Questioning of the murdered woman's neighbors in her apartment building revealed one person who had seen two women talking with the victim in front of the building at approximately 10:30 p.m. on the night she was killed. This person said that it appeared that an argument was taking place, with loud voices and some agitation. The apartment building was of new construction so there was no lawn as yet and only a few boards for walking.

Law officers returned to the homes of both Mrs. Strand and Ms. Mockridge and asked them to come to the police station for further questioning, and a search of both homes was conducted after warrants were issued. The following items were found and taken to the crime laboratory.

Both women had shoes in their possession that had soil adhering to the soles. Both had pens containing ink of a similar color to that in the note in the victim's apartment. Tubes of lipstick were collected from both women for comparison. Small fragments of glass were found in the cuffs of slacks in their soiled laundry, as well as stains that appeared to be either paint or blood. Both women's clothing had smudges of a white powdered substance that could be from many sources and may be insignificant.

Both women were fingerprinted and samples of their blood were taken for analysis. Samples of their hair were collected as well. Both women are now under suspicion of murder. Ms. Mockridge will be called suspect A and Mrs. Strand will be suspect B.

You are working as analysts in the crime lab, and your task will be to determine similarities or differences between the scene samples and those belonging to each suspect. Some of the evidence may serve to implicate one or the other of these two women; some may not be useful at all. After completing the work, summarize your findings and state the certainty upon which you base your conclusion, if you can make one.

We hope you will enjoy this exercise and that you will find it a worthwhile conclusion to the work you have done this term.

R. E. James (deceased)
C. E. Meloan
R. Saferstein
T. A. Brettell

Glossary

Abbe refractometer—an instrument used to measure refractive index.

Acid phosphatase—an enzyme found in high concentration in semen.

Agglutination—the clumping together of blood cells.

Agglutinin—an antibody in plasma that promotes agglutination.

Agglutinogen—a substance in red blood cells that acts as an antigen and incites the production of agglutinin.

Antibody—a substance in blood that reacts with a specific antigen, causing blood cells to clump together.

Antigen—a substance that incites the formation of antibodies.

Archimedes's principle—states that an object immersed in a fluid displaces a volume of fluid equal to its volume.

Atomic absorption spectrophotometer—an instrument used for determining the concentration of a particular metal element in a sample.

Becke line—when a transparent object such as a glass chip is immersed in a liquid, it is seen by the unaided eye or under a microscope as having a dark or colored boundary; a sort of "halo."

Cast—an impression formed in a mold.

Compound microscope—a light microscope that has two converging sets of lenses: the objective and the eyepiece.

Condenser—the part of a microscope that focuses the light collected by the mirror onto the sample.

Coronal—the scale structure characteristic of hairs of very fine diameter resembling a stack of paper cups. These scales are commonly encountered on small rodents and bats and only rarely in human hair.

Cortex—the main body of the hair shaft.

Cortical fusi—the irregularly shaped air spaces dispersed throughout the cortex of hair.

Counter immunoelectrophoresis—a laboratory technique in which an electric current is used to accelerate the migration of antibody and antigen through a buffered gel diffusion medium.

Crossover electrophoresis see **Counter immunoelectrophoresis**.

Cuticle—the scale structure covering the exterior of the hair.

Density—a physical property of matter that is specific to the sample being measured and that may be used as a means of identification or comparison, whichever is required. The equation for density is

$$\text{Density} = \frac{\text{Mass of object}}{\text{Volume of object}} \text{ expressed either as } \frac{g}{cm^3} \text{ or } \frac{lb}{ft^3}$$

Density gradient method—a comparative-density technique using a standard density gradient tube made up of layers of two liquids mixed in varying proportions so that each layer has a different density value.

Depth of focus—the thickness of the object that is simultaneously in focus on a microscope.

Emission spectroscopy—a spectroscopic technique that examines the wavelengths of photons emitted by atoms or molecules during their transition from an excited state to a lower-energy state.

Excited state—when a system (such as an atom, molecule, or nucleus) has a higher energy than the absolute minimum.

Field diaphragm—controls how much light enters the microscope.

Field of view—the area or diameter of the specimen that is in view on a microscope.

Fingerprint—an impression of the friction ridges on all parts of the finger.

Flotation—the simplest comparative-density technique based on the observation that a solid particle will float in a liquid medium of greater density, sink in a liquid of lower density, or remain suspended in a liquid of equal density.

Friction ridges—raised portions of the outer layer of the skin.

Gas chromatograph—an instrument used in gas chromatography to separate a sample of a volatile substance into its components.

Gas chromatography—separates mixtures of volatile compounds on the basis of their distribution between a stationary liquid phase and a moving gas phase.

Hemoglobin—the oxygen-carrying coloring matter of red blood cells.

Imbricate—overlapping scales with narrow margins. These scales are found on the hairs of humans and often of animals.

Improvised mixtures—low-order explosive mixtures made from commonly available chemicals.

Individual characteristics—evidence that can be associated with a common source with an extremely high degree of probability is said to posses individual characteristics.

Inked prints—fingerprints taken directly from a person's fingers through the use of an ink pad or block.

Iris diaphragm—a circular device with a variable diameter, commonly used on microscopes to regulate the amount of light admitted.

Instrument—a device used to make measurements.

Kohler illumination—a microscopic method to align the optics and focus all of the components so as to minimize distortion and to obtain uniform brightness.

Latent prints—invisible prints left on an object by a person.

Light source—the part of the microscope that provides light.

Magnification—in regard to a microscope, is determined by multiplying the magnification of the eyepiece by the magnification of the nosepiece.

Magnifying glass—the simplest microscope.

Medulla—the cellular column running through the center of the hair.

Metric system—a list of commonly used units of measurement—for example, **meter** (m), **gram** (g), **liter** (L).

Mobile phase—the phase that moves in a definite direction in a chromatographic system.

Mold—a frame or model around or on which something is formed or shaped.

Moulage—a death mask made of the deceased's face from wax so that relatives could identify the body at a later date.

Nitrates—chemical compounds found in unburned smokeless gunpowder.

Nitrites—chemical compounds found in burned smokeless gunpowder.

Objective lens—the lens in a microscope that is nearest the object being viewed.

Parfocal—means that once the image is brought into sharp focus under low power, it will remain in focus when the high-power objective is turned into position.

Plasma—the colorless fluid of the blood.

Precipitin test—a serologic test in which an antibody reacts with a specific soluble antigen to form a precipitate.

Refractive index—a measure of the bending of a ray of light as it passes from air into a solid or liquid.

R_f—the abbreviation for retardation factor, which is the distance a compound moves relative to the distance the mobile phase moves in a thin-layer chromatographic system.

Serum—the clear yellowish liquid part of blood after the fibrin and corpuscles have been removed.

Spatter—the spurting of blood in drops.

Spectroscope—the simplest instrument used to separate light into its component wavelengths.

Spectrum—a pattern of frequencies characteristic of a material's interaction with light.

Splatter see **Spatter**.

Spinous—the triangular-shaped scales that frequently protrude from the hair shaft. These scales are never found in human hairs.

Stationary phase—the substance that is fixed in place for the chromatography procedure. An example is the silica layer in thin-layer chromatography.

Stripping a dye—a process of either reducing or oxidizing a dye in a fiber, causing it to lose its color.

Working distance—the distance between the specimen and the tip of the objective lens of a microscope.

The Metric System

APPENDIX 2

The **metric system** of units is used in most scientific work, and a list of commonly used units follows. You should familiarize yourself thoroughly with these units, and with the relationship of these units to common units of the English system.

The fundamental unit of **linear** measurement is the **meter**, (m).

The fundamental unit of **mass** measurement is the **gram**, (g).

The fundamental unit of **volume** measurement is the **liter**, (L).

Commonly used prefixes of the foregoing fundamental units are

deci-	(d)	1/10 or 0.1
centi-	(c)	1/100 or 0.01
milli-	(m)	1/1000 or 0.001
deka-	(dk)	10
hecto-	(h)	100
kilo-	(k)	1000

Thus, 1,000 meters (m) is 1 kilometer (km), 0.1 gram (g) is 1 decigram (dg), 0.001 liter (L) is 1 milliliter (mL), and so on.

Some of the common English units and their approximate metric equivalents are

1 inch = 2.54 centimeters   1 meter = 39.37 inches
1 foot = 30.5 centimeters   1 liter = 1.06 quarts
1 pound = 453.6 grams   1 kilogram = 2.2 pounds
1 ounce = 28.35 grams   1 quart = 0.94 liters
1 fluid ounce = 29.6 mL

1.0 mL of water weighs 1.0 g; 1.0 liter (L) of water weighs 1.0 kg.

FACTOR LABEL SYSTEM FOR MAKING CONVERSIONS

A convenient method for converting from one set of units to another without getting mixed up is to use a **numerical factor** followed by a **units label**; this is called the **factor-label method**. A pattern that can be followed is:

$$\text{What you have plus its units} \times \text{Conversion factor(s)} = \text{What you want plus its units}$$

The factor(s) should be written so that the numerator (top) of one set of units will cancel the denominator (bottom) of another set of units.

EXAMPLES

1. A shoe imprint found at a scene was found to be 13.0 inches long. How many centimeters long is this shoe?

$$\frac{13.0 \text{ inches}}{1} \times \frac{2.54 \text{ cm}}{1.0 \text{ inch}} = 33.02 \text{ cm}$$

Notice that the factor here is arranged so that the units in the denominator cancel the units in the numerator of the initial term. You use as many factors as you need until the units on the left side of the equation equal the units on the right side of the equation.

2. I am 74 inches tall. How many meters tall am I?

$$\frac{74.0 \text{ inches}}{1} \times \frac{2.54 \text{ cm}}{1.0 \text{ inch}} \times \frac{1 \text{ meter}}{100 \text{ cm}} = 1.88 \text{ meters}$$

3. A bullet slug weighs 0.62 ounces. How many milligrams does it weigh?

$$\frac{0.62 \text{ ounces}}{1} \times \frac{28.35 \text{ grams}}{1.0 \text{ ounce}} \times \frac{1,000 \text{ mg}}{1.0 \text{ grams}} = 17,577 \text{ mg}$$

4. A room is 12 ft wide and 15 ft long. How many square meters (m²) is the floor in this room? Follow the same pattern, but convert each measurement, then multiply the results to find the answer.

$$\frac{12 \text{ ft}}{1} \times \frac{12 \text{ in}}{1 \text{ ft}} \times \frac{2.54 \text{ cm}}{1 \text{ in}} \times \frac{1 \text{ m}}{100 \text{ cm}} = 3.66 \text{ m}$$

$$\frac{15 \text{ ft}}{1} \times \frac{12 \text{ in}}{1 \text{ ft}} \times \frac{2.54 \text{ cm}}{1 \text{ in}} \times \frac{1 \text{ m}}{100 \text{ cm}} = 4.57 \text{ m}$$

$$3.66 \text{ m} \times 4.57 \text{ m} = 16.7 \text{ m}^2$$

SELECTED SOURCES FOR ADDITIONAL INFORMATION

Albanese, J., Eklics, G., and Tuck, A., "A metric method for sex determination using the proximal femur and fragmentary hipbone," *J. Forens. Sci.*, 53 (6), 2008, 1283.

Kemkes, A., and Gobel, T., "Metric assessment of the 'Mastoidal Triangle' for sex determination," *J. Forens. Sci.*, 51 (5), 2006, 985.

Spradley, M. K, Jantz, R. L, Robinson, A., and Peccerelli, F.," Demographic change and forensic identification: problems in metric identification of Hispanic skeletons," *J. Forens. Sci.*, 53 (1), 2008, 21.

EXERCISES

1. Add: 3.45 g, 0.06 kg, 0.67 g, 690 mg, 2 dg.

2. Add: 3.28 g, 8,604 mg, 6.20 dg, 0.780 kg, 5.62 g, 0.08 dg.

3. Add: 5.2 L, 5,300 mL, 0.44 L, 50 mL.

4. Add: 0.30 m, 450 cm, 4.2 m, 600 mm, 2.8 cm, 4 dm, 60 mm.

5. Add: 78 cm, 567 mm, 14 dm, 1.2 m, 0.023 km, 75 mm.

6. How many liters are contained in a 1.00-cubic-meter container, and what would it weigh if it were filled with water? Ignore the weight of the container (hint: 1 L of water weighs 1 kg).

7. Fill in the blanks.
   a. 1 centimeter (cm) = _____ inch (in)
   b. 1 pound (lb) = _____ kilogram (kg)
   c. 1 quart (qt) = _____ liter (L)
   d. 1 ounce (oz) = _____ grams (g)
   e. 2 ounces (oz) = _____ milliliters (mL)
   f. 100 meters (m) = _____ yards (yd)
   g. 1 mile (mi) = _____ kilometers (km)
   h. 1 gallon (gal) = _____ milliliters (mL)
   i. 1 square inch (in^2) = _____ square centimeters (cm^2)
   j. 1 cubic decimeter (dm^3) = _____ cubic centimeters (cc) or (cm^3)